CROSS-STRAIT RELATIONS SINCE 2016

Cross-Strait Relations Since 2016: The End of the Illusion examines the situation in the Taiwan Strait since the election of Tsai Ing-wen of the Democratic Progressive Party in the January 2016 general elections.

Tracking the pragmatic approach taken by the Tsai administration, this book positions the recent developments within a changing geopolitical context and analyzes Beijing's reactions to an environment that has become increasingly skeptical of its intentions. It shows that despite President Tsai's commitment to the "status quo" in the Taiwan Strait and pro-democracy policies, which have been well received by the international community, Xi Jinping continues to advocate for a unification policy that remains very unpopular in Taiwan. With in-depth, on-the-ground analysis based on access to various government actors in Taiwan and abroad, the author takes a deep dive into a highly complex relationship that is often misunderstood abroad, with stakes that have direct implications for the future stability of the Indo-Pacific region.

The first English language book to provide a full assessment of the four years of DPP rule since 2016, this book will be useful to students and scholars of Asian Studies and Taiwan Studies, as well as Security Studies, Politics, and International Relations.

J. Michael Cole is a Taipei-based senior non-resident fellow with the Global Taiwan Institute in Washington, D.C., the Macdonald-Laurier Institute in Ottawa, Canada, and the Taiwan Studies Programme at the University of Nottingham, U.K.

Routledge Research on Taiwan Series

Series Editor: Dafydd Fell, *SOAS, UK*

The *Routledge Research on Taiwan Series* seeks to publish quality research on all aspects of Taiwan studies. Taking an interdisciplinary approach, the books will cover topics such as politics, economic development, culture, society, anthropology and history.

This new book series will include the best possible scholarship from the social sciences and the humanities and welcomes submissions from established authors in the field as well as from younger authors. In addition to research monographs and edited volumes general works or textbooks with a broader appeal will be considered.

The Series is advised by an international Editorial Board and edited by *Dafydd Fell* of the Centre of Taiwan Studies at the School of Oriental and African Studies.

Positioning Taiwan in a Global Context
Being and Becoming
Edited by Bi-yu Chang and Pei-yin Lin

Young Adults in Urban China and Taiwan
Aspirations, Expectations, and Life Choices
Désirée Remmert

Taiwan Studies Revisited
Dafydd Fell and Hsin-Huang Michael Hsiao

Cross-Strait Relations Since 2016
The End of the Illusion
J. Michael Cole

For more information about this series, please visit: www.routledge.com/Routledge-Research-on-Taiwan-Series/book-series/RRTAIWAN

CROSS-STRAIT RELATIONS SINCE 2016

The End of the Illusion

J. Michael Cole

LONDON AND NEW YORK

First published 2020
by Routledge
2 Park Square, Milton Park, Abingdon, Oxon OX14 4RN

and by Routledge
52 Vanderbilt Avenue, New York, NY 10017

Routledge is an imprint of the Taylor & Francis Group, an informa business

© 2020 J. Michael Cole

The right of J. Michael Cole to be identified as author of this work
has been asserted by him in accordance with sections 77 and 78 of the
Copyright, Designs and Patents Act 1988.

All rights reserved. No part of this book may be reprinted or reproduced or
utilised in any form or by any electronic, mechanical, or other means, now
known or hereafter invented, including photocopying and recording, or in
any information storage or retrieval system, without permission in writing
from the publishers.

Trademark notice: Product or corporate names may be trademarks or
registered trademarks, and are used only for identification and explanation
without intent to infringe.

British Library Cataloguing-in-Publication Data
A catalogue record for this book is available from the British Library

Library of Congress Cataloging-in-Publication Data
A catalog record for this book has been requested

ISBN: 978-0-367-42828-0 (hbk)
ISBN: 978-0-367-42849-5 (pbk)
ISBN: 978-0-367-85553-6 (ebk)

Typeset in Bembo
by Apex CoVantage, LLC

For Ketty, as always. And to Bruce Jacobs (1943–2019).

CONTENTS

Introduction	*ix*
Acknowledgments	*xiii*

PART 1
The illusion is broken   1

1 The road to the "deep freeze"	3
2 The gloves come off: China's punitive strategy	25
3 Trouble in the green camp	69

PART 2
The regional and global context   77

4 Taiwan and China's greater ambitions: geopolitics and ideology	79
5 U.S.–Taiwan rapprochement	98
6 The future of the Japan–Taiwan partnership	122
7 Taiwan and the world: isolation vs. creative engagement	138

viii Contents

PART 3
The road ahead 149

8 Democracy under the DPP: a scorecard 151

9 Reinventing Taiwan for the 21st century 167

10 What's next? 2019 and beyond 177

Index *194*

INTRODUCTION

When this book goes to print, about four years will have elapsed since the release of *Convergence or Conflict in the Taiwan Strait: The Illusion of Peace?* (Cole 2016). Although most of the fundamentals discussed in the first book still apply, a number of important variables have changed since then. Chief among them is the fact that Tsai Ing-wen (蔡英文) and her Democratic Progressive Party (DPP, 民進黨) have been the government since May 2016. Released weeks after the DPP's landmark victory in the 16 January 2016 general elections, *Convenient* could only speculate as to the direction that the relationship across the Taiwan Strait would take. Ma Ying-jeou (馬英九), president since 2008, was still in office, and his Kuomintang (KMT, 國民黨) administration would be in power for another three months before the new DPP government took over, both in the executive and legislative branches – a first in the nation's democratic history.

With the present volume, we now have the benefit of more than four years of developments upon which to test, and in some cases revise, the hypotheses I put forward in *Convenient*. One of the concluding chapters in *Convenient*, titled "The 2016 Elections: A Return to Uncertainty?" proposed a number of scenarios for the future; one of those speculated that Beijing would decide to "punish" the Taiwanese for the choices they made in the elections and therefore would ramp up its coercive approach to cross-Strait relations. That scenario has come to pass, and for better or worse uncertainty has been replaced by clarity. The first section of this book (Chapter 1 and Chapter 2) brings us up to date on what Beijing has done since Inauguration Day on May 20, 2016. It discusses why the Chinese regime felt compelled to act in such a manner, and details the various forms – from "sharp power" to military threats and diplomatic isolation – that this punitive strategy has taken.

It also assesses (Chapter 3) how incessant Chinese pressure on Taiwan has energized the "deep green" camp, which has been dissatisfied with President Tsai's "lax" response to Beijing. Among other things, this has led to efforts by such organizations and to launch a referendum campaign to rectify Taiwan's official name. I make the case that maintaining and strengthening the "status quo" remains the best policy for Taiwan under current circumstances and that pursuing campaigns such as a referendum would risk alienating the United States, deepen divisions within Taiwan, and unnecessarily give Beijing justification to further intensify its crackdown on Taiwan.

The next section (Chapter 4) looks at democratic Taiwan as a first line of defense in the global battle that is being waged between autocratic, revisionist forces, and the liberal-democratic order that has underpinned international relations since the conclusion of hostilities in World War II. It looks at the rapidly changing circumstances in the Indo-Pacific amid greater Chinese assertiveness under Xi Jinping (習近平), arguably the most powerful – and paranoid – Chinese leader since Mao Zedong (毛澤東). This section also analyzes China's regional, and increasingly global, ambitions, the ideological underpinnings of this new expansionist outlook, and positions Taiwan as one element in that context. It also argues that demographics in Chinese society could force the regime to act soon to grab as much as it can before the window of opportunity closes. Finally, this chapter looks at internal politics in China in the wake of the 19th Party Congress, where one key development was the removal of term limits on the presidency, and highlights other recent developments in Chinese politics that are expected to have an impact on Beijing's relations with Taiwan.

Another "prediction" made in *Convenient* that also became reality was the expectation that ties between Taiwan and the United States would deepen. Chapter 5 explains how and why this has occurred, and demonstrates that this held true both during the remaining months of the Obama administration and after Donald J. Trump assumed office. It also argues that this rapprochement was made necessary for a variety of reasons, among them the intensifying Chinese assault on the "status quo" in the Taiwan Strait after May 2016, and a somewhat reinvigorated, if uneven, U.S. commitment to working with democratic allies in the region. It also looks at the effects the U.S.–China trade war could have on the triangular relationship.

In Chapter 6 we turn to Japan, a natural and increasingly important ally of Taiwan, which received little mention in *Convenient*. Informed by the author's interviews with government officials, military officers, and analysts in Japan and Taiwan, this chapter also sheds light on Japanese perceptions of Taiwan, and seeks to establish the extent of Tokyo's commitment to Taiwan's status as a *de facto* independent state, the role of the Treaty of Mutual Cooperation and Security between the United States and Japan (日本国とアメリカ合衆国との間の相互協力及び安全保障条約), and what preparations Taiwan's northern neighbor has been making to address various scenarios in the Taiwan Strait.

We then analyze (Chapter 7) how Beijing's assault on Taiwan and international norms has created incentives for the international community (primarily the community of democracies) to reach out to Taiwan and create opportunities for Taipei to counter Beijing's efforts to isolate it diplomatically. This chapter debunks the notion that Taiwan's loss of official diplomatic allies (at this writing, seven since Tsai Ing-wen assumed the presidency, with others likely to follow) has exacerbated Taiwan's international isolation and argues that Taiwan has in fact strengthened its ties with the global community through various, albeit often unofficial, channels.

This section next zooms in on Taiwan with an assessment of the current status of its democracy (Chapter 8), which arguably remains one of the key "firewalls" against Beijing's attempts to subjugate it. *Convenient* was critical of the Ma administration on some human rights issue, and demonstrated why it was essential for civil society, an essential component in any consolidated democracy, to take corrective action, culminating in the Sunflower Movement's (**太陽花學運**) occupation of the Legislative Yuan in March/April 2014. This section asks whether the DPP has performed better on the democracy front and whether it has succeeded in responding to the demands of civil society, especially among young Taiwanese who voted for the DPP in 2016 with the hope that the party would perform better on this front.

Finally, the book revisits an argument made in *Convenient* by drawing further attention (Chapter 9) to the persistent dangers of divisive politics in Taiwan, and restates the case for the essentiality of a mainstream "blue-green" united front against China. Through the author's work and privileged access over the years, and perhaps more apparent due to his status as an "outsider," it is clear that Taiwanese have every advantage in transcending the age-old ethnopolitical divide within their society. This chapter argues that the very survival of this nation is contingent on the eradication, once and for all, of a divisiveness that has been kept on life support for far too long. This is followed by a discussion on some of the challenges that continue to plague Taiwan in the 21st century, with recommendations on how to address those deficiencies in order to strengthen Taiwan's ability to retain its independent sovereignty and democracy in the long term. The book concludes (Chapter 10) with a list of possible scenarios for the future and a discussion on the 2020 general elections.

A final note on the author's professional affiliations: at the time of writing *Convenient*, the author was an employee at the Thinking Taiwan Foundation (**小英教育基金會**), a think tank that was launched by Tsai Ing-wen following her defeat in the 2012 general elections. Ms. Tsai's offer to join the Foundation in early 2014 allowed the author to continue his work in Taiwan and presented many opportunities for interactions with people who would eventually become top officials in her administration. To her credit, Ms. Tsai never broke her agreement with the author that his employment at the Foundation should in any way influence what he wrote or published on the Internet platform he ran for the Foundation. What's more, Tsai and management at the Foundation did not know that the author was writing a book about Taiwan, and so the views and opinions expressed in *Convenient* were the author's alone. The author's relationship with the Foundation ended in

xii Introduction

May 2016, and since then the author has had no employment with any agency tied with the administration, although he has collaborated on some projects with the government-funded Taiwan Foundation for Democracy (**臺灣民主基金會**) and Prospect Foundation (**遠景基金會**). As with *Convenient*, the opinions expressed herein, as well as any remaining errors, are therefore entirely the author's.

Reference

Cole, J. Michael (2016) *Convergence or Conflict in the Taiwan Strait The illusion of Peace?* London: Routledge.

ACKNOWLEDGMENTS

The mere listing of names does injustice to the countless number of people who, in various ways, have contributed over the years to the views and conclusions discussed in this book. Below are the individuals who had the greatest impact on my professional journey in the years between the publication of *Convenient* and the completion of the present manuscript. Naming them all would be impossible. A few people deserve specific mention, however, and these come first.

To Dr. Hsu Szu-chien (徐斯儉), former president of the Taiwan Foundation for Democracy and now deputy minister of foreign affairs. Shared professional pursuits aside, Dr. Hsu has been a close friend and opened many doors for the author. To Dr. Dafydd Fell (羅達菲) at SOAS, University of London, for his support and turning SOAS into a familiar space where the author could share his research with young academics. Dr. Fell also played an instrumental role in facilitating the publication of *Convenient* in English and invited the author to contribute a chapter in his book *Taiwan's Social Movements under Ma Ying-jeou*.

In Taiwan: Lu Yeh-chung (盧業中), Olivia Yang (楊斯茜), Alison Hsiao (蕭仔君) and Chou Ya-wei (周雅薇) at the Taiwan Foundation for Democracy; Lai I-chung (賴怡忠), Mark Chen (陳唐山), Alvin Yao (姚源明), Norah Huang (黃美鳳), Annie Chen (陳怡安) and Liu Wei-min (劉維民) at the Prospect Foundation; Lin Cheng-yi (林正義), Wu Jau-shieh (吳釗燮), President Tsai Ing-wen (蔡英文), Sylvia Feng (馮賢賢) for her invaluable help making *Taiwan Sentinel* (台灣守望) possible, Eli Huang (黃引珊), Michael Hsiao (蕭新煌), "Jerry" Huang Kuo-cheng (黃國城) for the legal help when the Chinese took legal action, Lii Wen (李問), Antonio Chiang (江春男), Vincent Yao (姚金祥), Fan Yun (范雲), Alexander Huang (黃介正), Tao Yi-feng (陶儀芬), Chen Ming-chi (陳明祺), Lin Lianron (林良蓉), Chen Mu-min (陳牧民), Andrew Yang (楊念祖), Eric Yu (俞振華), William Stanton, Ho Ming-sho (何明修), Wu Jieh-min (吳介民), Tsai Hung-jeng (蔡宏政), Manohar Thyagaraj, Sandeep Jakhar, Asher Yarden, Jojje Olsson, Arthur

xiv Acknowledgments

Ding (丁樹範), Liu Chang-cheng (劉長政), Stacy Hsu (徐薇婷), Michelle Wang (王美琇), Nicola Smith; the good people at the American Institute in Taiwan, the Australian Office Taipei, the Japan–Taiwan Exchange Association, and the Canadian Trade Office in Taipei; and to Denny Chen (陳玳妮) at *Business Weekly* in Taipei for handling the publication of an earlier version of this book, 《島嶼無戰事2：難以迴避的價值抉擇》 in July 2019.

In North America: Winston Chen (陳文儀), Simon Sung (宋申武), Vincent Chao (趙怡翔), Mark Stokes, Randall Schriver, Peter Mattis, Richard Bush, Scott Harold, Ian Easton, Abraham Denmark, Steve Yates, Russell Hsiao, Marzia Borsoi-Kelly, Marc Bennett, Zachary Riskind, Michael Mazza, Derek Grossman, Harry Kazianis, Natasha Hassan at the *Globe and Mail*, Clayton Dube, Mike Chinoy, Rupert Hammond-Chambers, Jerome Cohen, Brandon and Su Yun Geithner, Victor Radujko, Shelley Rigger, Isaac Stone Fish, Scott Urbom, Christian Marchant, Natalie Liu, Janice Chen, Mike Fonte, Timothy Rich, Charles Burton, Brian Lee Crowley, David McDonough, David Watson, Jonathan Miller and Brett Byers-Lane at the MacDonald-Laurier Institute in Ottawa, Aaron Friedberg, Nadège Rolland, André Laliberté, Doris Liu, Sarah Cook, Louisa Greve, and Shanthi Kalathil.

In Europe/Middle East: Steve Tsang (曾銳生), Lee Chun-yi (李駿怡), Jonathan Sullivan, Ernest Caldwell, Chang Bi-yu (張必瑜), Gunter Schubert, Stéphane Corcuff, Wang Chung-I (汪忠一), Lin You-hung (林祐宏), Jean-Pierre Cabestan, Gary Rawnsley, Ming-yeh Rawnsley (蔡明燁), Martin Hala, Michal Thim, Juan Pablo Cardenal, Peter Enav, Nick Payne, Barak Kushner, Laura E. Anderson, and Gabriella Faerber at Al Jazeera.

Elsewhere in Asia/Oceania: Ian Ja Ian Chong (莊嘉穎), John Garnaut, Anne-Marie Brady, David Bostwick, Ogata Makoto, Oiso Mitsunori, Sato Yoshitaka, Simon Denyer, Jerome Taylor, James Palmer, Nathan VanderKlippe, Josh Spero, Bruce Jacobs, Andrew Tan, Ben Schreer, Richard McGregor, Richard Rigby, Alex Neill, Kristie Lu Stout, Sam Roggeveen, and Mark Harrison.

To the members of Chinapol (C-POL) around the world, an online forum that serves as an indispensable tool for China-watchers.

To the two anonymous reviewers who gave their mark of approval for this project and made highly useful recommendations on how to improve the manuscript.

As always, to my parents in Canada for their unflagging support and love, with the usual apologies for not visiting home more often, but I know they understand.

To Hanji, our beautiful Formosa Mountain Dog (a breed now officially recognized worldwide), for the unconditional love and the much-needed daily dose of silliness.

To the Taiwanese people, who have been so movingly welcoming, who have opened their doors and hearts to me for 14 years. What an extraordinary country you have!

Finally, none of this would have been possible without the encouragement, help, love, and understanding of Dr. Ketty W. Chen (陳婉宜), who during the period covered in this book made tremendous contributions of her own to Taiwan's democracy and position within the international community. Therefore, here again, this book is dedicated to her, to my wonderful in-laws, and to those who, every day, fight for the maintenance of a free, prosperous, and democratic Taiwan.

PART 1
The illusion is broken

1

THE ROAD TO THE "DEEP FREEZE"

Under a blistering sun, thousands of people were gathered in front of the Presidential Office in Taipei on 20 May 2016 to celebrate the inauguration of Tsai Ing-wen. Four months earlier, in the 16 January general elections, Tsai had defeated her opponent, Eric Chu (朱立倫), of the Kuomintang (KMT), ending eight years of KMT rule and creating uncertainties about Taiwan's future relationship with China. Compounding the uncertainty was the fact that in the same elections, Tsai's Democratic Progressive Party (DPP) had, for the first time in the nation's history, won a majority of seats in the Legislative Yuan (立法院), the nation's parliament.

Struggling to remain hydrated, many of the people in attendance must have wondered whether the oppressive heat on that day was a warning that cross-Strait relations were about to heat up. Around us, dozens of staffers, many of them from Tsai's victorious campaign team, were busy guiding foreign diplomats and other attendees to their respective sections. Several employees went hours without water, and were it not for the intervention of foreign diplomats, who ventured into nearby tents and collected bottles, some of them would probably have fainted from the extreme heat. That small gesture would come to symbolize the new relationship that Taiwan would form with its many "unofficial" allies in the international community.

Most international media were primarily interested in the signal that the newly installed president would send to Beijing. Since election night, Tsai had stuck to a conciliatory tone when discussing cross-Strait relations, maintaining that her administration would seek continuity with Beijing, however skeptical the CCP might be of the DPP's intentions.

Tsai's inaugural address was aimed at two principal audiences – the Taiwanese public, which had elevated her to the nation's highest office, and Beijing, which would scrutinize every word for signals and hidden meanings. She was, therefore, walking a tightrope, on the one hand needing to respect the democratic aspirations

4 The illusion is broken

of the people who had voted her into office *and those who did not*, and on the other needing to ensure that the cross-Strait environment remained stable enough that she could accomplish the many tasks she had set for her administration domestically. The first she could control; the second, however, was a leap of faith and ultimately the future direction of cross-Strait relations would be largely determined by Beijing. Like her predecessors, the new president was facing an extraordinarily complex balancing act in a game whose rules are constantly being rewritten by the opposing camp.

The first and longest part of Tsai's address (Office of the President, Republic of China (OPROC) 2016) touched on the various issues that mattered most to ordinary Taiwanese. Those, as had been demonstrated during the election campaign, were the same pragmatic, everyday concerns that animate people worldwide: the economy, education, food safety, reform, and so on. As one ordinary Taiwanese told this author in an interview, a motorcycle repairman surnamed Wu, what mattered most to him was that President Tsai fixes the economy. "It's been bad," he said (Cole 2016a).

Like many Taiwanese, Mr. Wu didn't obsess much about cross-Strait relations, though an incident involving Chou Tzu-yu (周子瑜), a teenage Taiwanese K-Pop artist, who on election day had been forced by her South Korean agent to issue a videotaped "apology" to China for holding a ROC flag in a picture, caused a major controversy and may have convinced undecided voters to take action. Mr. Wu barely mentioned China during the interview. When pressed, he said almost as an afterthought that he trusted the government to deal with those issues accordingly.

For some, the early criticism focused more on the fact that the new president had created a Cabinet that was regarded as old, technocratic, and male-dominated, in other words, not progressive enough to bring about the change the DPP had promised during the campaign.

For the rest of the international community, and for China most specifically, it was the latter part of President Tsai's inaugural address that mattered most. In it, and continuing on earlier themes she had used during the election, Tsai struck a measured tone, one that sought to reassure the Taiwanese people and the international community that she could handle the complicated relationship with China. Among other things, Tsai said she would not dismantle any of the existing channels for communication between the two sides of the Taiwan Strait and promised that her administration would "work to maintain peace and stability in cross-Strait relations."

"The new government will conduct cross-Strait affairs in accordance with the Republic of China Constitution, the Act Governing Relations Between the People of Taiwan Area and the Mainland Area [臺灣地區與大陸地區人民關係條例], and other relevant legislation," Tsai said. "The two governing parties across the Strait must set aside the baggage of history, and engage in positive dialogue, for the benefit of the people on both sides."

The catchall term for her cross-Strait policy was the maintenance of the "status quo" of no de jure independence and no unification. This signaled the continuation of an official policy espoused by her predecessor, even though many critics in the green camp have argued that the "status quo" is in fact ever shifting, and that under the Ma administration it had drifted dangerously closer to China.

The ceremony, whose visuals and themes emphasized unity and democracy, concluded with a choir that sang "Ilha Formosa," a poetic song that served as an anthem for pro-democracy groups during the Martial Law era. For the people in Taiwan, the ceremony, and President Tsai's address, had struck all the right notes. It exuded confidence, spoke of unity, and extended an olive branch to Beijing, whose reaction remained to be seen.

In the months since the election, there had been reason for guarded optimism that relations across the Taiwan Strait would be characterized by continuity rather than revert back to the kind of animosity that had marked much of the Chen Shui-bian (陳水扁) presidency (2000–2008). Already in her victory speech on the night of 16 January, the future president had reached out to Beijing and vowed to keep the relationship on the right course – provided, of course, that the other side agreed to cooperate. On the night of her election victory, Tsai had already struck what many observers believed was the right tone vis-à-vis China:

> During this election, I had promised on many occasions that I will build a consistent, predictable, and sustainable cross-strait relationship. As the 14th president-elect of the Republic of China, I reaffirm that after my new administration takes office on May 20, the Republic of China constitutional order, the results of cross-strait negotiations, interactions and exchanges, and democratic principles and the will of the Taiwanese people, will become the foundation for future cross-strait relations. My position will move past partisan politics. Following the will and consensus of the Taiwanese people, we will work to maintain the status quo for peace and stability across the Taiwan Strait, in order to bring the greatest benefits and well-being to the Taiwanese people.
>
> I also want to emphasize that both sides of the strait have a responsibility to find mutually acceptable means of interaction that are based on dignity and reciprocity. We must ensure that no provocations or accidents take place. The results of today's election showcase the will of the Taiwanese people. It is the shared resolve of Taiwan's 23 million people that the Republic of China is a democratic country. Our democratic system, national identity, and international space must be respected. Any forms of suppression will harm the stability of cross-strait relations.
>
> (Focus Taiwan 2016a)

In the expression of her China policy, the continuity and similarities between her victory speech and her inaugural address were hard to miss:

> The new government will conduct cross-Strait affairs in accordance with the Republic of China Constitution, the Act Governing Relations Between

the People of Taiwan Area and the Mainland Area, and other relevant legislation. The two governing parties across the Strait must set aside the baggage of history, and engage in positive dialogue, for the benefit of the people on both sides.

By existing political foundations, I refer to a number of key elements. The first element is the fact of the 1992 talks between the two institutions representing each side across the Strait (Straits Exchange Foundation and Association for Relations Across the Taiwan Straits), when there was joint acknowledgement of setting aside differences to seek common ground. This is a historical fact. The second element is the existing Republic of China constitutional order. The third element pertains to the outcomes of over twenty years of negotiations and interactions across the Strait. And the fourth relates to the democratic principle and prevalent will of the people of Taiwan.

Later on, in her National Day addresse on 10 October, President Tsai would again revisit similar themes. The 2016 version of her speech said:

On cross-strait relations, I once again reiterate the immovable position of the new government, and that is to establish a consistent, predictable and sustainable cross-strait relationship, and to maintain both Taiwan's democracy and the status quo of peace across the Taiwan Strait.

Maintaining the status quo is the pledge I made to voters. Not a single sentence from my inaugural address on May 20 has ever changed. The new government will conduct cross-strait affairs in accordance with the Constitution of the Republic of China, the Act Governing Relations between the People of the Taiwan Area and the Mainland Area, and other relevant legislation. And we will spare no effort in maintaining mechanisms for dialogue and communication across the Taiwan Strait.

We respect the historical fact that in 1992, the two institutions representing each side across the strait (SEF & ARATS) met, and we advocate that both sides must collectively cherish and sustain the accumulated outcomes enabled by over twenty years of cross-strait interactions and negotiations since 1992, and continuously promote the stable and peaceful development of the cross-strait relationship based on such existing political foundations. I also call on the two governing parties across the strait to set aside the baggage of history, and engage in positive dialogue for the benefit of people on both sides.

Although cross-strait relations have seen certain ups and downs in the past months, our position remains consistent and firm. Our pledges will not change, and our goodwill will not change. But we will not bow to pressure, and we will of course not revert to the old path of confrontation. This is our fundamental attitude toward maintaining the status quo, and it is based on the collective hope for peace across the Taiwan Strait.

I want to stress that maintaining the status quo has a more proactive meaning: With deepening democracy as foundation, we will take proactive and

The road to the "deep freeze" **7**

forward-looking measures to promote constructive exchanges and dialogue across the strait, in order to build a peaceful and stable cross-strait relationship that endures.

I call upon the authorities of mainland China to face up to the reality that the Republic of China exists, and that the people of Taiwan have an unshakable faith in the democratic system. The two sides of the strait should sit down and talk as soon as possible. Anything can be included for discussion, as long as it is conducive to the development of cross-strait peace and the welfare of people on both sides. Leaders on both sides should jointly display wisdom and flexibility, and together bring a divided present toward a win–win future.

(Focus Taiwan 2016b)

And in her 2017 address:

Cross-strait relations are an issue that affects Taiwan's future and the long-term welfare of our 23 million people. Since May 20 last year, we have exerted maximum goodwill in order to safeguard the peaceful and stable development of cross-strait relations. Although political differences between the two sides have led to some complications, we have nevertheless worked to maintain the basic stability of cross-strait relations.

As I have stated on many occasions: "Our goodwill will not change, our commitments will not change, we will not revert to the old path of confrontation, and we will not bow to pressure." This has been my consistent position on cross-strait relations.

This year marks the 30th anniversary of cross-strait exchanges. Over the past 30 years, hostility between the two sides of the strait has been replaced by peaceful development. A new chapter has been written in cross-strait relations. Key to this was that both sides were able to put aside political differences in order to be pragmatic and realistic. In the course of exchanges and interactions, both sides accumulated goodwill and established new interactions and ways of thinking.

We should treasure these hard-fought results and the accumulated goodwill from the past 30 years. On this existing basis, we hope for more breakthroughs in the cross-strait relationship.

This year also marks the 30th anniversary of Taiwan allowing familial visits to the mainland. Even today, footage of family members reuniting for the first time continues to be emotional. In 2011, Taiwan also opened up to students from the mainland. Since then, young people from both sides of the strait have started to live, study, and think together. In this process, they started to gradually understand the differences in each other's backgrounds. They have started to develop mutual understanding, so that they can work together to build a more prosperous and peaceful world.

As we face new circumstances in cross-strait and regional relations, leaders from both sides should together work to display the political wisdom that has

8 The illusion is broken

carried us through over the years. We should search for new modes of cross-strait interactions with determination and patience. This will lay a more solid basis for long-term peace and stability in the cross-strait relationship.

(Focus Taiwan 2017)

Despite the overtures, one crucial question which arose in the months following her inauguration was whether Beijing would insist that the Tsai administration go beyond her reference to the 1992 talks and abide by the so-called "1992 consensus" (九二共識) and "one China" (一個中國) framework. More construct than an actual consensus, and a term which former KMT legislator Su Chi (蘇起) admitted he had coined in order to facilitate dialogue, the "1992 consensus" had become a prerequisite for cordial relations in the Taiwan Strait. Under the Ma Ying-jeou administration, Taipei had agreed to recognize the term, in return for which Beijing had permitted the relationship to develop along "peaceful" lines and ceased most, though never all, of its efforts to isolate Taiwan internationally. Beijing used that period of détente to sign various cross-Strait agreements with Taiwan and to tighten its neighbor's dependence on the Chinese economy so as to further its political aims. Back in Taiwan, President Ma was able to convince a majority of Taiwanese of the benefits of agreeing to the "consensus" by insisting that both sides had "different interpretations" of what "one China" means, and arguing that closer ties with China, and pacts such as the Economic Cooperation Framework Agreement (ECFA, 兩岸經濟合作架構協議), would help resuscitate Taiwan's moribund economy. After years of slow growth, exacerbated by the Asian Financial Crisis of the late 1990s and the global economic recession which deepened after the 11 September 2001 terrorist attacks in the United States, it was understandable that many voters in Taiwan would agree with the contention that closer economic ties with China, whose economy had grown by leaps and bounds while the rest of the world struggled, constituted wise policy.

As people would eventually realize, President Ma's gamble was not an unmitigated success. Although relations with China indeed seemed to have become more "peaceful" during his two terms in office (2008–2016), the economic benefits of closer ties were generally only felt by a small segment of the population, such as the tourism industry, which at its apex saw 4.1 million tourist arrivals from China in 2015. Moreover, the risks and costs of closer engagement with China – the rentier economy that primarily benefited the politically connected on both sides of the Taiwan Strait, economic over-reliance on China, and the feared erosion of Taiwan's sovereignty – became more significant as the relationship deepened. The "black box" nature of the negotiations surrounding cross-Strait agreements, not to mention the conflicts of interest that arose as negotiators on the Taiwanese side stood to benefit personally from those pacts, gave rise to apprehensions, which eventually led to the Sunflower Movement's occupation of the Legislative Yuan in March and April 2014 over the Cross-Strait Services Trade Agreement (CSSTA, 海峽兩岸服務貿易協議). As discussed in *Convergence*, the Sunflower Movement stemmed primarily from a loss of confidence in the Ma administration's willingness to respect democratic norms in its engagement with China, and the demand that the system as a whole be held accountable to ensure a return to good governance. The Sunflower Movement marked a turning point in the Ma presidency, and its aftereffects contributed largely to the outcome of the 2016 elections, by which time many of the movement's participants had joined political parties and run for election.

There was no doubt that whoever prevailed in the 2016 elections would have to adopt a more careful approach to cross-Strait relations. The fate of Hung Hsiu-chu (洪秀柱), the former KMT chairwoman and the party's initial presidential candidate in the elections, perfectly exemplified the new political environment in the wake of the 2014 occupation. Politically tone-deaf, Hung had behaved as if the Sunflower Movement had not occurred. Rather than move her party to a position that was more acceptable to the general public, Hung called for a relationship with Beijing that went beyond that which her predecessor had allowed, and in the process sparked an exodus from her party. Basically, her policy was to offer more of something that, after eight years, had proven a failure. And she did so at a time when China under Xi Jinping was becoming more self-confident and assertive. As a result, the KMT sidelined Hung at the eleventh hour and replaced her with a new candidate, Eric Chu, who hewed to a policy that, it was hoped, would have greater appeal among voters. It was, however, too late in the game, and it is unlikely that anyone could have saved the KMT from electoral defeat in 2016. Too much damage to the party's image had been done, and the public, after giving the blue camp eight years to demonstrate the wisdom of its policies, wanted a course correction.

Armed with the experience of her unsuccessful presidential bid in 2012, Tsai Ing-wen entered the 2016 presidential campaign with a major advantage. Her announcement, early on, that she would not seek to undo any of the agreements signed between Taiwan and China during the Ma years, her determination to abide by the "Republic of China constitutional order," and her emphasis on continuity and stability in cross-Strait relations were also determinant factors in her electoral success. Under her watch, Taiwan would not be a "troublemaker" and would seek cordial, pragmatic, and respectful relations with Beijing, language that would reassure skeptics of the DPP abroad as well as much of the blue camp in Taiwan.

Where Tsai departed from her predecessor was on the question of the "1992 consensus," which she refused to embrace. Cognizant of the slippery slope of the "one China," which lies at the core of the "consensus," added to the fact that, under Xi Jinping, it had become increasingly difficult to believe in the viability of "different interpretations" – a view that was exacerbated by developments in Hong Kong – Tsai knew that "one China" was no longer acceptable to the Taiwanese public. Trends in self-identification and support for unification, which, notwithstanding Beijing's supposed "goodwill," had shifted against Beijing under President Ma, made it clear that a new formula was necessary. Rather than negate the "consensus" altogether, however, Tsai stated that she recognized the "historical fact" that the two sides had held a round of negotiations in 1992 and in that spirit would build upon the accomplishments made since then while shelving differences as a way to continue building a relationship that is mutually beneficial, stable, and

10 The illusion is broken

predictable. Tsai's formula was therefore a test and an invitation for Beijing to meet her halfway.

Early on, there was reason to believe that Beijing would relax its insistence on the "consensus." A handful of academics in China had already called for pragmatism and stated publicly that Taiwan did not need to recognize the "1992 consensus" for relations to remain stable and constructive. For example, Zhang Nianchi (章念馳), a scholar at the Shanghai Institute for East Asia Studies and intellectual heir to former Association for Relations Across the Taiwan Straits (ARATS, 海峡两岸关系协会) chairman Wang Daohan (汪道涵), had told the *Washington Post* that Beijing "shouldn't be unsatisfied with her not accepting the 1992 consensus. Tsai was chosen by Taiwanese people, and that is a reality we have to face, too." Another Chinese academic, this time speaking on condition of anonymity, was quoted in the same article saying, "maintaining the current relationship is what really matters, not the 1992 consensus" (Denyer 2016). In other words, what Tsai argued, and what some intellectuals in China averred, was that a constructive relationship between Taiwan and China was possible even in the absence of the overly symbolic "1992 consensus."

Moreover, it was believed that the two sides had trusted emissaries who, quietly, ensured that the right signals were sent in public statements, even if this meant that the public had to read between the lines to see what was going on.

It was in that context, therefore, that the new president delivered her address on 20 May. It was perceived as a test, and a few hours later, after the streets in front of the Presidential Office had been cleared, Beijing passed its judgment: President Tsai had provided an "incomplete answer." In a statement, the State Council's Taiwan Affairs Office (TAO, 國務院台灣事務辦公室) said that Tsai's speech had been "vague" and provided "an incomplete answer sheet," adding that Tsai "didn't come up with specific ways to ensure peaceful and stable development of the cross-Strait relations . . . She was vague on the nature of cross-Strait relations that concerns people on both sides the most" (Peng 2016).

"Only by confirming adherence to the common political foundation of the '1992 consensus' that embodies the 'one China' principle can cross-Strait affairs authorities continue their regular communication," Ma Xiaoguang (馬曉光), a TAO spokesman, declared one day after the inauguration (Chung 2016).

As developments in the months that followed would make clear, Beijing was continuing to insist on the symbolism of the "1992 consensus," not so much because of the language it contained, but rather because recognition of the "consensus" by Taipei was the necessary genuflection by what Beijing regards as the weaker, and by necessity subservient, party in the cross-Strait hierarchy. By seeking to reformulate the symbols that serve as the foundations of that relationship, President Tsai was overstepping the boundaries as defined by Beijing. And in doing so, she was challenging the leadership in Beijing by treating it *as an equal*, which in the CCP worldview was unacceptable. Symbolism and hierarchy trumped pragmatism, even if this meant a return to tensions in the Taiwan Strait. To permit the emergence of an equal interlocutor in what China regards as its peripheries would violate the core principles of the Chinese imperial architecture. From that point on, President Tsai and her DPP were anathema, a band of "separatists" who needed to be taught a lesson for their obstinacy. The "1992 consensus" became a convenient instrument and provided the justification for the crackdown that ensued.

Taiwan and China could arguably have a cordial relationship without the "1992 consensus," which serves little other purpose than to suggest that an agreement was reached between the two sides. The "consensus" is not an agency, nor it is a mechanism or even an *ad hoc* working group. In other words, it has no power, no institutional value, and is by no means indispensable to constructive dialogue between the two sides. It only became an impediment to good relations because Beijing insisted on adherence to its symbolism. The Chinese academics who expressed the view that it was not necessary to recognize the "consensus" were correct. But soon after 20 May, those pragmatic voices – the voices that will be needed if Taiwan and China are ever to find a way out of this political impasse – were soon silenced as the intellectual environment in China tightened amid a renewed ideological campaign meant to bolster Xi Jinping's and the CCP's control over every aspect of Chinese society.

Despite her efforts to foster a workable relationship from the outset, President Tsai quickly found herself in a situation that was reminiscent of that which Chen Shui-bian had found himself in during the first term of his presidency. Like her, Chen had made early concessions to Beijing, including his "three noes and one without" (四不一沒有) during his inaugural speech on 20 May 2000. What Chen promised then – no declaration of independence, no change from Republic of China to Republic of Taiwan, no inclusion of the special state-to-state (特殊的國 與國的關係) formulation[1] in the ROC constitution, and no referendum on unification or independence – was in many aspects similar to what President Tsai was now offering, although in her case President Tsai also vowed not to undo any of the agreements that had been signed between the two sides during the Ma presidency. (Chen's "one without," under which Taipei would refrain from abolishing the National Unification Council [國家統一委員會], was broken in 2006 after the relationship had soured. Once it became clear that Beijing would not reciprocate its goodwill, the Chen administration also eventually flirted with referenda, which caused apprehensions in Washington, D.C., and in the process made it easier for Beijing to depict Taiwan as the "troublemaker" in the Taiwan Strait.)

Another reason why Beijing decided to crack down on President Tsai was the greater clarity with which she characterized the current status of Taiwan. Given, as mentioned above, that the power imbalance in the Taiwan Strait has allowed Beijing to move the goalposts and constantly redefine the "status quo" between Taiwan and China, it should not be surprising that a new president would state more clearly what Taiwan is, and what it is not. Under Tsai, gone was the ambiguity of "one China, different interpretations," which hitherto had allowed both sides to "agree to disagree." While one can argue for the utility of ambiguity, that tool of diplomacy lost much of its currency as China under Xi increasingly made it clear that there is only one China – the People's Republic of China. Rhetorically, this has always

12 The illusion is broken

been Beijing's position, and we should note that references to "different interpretations" were only made on the Taiwan side under Ma. However, things had changed during Xi: China's behavior and assertiveness were whittling away at the illusion that two Chinas were perhaps overlapping. Whatever ambiguity had existed in the past had died with the emergence of Xi Jinping in 2012 as the leader of China.

Needing to assuage the fears of the Taiwanese public and to set the tone for her incoming administration, Tsai therefore had little choice but to dispense with ambiguity, which in the process took her closer to the "special state-to-state" formulation. Under this view, Taiwan exists as a sovereign state whose official name is the Republic of China. Moreover, despite a constitution that continues to lay claim to the entirety of the Chinese territory prior to 1949, Taipei has made it clear that the territory of Taiwan/ROC is limited to Taiwan proper and its outlying islands. This also includes the ROC claim on the South China Sea, which overlaps with Beijing's, although few Taiwanese today believe in the viability of those claims and most recognize it is a legacy of an old constitution and that it is intrinsically related to cross-Strait relations: abandoning the claim to the South China Sea would be perceived by Beijing as a change to the ROC constitution and therefore a move toward *de jure* independence, which under the Anti-Secession Law (反分裂國家法), adopted on 14 March 2005, could constitute justification for military intervention by the People's Liberation Army (PLA, 中國人民解放軍). As part of her concessions to Beijing, President Tsai has retained the ROC's official designation and symbols, and thereby maintained an illusion that often is a source of confusion within the international community, not to mention a source of resentment among the deep-green elements within Taiwanese society.

Although relations in the Taiwan Strait have entered what could be called a "deep freeze" since 2016, we should point out that this state of affairs was probably inevitable, regardless of who sits in the Presidential Office. Barring capitulation on Taiwan's side, it is difficult to imagine an administration in Taipei that could come to power via democratic means while advocating Beijing's position, which has become more rigid over the years. The principal reason for an inevitable clash – a clash that never ceased, even at the height of rapprochement during the Ma presidency – is nationalism and the different histories that have shaped the Taiwanese and Chinese nations.

Despite the CCP's use (and abuse) of history, China's claim of inalienable sovereignty over Taiwan is highly contentious. Beijing's annexationist ideology flies in the face of the more than one century of separate rule, first under 50 years of Japanese colonialism (1895–1945) and subsequently KMT rule after World War II and following its defeat in the Civil War in 1949. In Beijing's view, the PRC is a successor state to the ROC and therefore the ROC ceased to exist in 1949. However, having first transplanted itself on Taiwan, where it ruled with ruthlessness for decades, the ROC was eventually transformed and in many respects absorbed by Taiwan, leading to phases of liberalization and, in the 1980s, democratization. Thus, the state/regime continued to exist outside what was now the PRC, and over time was reborn, imperfect and sometimes bound by old reflexes, as democratic Taiwan.

As will be discussed in subsequent chapters and more directly in Chapter 9, a sizable number of people in the green camp have a deep resentment for any notion that the ROC is synonymous or coterminous with Taiwan, and continue to regard the former as an "illegitimate colonial regime" that needs to be eradicated. And indeed, many of the legacies of the ROC/KMT party-state still exist today in government institutions and the education system, for example. But gradually, those have been upended, and the everyday experience and way of life of people living in Taiwan today are a distant echo of the ROC that existed seven, or even four decades ago. To argue otherwise, as some Taiwanese do, is to deny the extraordinary achievements that have been made by Taiwan in the past four decades, the results of which constitute Taiwan's strongest defense against the claims of authoritarian China. Although some have disagreed on this point, one could argue that Beijing today is facing not *one* form of independence in Taiwan but rather *two* (Cole 2016b). Those two independence movements – *taidu* (台獨) and *huadu* (華獨) – while overlapping on most matters (e.g., the mores and democracy that define Taiwan today), will exist simultaneously as long as Taiwanese society does not resolve, once and for all, the question of whether the ROC and Taiwan are (1) now coterminous or (2) mutually exclusive and fundamentally antithetical, resulting in a prolonged "mainlander" versus "Taiwanese" ethnic divide. While that divide has more traction among older generations of people in Taiwan who went through first contact with "mainlanders" after World War II, and whereas "ethnicity" is no longer regarded as a determinant factor in Taiwan's national identity and membership in its polity, the alienation that results from this lingering phenomenon continues to undermine Taiwan's ability to formulate a coherent strategy to counter China.

Despite the unresolved issues of ethnicity in Taiwan, decades of interactions between the citizens of Taiwan and democratic allies elsewhere have indubitably contributed to Taiwan's idiosyncratic existence, so much so that the country can now be regarded "as intrinsically modern and Western as are Sweden, France, and Canada." According to Bill Emmott (2017), the former editor in chief at *The Economist*, that is because Taiwan shares with those countries "not geography, not history, but an idea."

And that idea is democracy.

For all the divisions that continue to plague Taiwanese politics, it is clear that democracy is now intrinsic to the way of life of its people, no matter which party they identify with. Even parties like the New Party (新黨) and the China Unification Promotion Party (CUPP, 中華統一促進黨), which are decidedly pro-unification, pro-Beijing and for all intents and purposes anti-democracy, must operate in a multiparty, democratic environment by participating in the battle of ideas and fielding candidates in elections (though, as will be shown in Chapter 2, the principal role of those two parties, and the CUPP more specifically, has very little to do with electoral politics and is more related to China's "sharp power" activities). The CUPP and NP's unenvious performance in recent elections is clear evidence that desire for unification has little traction in Taiwan, and that any of the major parties that embraced such an ideology, as Hung Hsiu-chiu came close to

14 The illusion is broken

doing before she was removed as the KMT candidate in late 2015, would ensure defeat in future elections.

The democratic ideal runs deep. A poll, conducted by the National Chengchi University Election Study Center on behalf of the Taiwan Foundation for Democracy (TFD, 臺灣民主基金會), whose results were first unveiled in April 2018, revealed that despite dissatisfaction with the health of Taiwan's democracy, 94 percent of respondents said living in a democratic society is "important," and 65.8 percent said it is "very important." Close to 70 percent agreed with the statement that "There exist some problems in democracy, but it is still the best political system" (that number rose to 86.2 percent in the 20–39 age category, up from 75.9 percent in 2011). Also, nearly 70 percent of Taiwanese respondents in the same survey said they would be willing to fight to defend their nation's democratic way of life if China attempted to annex it by force (TFD 2018).

Ironically, the emergence and consolidation of the shared value of democracy over the years has often gone unacknowledged due to the scorched-earth battles that are waged, in part due to electoral politics, by the green and blue camps. However, with the exception of CUPP and NP members and adherents to even more marginal political parties, an overwhelming majority of Taiwanese agrees that the rules of the game are democratic, and that a reversal would not be in Taiwan's best interest. While the CCP and some of its apologists in Western academia have proposed an alternative to democracy, namely Chinese "meritocracy" (Bell 2016), and although the virtues of that alternative model have been discussed on university campuses in Taiwan, recent developments in China — chief among them the removal of term limits on the presidency and the elevation of Xi Jinping to near-emperor status — have highlighted the limits, and destabilizing effects, of this model.

Furthermore, the experience of Hong Kong since Retrocession in 1997 has shown the consequences of annexation by China and brought clarity to the effects that the "one country, two systems" (一國兩制) formula proposed by Beijing would have on Taiwan's democratic institutions. It would be dangerously naive to believe that Beijing would somehow show greater flexibility with a Taiwan Special Administrative Region (SAR) than it has thus far with Hong Kong SAR, where civil liberties, freedom of expression, and even border controls have been eroded as the central government in Beijing shows who is ultimately the arbitrator of all Chinese citizens. The centrality of governance was moreover reinforced on 1 July 2015 with the passage by the National People's Congress (中華人民共和國全國人民代表大會) of the New National Security Law (中華人民共和國國家安全法), which among other things extended highly restrictive domestic laws in China proper to the "peripheries," including Macau, Hong Kong and, in theory at least, Taiwan. If the erosion of freedoms and autonomy of the Hong Kong Special Administrative Region (HKSAR) wasn't enough to convince the Taiwanese that Beijing will never countenance true autonomy, the chaos that engulfed the city in 2019, not to mention the growing evidence of mass human rights violations in the Muslim-majority Xinjiang Autonomous Region (新疆維吾爾自治區), with claims of rampant re-education camps and social controls that belong in a dystopian

The road to the "deep freeze" **15**

science-fiction novel, are providing a stark reminder of the fundamentally racist, and irrevocably abusive, nature of the CCP, and of what could happen in Taiwan should it be annexed by China.

All of this has contributed to a legitimate desire for self-determination on the part of the Taiwanese. Admittedly a Western concept, this idea also explains why most Taiwanese (with the exception of aborigines, of course) see no contradiction between embracing their ethnic, linguistic and cultural origins in China on the one hand, and a desire for a sovereign, Westphalian and democratic state of their own. As Syaru Shirley Lin (林夏如) observes in her book *Taiwan's China Dilemma* (2016),

> After more than twenty years of democratization, contestation over Taiwanese national identity has largely been resolved; the identity that has emerged is no longer defined on the basis of ethnicity, but rather on common residence on Taiwan and a strong commitment to Taiwanese civic values and institutions, which are very different from China's.

This is what the political scientist and philosopher Yaron Ezrahi has termed *political imaginaries* – the "configurations, imagined authorities, individual and collective agencies, actions, events, and situations that have acquired regulatory powers and causal links to processes of shaping, enacting, and maintaining the political order" (2012).

Put more simply, it is the combination of principles and aspirations, such as personal freedoms, equality and liberty, judicial independence, and opposition to tyrannical powers, that defines Taiwan today and which sets it apart from other nations across Asia. In fact, Taiwan's democratic achievements, and the state of what is defined as permissible by society, becomes all the more apparent when it is contrasted with other democracies in the region, such as Japan and India, which remain far more deeply attached to concepts such as social stability and harmony. None of this, we should add, supports in any way a denial of the existence, or a challenge to the legitimacy, of the People's Republic of China, where the polity of 1.3 billion people also has at its disposal the means to define its *political imaginaries*. For the great majority, if not all, of the Taiwanese, the PRC is a recognized fact of life, a large neighbor which serves both as a source of risks *and* opportunities. The embracing of a distinct, sovereign Taiwan is an *affirmation*; it is not a *denial* of China. In other words, it is non-zero-sum – at least for the Taiwanese side. However, the concept of self-determination and the Westphalian nation-state clashes directly with the "civilizational" worldview that has existed in China for centuries, and which does not allow for the emergence of "equal" states in what Beijing considers to be its historical territory or sphere of influence. Thus, for China, the equation is very much zero-sum.

Consequently, despite all the propaganda, "peaceful unification" ceased long ago to exist as a feasible scenario for the Taiwan Strait. The contradictions between the two sides, and the diametrically opposed values that govern the two societies, shared language and cultural elements notwithstanding, have ensured that unification

16 The illusion is broken

would not be "peaceful," but would rather be coercive, overwhelmingly one-sided in the inevitable concessions made, and would by necessity be transformative of the way of life which Taiwanese of all colors and persuasions currently enjoy. As discussed in *Convergence*, the CCP has put itself in a corner on the Taiwan "question" and is now unable to de-escalate, lest this be viewed by hardline elements in the Party as weakness. Another consequence of this is that Beijing has left itself no room to propose alternatives to "one country, two systems," which itself has little, if any, appeal among the Taiwanese. However, making a better, more flexible offer to Taiwan would invite similar demands by other regions of China, which could prove destabilizing and threaten the regime's ability to keep the country together.

As a result of all this, it does not really matter which party governs Taiwan today: whether the DPP or KMT occupies high office, Taiwanese society is overwhelmingly opposed to unification and will not hesitate to use the full provisions of democracy – from retribution at the polls to a politicized civil society that takes action whenever the government is perceived to be failing in its mandate – to ensure the continued survival of the democratic state. To win elections, and in order to maintain the support of voters, governments in Taiwan are thereby compelled to aim for the middle ground, as Tsai successfully did in 2016. This process not only eliminates extremists on both sides, it also makes it impossible for a government – any government – to collaborate with China toward realizing unification against the public's will. When the Ma administration was seen to be flirting with that idea, the Sunflower Movement struck and the repercussions of that adventurism were very much felt in the elections in 2014 and 2016.

While Beijing has sought to blame the current "deep freeze" in the Taiwan Strait on President Tsai's supposed intransigence on the "1992 consensus," in reality the Chinese leadership understood well before Tsai's election victory that it could not achieve its political objectives as long as Taiwan remained a democracy. For the "firewall" which democracy confers upon Taiwan acts as the regulator of cross-Strait relations and limits the ability of anyone in government to dictate terms which are unappealing to the large majority of Taiwanese. That is why, well before the 2016 elections, Beijing had already begun to bypass central government institutions and sought to deal directly with compromised local officials, the private sector, and ideological partners such as the NP and CUPP proxies. Although it won't admit it and continues to argue that only a small group of "separatist elements" within the DPP remain opposed to the "historical trend" of the unification of the Chinese people – to say otherwise would be to admit that the entire CCP approach to Taiwan has been a failure – Beijing also realized some time ago that it cannot win the hearts and minds of the Taiwanese, nor can it "buy" enough of them to generate momentum for unification. One reason for this is that China remains largely incompetent when it comes to "soft power." Despite investing billions of dollars in recent years building a global media presence and acquiring film studios in Hollywood, the propagandistic nature of China's "soft power" initiatives remains starkly evident, so much so that it is counterproductive. Admittedly, China's "soft power" and alternative to liberal democracy may have appeal with underdeveloped

The road to the "deep freeze" **17**

countries in need of rapid infrastructure investment and guided development, that appeal is almost entirely powerless when it is wielded against modern, developed industrialized societies like Taiwan. Unable to use its model to win over adherents in Taiwan, China has instead used what is now known as "sharp power" – a combination of activities that seek to pierce, penetrate, or perforate the political and information environments in the targeted countries – to shape the environment in its favor (NED 2017). Part of this endeavor involves undermining democratic institutions and eroding public support for them. "Sharp power" is one of the many punitive strategies discussed in the next chapter.

Some would argue, as former president Ma did on 21 August 2018 after Taiwan lost its fourth official diplomatically, El Salvador, to China since Tsai had assumed office, that the Tsai administration should recognize the "1992 consensus" in order to repair the relationship. The same people would also claim that Tsai's "obstinacy" has cost Taiwan too much and that a more deferential approach to Beijing would help resolve the matter.

If we take a short-term view of the cross-Strait situation, it is indeed possible that a shift in Taipei's stance on the "consensus" could reduce the pressure that China has exerted on Taiwan, and perhaps even reactivate the "diplomatic truce" that existed under Ma, under which both sides agreed to refrain from efforts to lure each other's allies. However, the longer view of all this – and China always thinks in the long-term – should alert us to the inevitable fact that, "1992 consensus" or not, Beijing's ultimate aim is the subjugation and annexation of Taiwan. Whoever governs Taiwan, DPP or KMT, should operate with this in mind. Therefore, while yielding to Beijing's demands could reduce tensions for a while, such an outcome would be temporary, a mere hiatus in China's strategy of unification. Put differently, recognizing the "1992 consensus" would simply shift Beijing's attention to other areas where it can erode Taiwan's sovereign existence and democracy, just as it did during the Ma era via economic and social means. From a DPP perspective, giving in to Beijing on the issue of the "consensus" would engage the administration on a slippery slope: seeing an opening, Beijing would simply begin to ask more concessions on other issues.

As we shall see in Chapter 4, the current "deep freeze" was inevitable. If it comes as a surprise to some, that is because they have been asking the wrong question. Notwithstanding the rhetoric of unification, of the rejuvenation of the Chinese nation and the rectification of "historical grievances," the fact of the matter is that China's claim to Taiwan is all about territory and the CCP's need to bolster its legitimacy as the only possible architect of China as a great global power. Everything else is mere justification. Given this, whosoever governs in Taiwan, and regardless of how many concessions an administration makes to Beijing, such as acknowledging the "1992 consensus," China's hunger for territory will remain the same. Anyone who argues otherwise should remember that even when the Ma administration was in office and recognized the "consensus," Beijing still acted unilaterally in some instances, such as with the surprise declaration of the M503 route (M503航路事件) on 12 January 2015 which ostensibly caught Ma administration

18 The illusion is broken

officials unawares (LY 2015), or the deporting to China by Kenyan authorities of 45 Taiwanese nationals suspected of telecom fraud, over the protests of Taiwanese officials, in April 2016 (Blanchard 2016).

Beijing's insistence on the "1992 consensus" can only be described as utilitarian: it is part of the regime's hopes of winning without a fight; barring that, it is a means by which to create pressure toward unification while Beijing buys time and strengthens itself so that, should use of force be deemed necessary at some point, it will have the capability to do so, and will have shaped the environment in a way that is conducive to such actions.

Xi Jinping's intransigence on the "1992 consensus" is also meant to serve as a lesson for other restive parts of China. It is meant to indicate that persuasion will come first; failing that, Beijing will not hesitate to engage in coercion. Once again, the crisis in Hong Kong in 2019 is a clear example of this dynamic. Beijing's unyielding position on the matter is also about saving the CCP from its own rhetoric. Having insisted on the indispensability of the "1992 consensus" for dialogue across the Taiwan Strait, the Party cannot back down. Suddenly showing more flexibility on the issue would be to admit that Beijing's Taiwan policy has failed. It would concede that all the "goodwill" that China has extended to Taiwan, especially during the Ma administration, has not yielded the expected results promised by a supposedly infallible CCP. And it would constitute an admission that economic determinism, the idea that economic incentives will eventually shape minds and translate into political change, has failed, which could have serious ramifications for stability in territories such as Tibet and Xinjiang.

Throughout the many phases of cross-Strait relations, China has stubbornly stuck to its Taiwan policy because that policy is a dogma; any change would be a repudiation of ideology, which, like the party, is sacrosanct. It is the same phenomenon that, for example, made it impossible for Deng Xiaoping (鄧小平) to frame the reforms he initiated in the 1980s, after he had prevailed upon the Gang of Four, as criticism of Mao's policy during the catastrophic Great Leap Forward and the chaos of the Cultural Revolution. The ideological rigidity that is so characteristic of the CCP makes adaptation to new situations difficult, especially on what the Party regards as "core issues." Already rigid by nature, the Party has only become more so under Secretary-General Xi.

The continuation of China's Taiwan policy was emphasized again when Xi Jinping presented his report to the 19th Party Congress in Beijing on 18 October 2017 (EEO 2017), during which he said that "We will resolutely uphold national sovereignty and territorial integrity and will never tolerate a repeat of the historical tragedy of a divided country. All activities of splitting the motherland will be resolutely opposed by all the Chinese people." He then added,

> We have firm will, full confidence, and sufficient capability to defeat any form of Taiwan independence secession plot. We will never allow any person, any organization, or any political party to split any part of the Chinese territory from China at any time or in any form.

The road to the "deep freeze" **19**

This was followed by a more direct reference to policy continuity, in the form of six points:

(1) The guiding principle (*fangzhen*) of peaceful reunification [sic] of Taiwan according to the "one country, two systems" formula and the eight-point proposal[2] enunciated by Jiang Zemin (江澤民) in 1995.
(2) Adherence to the "one China" principle, the key point of which is that the territory of Taiwan is within the sovereign territory of China.
(3) Strong opposition to separatism and Taiwan independence.
(4) Willingness to have dialogue, exchanges, consultations, and negotiations with any political party that adheres to the "one China" principle.
(5) Stress on the idea that the people on Taiwan and people on the mainland [sic] are "brothers and sisters of the same blood."
(6) Establishing a connection between unification and the cause of "the great rejuvenation of the Chinese nation."

Interestingly, the last omitted three points had hitherto constituted China's approach to the Taiwan "issue." Those were:

(7) Placing hopes on the Taiwan people as a force to help bring about unification.
(8) A promise that progress toward unification, and unification itself, will bring material benefits to Taiwan.
(9) An expression of "utmost sincerity" by Beijing toward the unification project.

As Richard Bush (2017), a former chairman of the American Institute in Taiwan (AIT) now at the Brookings Institution in Washington, D.C., observed, the removal of the seventh point was most worrying, as it suggested that popular opinion in Taiwan would no longer be taken into consideration. Needless to say, this would be as clear an admission that democracy was standing in the way of Beijing's aspirations as one could get.

All of this, therefore, means that real, durable de-escalation is probably impossible. Consequently, Taiwan has two choices: either it gives up, or it continues to defy China. The first will ensure lesser hostility but would inevitably result in a loss of sovereignty and the high likelihood, as the Hong Kong example has shown, that the freedoms and liberties that Taiwanese have come to expect and which define who they are would come under pressure and face curtailment. The defiant path, meanwhile, has no assurance of success and makes it certain that the relationship will remain conflictual for the foreseeable future. The Tsai administration has adopted the latter option, and despite the costs that this has entailed for Taiwan – suspended cross-Strait communication, the loss of official diplomatic allies, blocked participation in multilateral organizations, threatening PLA exercises, and an assault on Taiwan's visibility in the private sector, among other things – the Taiwanese public has, in general, so far stood by her administration's decisions. It remains to be seen whether the Taiwanese will remain willing to pay the price. That decision

20 The illusion is broken

was made in the 2020 elections, when Taiwanese had a chance to use their votes to give Tsai a second term or – Beijing's preferred outcome – replace her with someone else. Chinese pressure could either convince the Taiwanese that all the pain is not worth it and that some accommodation should be considered, even if this creates uncertainty regarding Taiwan's future; conversely, continuing pressure on Taiwan could spark a rally-round-the-flag phenomenon whereby Taiwanese decide to deepen their resistance to China, come what may, as happened during the 1995–96 Third Taiwan Strait Crisis. The aforementioned TFD poll seems to suggest this is the case.

Taiwanese voted for a leader in the 2016 elections whose stance on China, pragmatic yet more resolute in its assertiveness on matters of sovereignty and democracy, was already well established. The Taiwanese public made a choice, and so did President Tsai in her refusal to defer to Beijing's wishes on the "1992 consensus" and "one China." President Tsai sought to meet Xi Jinping halfway by making some concessions on the "status quo" and expressing her willingness to build upon to cross-Strait political infrastructure that had been erected by her predecessor. Those concessions were not without political risk, as her administration's retention of the name and symbols associated with the ROC, its refusal to consider calls for a referendum on name rectification, and her "soft" response to Chinese pressure has alienated a segment of the green camp. And yet, faced with her decision, Xi Jinping made his own choice. Despite the belief expressed by some moderates in China that Beijing should show some flexibility, Chinese authorities remained adamant that Taipei had to recognize the "consensus." Impatient and increasingly authoritarian, Xi exhibited stubbornness, which resulted in increased tensions in bilateral ties. (As we will see later, the Chinese leader's impatience on many other issues has also created a more difficult external environment for China and sparked criticism in some segments of the Chinese intelligentsia.) President Tsai's signal that she was willing to meet President Xi, as long as there were no preconditions, understandably went unanswered.

Xi's reaction constituted a departure of sorts from Beijing's grand strategy since Deng Xiaoping. Before him, Beijing normally made it a virtue to "not let specific disagreements hamper the development of a sound overall relationship" (Khan 2018). Such flexibility had arguably paid dividends in the cross-Strait relationship since 2008, even when, under President Ma, the two sides still had disagreements on specific issues. In the past, this ability to focus on the greater picture had allowed China, for example, to develop healthy relationships with the U.S. even if it vehemently disagreed with Washington's continued arms sales to Taiwan or the Taiwan Relations Act (TRA). The same applies to its relations with Japan and other countries. By keeping its eyes on the larger picture, Beijing would act pragmatically. Consequently, despite its disagreement with the U.S. on Taiwan, China was nevertheless able to secure Washington's support for its accession to the World Trade Organization (WTO).

One reason for Xi's breaking with past practices could be that, more than his predecessors, he understands that Beijing cannot make more strategic gains with Taiwan by setting aside its dispute on the specifics (the "1992 consensus"), because

The road to the "deep freeze" **21**

the only thing that Beijing wants from it – unification – is something that the Taiwanese people will not give. Another possibility is that Taiwan tends to elicit much more emotional reactions within the CCP, as became clear during the Third Taiwan Strait Crisis, when the PLA bracketed Taiwan with missile tests. This form of coercion prompted a humiliating intervention by the U.S. military, which dispatched two carrier battle groups to the region, and had counterproductive effects on the electoral outcome Beijing was seeking to manipulate. Taiwan is a trigger point for the CCP, and the associated emotions can mean that China will occasionally forget its grand strategy. While Beijing appeared to have learned a lesson from the 1995–96 missile crisis, under Xi amnesia appears to have set in.

So an era ended. After eight years of deepening ties and exchanges which, in Beijing's view, supported its political objectives on Taiwan, and mere months after Xi and Ma had made history by holding a highly publicized, if merely symbolic, summit in Singapore, Beijing closed the door shut. It suspended the "hotline" that had been activated during the Ma years which had served as a channel for direct communication between Taiwan's Mainland Affairs Council (MAC, 大陸委員會) and the TAO. One month after President Tsai's inauguration, An Fengshan (安峰山), spokesman for the TAO, said that "The cross-Strait communication mechanism has been suspended because Taiwan did not recognize the '1992 Consensus,' the political basis for the 'one China' principle" (TAO 2016). He continued: "The position of peaceful development of cross-Strait relations remains the same. It is the Taiwan side that has changed this situation. The new Taiwan authorities have not yet acknowledged the '1992 consensus' or agree with its core meaning, which has shaken the political foundations of cross-Strait interactions and the communication mechanism between the TAO and MAC, and negotiations between ARATS and its Taiwanese counterpart, the Straits Exchange Foundation (SEF, 海峽交流基金會). The shutdown of the mechanism is therefore entirely the fault of the Taiwan side. People cannot help but ask: Why should the Taiwan side change the status quo of peaceful development of cross-Strait relations since 2008? What is the purpose?"

Part of that decision was meant to signal that Beijing would not recognize the legitimacy of any agency that is associated with the central government in Taipei. Beijing's directives to Chinese media on how to refer to the Taiwanese government ("authorities") and president ("leader"), and so on, were also meant to eliminate, in the Chinese view, any notion of the existence of a central government in Taiwan. Although trusted aides would be used by both sides to carry messages back and forth, the "deep freeze" also affected academic exchanges. It became increasingly difficult for Taiwanese deemed to be close to the Tsai administration to travel to China, and Beijing also imposed restrictions on Chinese academics seeking to participate at conferences in Taiwan. Track 2, or semiofficial exchanges, between the aforementioned ARATS and the SEF, as well as exchanges at the municipal level, did not end altogether, but also became less regular and more ad hoc. Thus, in a time of rising tensions, reduced dialogue encouraged miscommunication and made miscalculation likelier.

22 The illusion is broken

Ironically, and in a sign that Beijing could be pragmatic when needed, it was to the very same communication channel that the TAO turned to contact its Taiwanese counterpart when it sought assistance following a deadly bus crash on the No. 2 National Highway in Taoyuan County in July 2016, in which 24 Chinese tourists lost their lives.

Throughout all this, Beijing may also have sought to recreate the perception that Taiwan is a "troublemaker" and thereby damage Taiwan's reputation within the international community. Such a tactic had paid dividends during the Chen Shui-bian era and Beijing appears to have hoped that President Tsai's image would suffer a similar fate. But if that was the intention, that endeavor has failed – in fact, as we shall see in Chapters 5, 6 and 7, it appears to have backfired. Although some international media retained old habits and reflexes which, often out of ignorance, inadvertently put Taiwan at a disadvantage – for example, the tendency to report anything that Taiwan does as "angering" China, or references to "re-unification" and "the mainland," all of which unjustly impose strict parameters in the discussion on the conflict – sympathy for democratic Taiwan has trumped any effort by Beijing to place Taiwan in an unfavorable light.

Much of this, as we shall discuss later, can be attributed to a markedly changed global context from the first decade of the 21st century, due in large part to Chinese assertiveness following the 2008 economic crisis and the emergence of Xi Jinping, whose style of leadership has largely dispensed with the more cautious and patient approach to China's external relations. Under, Xi's predecessor, the "dull" Hu Jintao (胡錦濤), it was still possible to believe in a peaceful Chinese rise, or to hold on to hopes that greater engagement would somehow help democratize China or, at a minimum, ensure it behaved as a responsible stakeholder. As long as such hopes existed, it was possible for democracies to justify engagement with China and to regard democratic Taiwan as an irritant whose aspirations risked derailing more important relationships. Under Xi, such hopes have been dashed. Rather than become more like us, China has used its accumulated power to challenge the rules of the international order while deepening authoritarian controls, not to mention the removal on the limits on the president's term – implemented by Deng to avoid the emergence of a new dictator for life – at the 19th Party Congress.

As Khan wrote in his recent book on China's external relations, "dullness can be a virtue – and it was a virtue that would shine all the brighter in the days of Xi Jinping."

Due to all these developments, sympathy for China (or for the CCP, to be more exact) has dwindled; conversely, the rise of a revisionist authoritarian regime whose influence, what with the Belt and Road Initiative (一帶一路), its so-called "sharp power," Confucius Institutes, cyberattacks and high-tech industrial espionage, seems to extend to every corner of the planet, has contributed to a more positive image in global media, within academia and in government circles, of peaceful and democratic Taiwan.

Moreover, Beijing's constant assault on the island-nation has had the unintended effect of generating more sympathy for Taiwan while ensuing more sustained coverage of cross-Strait relations. Due to renewed tensions in the Taiwan Strait and a greater collective awareness of the challenges that are posed by an assertive China, Taiwan has become "newsworthy" again, which has been reflected in the number of news articles and commentaries that are written about it, as well as in the number of foreign correspondents who are posted to Taiwan (that number is still too low, but it has improved slightly from the Ma Ying-jeou years, when several bureaus downsized or closed shop altogether). In other words, having invested billions of dollars in its "soft power" and public diplomacy, Beijing's behavior only succeeded in generating more sympathy for the target it hoped to isolate. Democracy, once again, has proven a solid ally of the embattled Asian nation of 23 million souls.

In a narrative that has been written since 2016, Tsai remains the hero for most, while Xi is more and more the villain. Of course this does not prevent the international community from seeking to increase its trade relations with the market of 1.3 billion consumers, or to argue that on many of the challenges the world faces today, from global warming to weapons of mass destruction, China's cooperation is indispensable.

Xi could have taken a different approach to cross-Strait relations, but he chose not to. Under his watch, Beijing has adopted an overwhelmingly confrontational approach, which in turn has emboldened not only the more extremist elements in the Party, but also an increasingly nationalistic Chinese society that instigates its own bottom-up pressures on the CCP to adopt a more hawkish stance on Taiwan. Having decided on this path, the Chinese leadership made de-escalation nearly impossible. The outcome of this decision, made hours after President Tsai's inauguration speech, is the subject of the next chapter.

Notes

1 Tsai Ing-wen is said to have helped then-president Lee Teng-hui (李登輝) draft the "special state-to-state relationship" formulation. Here I refrain from referring to this as a "theory," as it is often described in academic works and in the media, in response to the China's "one China" principle. Using "theory" on one side and "principle" on the other gives unwarranted legitimacy to the claims made on the Chinese side, while relegating Taiwan's claim to statehood to a mere "theory."
2 See http://en.people.cn/90002/92080/92129/6271625.pdf

References

Bell, Daniel (2016) *The China Model: Political Meritocracy and the Limits of Democracy*, Princeton: Princeton University Press.

Blanchard, Ben (2016) "Taiwanese Deported from Kenya 'Suspected of Fraud in China'," *Reuters*, 13 April. www.reuters.com/article/us-china-taiwan-kenya-idUSKCN0XA05E.

Bush, Richard (2017) "What Xi Jinping Said About Taiwan at the 19th Party Congress," *Brookings Institution*, 19 October. www.brookings.edu/blog/order-from-chaos/2017/10/19/what-xi-jinping-said-about-taiwan-at-the-19th-party-congress/.

Chung, Lawrence (2016) "Beijing Threatens to Suspend Talks with Taipei Until Tsai Ing-wen Acknowledges '1992 Consensus'," *South China Morning Post*, 21 May. www.scmp.com/news/china/policies-politics/article/1949425/beijing-threatens-suspend-talks-taipei-until-tsai-ing.

24 The illusion is broken

Cole, J. Michael (2016a) "Taiwan's First Female President Walks Tightrope as She Takes Office," *CNN*, 20 May. https://edition.cnn.com/2016/05/19/asia/taiwan-president-tsai-ing-wen-takes-office/index.html.

Cole, J. Michael (2016b) "China Faces Not One but Two Forces for Independence in Taiwan," *Asia Dialogue*, 22 March. http://theasiadialogue.com/2016/03/22/90972/.

Denyer, Simon (2016) "Opposition Leader's Landslide Win in Taiwan Puts Onus on China to Respond," *Washington Post*, 17 January. www.washingtonpost.com/world/asia_pacific/opposition-leaders-landslide-win-in-taiwan-puts-onus-on-china-to-respond/2016/01/17/1f2fec52-b954-11e5-85cd-5ad59bc19432_story.html?utm_term=.2324efded021.

Economic Observer (EEO) (2017) "習近平作十九大報告, 新華網直播全文實錄," 18 October, www.eeo.com.cn/2017/1018/314936.shtml.

Emmott, Bill (2017) *The Fate of the West: The Battle to Save the World's Most Successful Political Idea*, London: The Economist, p. 1.

Ezrahi, Yaron (2012) *Imagined Democracies: Necessary Political Fictions*, New York: Cambridge University Press, pp. 38–39.

Focus Taiwan (2016a) "Full Text of Tsai's Victory Speech at International Press Conference," 16 January. http://focustaiwan.tw/news/aipl/201601160053.aspx.

Focus Taiwan (2016b) "Full Text of President Tsai Ing-wen's National Day Address," 10 October. http://focustaiwan.tw/news/aipl/201610100004.aspx.

Focus Taiwan (2017) "Full Text of President Tsai Ing-wen's National Day Address," 10 October. http://focustaiwan.tw/news/aipl/201710100004.aspx.

Khan, Sulmaan Wasif (2018) *Haunted by Chaos China's Grand Strategy from Mao Zedong to Xi Jinping*, Cambridge: Harvard University Press, p. 152.

Legislative Yuan (LY) (2015) "立法院第 8 屆第 7 會期內政委員會第 2 次全體委員會議紀錄," https://lis.ly.gov.tw/lgcgi/lypdftxt?10401501;381;430.

Lin, Syaru Shirley (2016) *Taiwan's China Dilemma: Contested Identities and Multiple Interests in Taiwan's Cross-Strait Economic Policy*, Stanford: Stanford University Press, pp. 208–209.

National Endowment for Democracy (NED) (2017) "Sharp Power: Rising Authoritarian Influence." www.ned.org/wp-content/uploads/2017/12/Sharp-Power-Rising-Authoritarian-Influence-Full-Report.pdf.

Office of the President, Republic of China (OPROC) (2016) "Inaugural Address of ROC 14th-Term President Tsai Ing-wen," 20 May 2016. https://english.president.gov.tw/News/4893.

Peng, Hsian-wei (2016) "蔡就職演說 中國國台辦：一份沒完成的答卷, 自由時報," *Liberty Times*, 21 May. http://news.ltn.com.tw/news/focus/paper/991944.

State Council Taiwan Affairs Office (TAO) (2016) "國台辦新聞發布會輯錄," 29 June. www.gwytb.gov.cn/xwfbh/201606/t20160629_11495077.htm.

Taiwan Foundation for Democracy (TFD) (2018) "臺灣民主價值與治理," www.tfd.org.tw/export/sites/tfd/files/download/PDF-2.pdf.

Tsai, Xiaoying (2016) "周子瑜事件：中國國台辦與台陸委會分別回應," *BBC Chinese*, 16 January. www.bbc.com/zhongwen/trad/china/2016/01/160116_taiwan_chou_tzu_yu_reax.

2

THE GLOVES COME OFF

China's punitive strategy

Hours after Tsai Ing-wen won the 16 January 2016 presidential election, her official Twitter and Facebook accounts were swarmed by what the authors of a report on computational propaganda politely described as "suspicious Chinese accounts" (Monaco 2017). In the days and weeks that followed the elections, thousands of messages were posted on her social media by accounts which in common usage are known as trolls. Having jumped over the Great Firewall (Twitter and Facebook are officially banned in China), these suspicious accounts used the telltale simplified Chinese to bombard the president-elect's accounts.

Although analysts did not see conclusive evidence of automated, or "bot," behavior, there was little doubt that the campaigns were heavily coordinated and overlapping (this, however, did not rule out the possibility of a "cyborg approach," in which some automation is used in tandem with human intervention). In one campaign, known as the "Diba Facebook Expedition" – Diba is an online forum similar to Reddit, and is hosted on China's Baidu Tieba (百度貼吧) – purported Chinese patriots posted pro-Beijing comments on President Tsai's Facebook account and also bombarded the official fan pages of the *Apple Daily* newspaper. One targeted post on the Tsai Facebook page garnered a total of 49,541 comments and replies between 20 January and 4 April, which "was a disproportionate number in comparison with all other posts on her wall."

According to the authors of the report, "Most of these posts expressed opposition to Taiwanese independence and extolled the Communist Party's rule in mainland China." One phrase in particular was repeatedly used among pro-China commenters, 八榮八恥 – "Eight Honors and Eight Shames." These eight principles of morality were penned by former Chinese president Hu Jintao and were part of his Socialist Conception of Honors and Shames (社會主義榮辱觀), a document released in 2006 that was meant to serve as a moral guide for Chinese citizens. As the report notes, "in the 24 hours following the original post, the highest rate of posting by a single user was 2.3 posts per minute. The user with the greatest number of contributions posted 825 times within the observed period." Such frequency of posting, the authors wrote, represented "extraordinary engagement" though still within the realm of human feasibility.

The constant trolling of President Tsai's accounts would continue over the following two years, and the tone, which immediately after the election had not been altogether acrimonious, would harden as the "deep freeze" deepened. Not particularly damaging in itself, the coordinated bombardment of social media in Taiwan that are banned in China nevertheless was indicative of the ultranationalism that now pervaded Chinese society and which, like other developments, would exacerbate the desire to punish Taiwan for its refusal to bend to Beijing's will. There is still debate, however, on the extent to which the online trolling is self-initiated or whether some guidance is being provided by the CCP.

As we saw in the previous chapter, once President Tsai made it clear that her administration would not prostrate itself before the altar of the "1992 consensus" and "one China" principle – in other words, after Taipei broke with what the CCP holds sacrosanct – President Xi Jinping abandoned all pretense of cordiality and launched his country upon a campaign of punishment. To add insult to injury, President Tsai insisted on the inviolability of Taiwan's democratic principles and called on Beijing to respect the reality of the Republic of China's existence, two things, which the CCP, mired in an ideological ice age of its own making, simply could not admit openly. The "1992 consensus" therefore became a point of contention: for President Tsai, a line that she would not cross; and for Xi, an unavoidable prerequisite for the resumption of dialogue. As both leaders did not budge, the relationship soured. Early on, Beijing suspended the TAO-MAC communication mechanism, and contact between the two sides, both at the official and unofficial level, was reduced markedly.

In the months and years that followed, Beijing would launch an all-out, multifaceted and sustained effort to narrow Taiwan's international space, scrub its visibility, undermine its economy, exacerbate its sense of vulnerability, and corrode its democratic institutions through a combination of "sharp power" and united front activity. It would also relaunch its strategy, suspended during the "diplomatic truce" that prevailed during the Ma Ying-jeou presidency, of luring Taiwan's official diplomatic allies. It would even now seek to compel Taiwan's non-official diplomatic partners to distance themselves from Taipei.

Besides aiming to isolate Taiwan, this punitive campaign was meant to break Taiwan's morale and reinforce the sense of historical inevitability Xi Jinping and other CCP luminaries often alluded to in their speeches. It was meant to overwhelm, to create a sense of embattlement and a state of perpetual crisis, which Beijing can dial up and down as it sees fit. Another objective was to undermine public support for President Tsai and her Democratic Progressive Party, with hopes of limiting her presidency to a single, four-year term. We now turn to the many forms that Beijing's punitive strategy against Taiwan since 2016 has taken and assess the effectiveness of those measures in furthering Beijing's political objectives.

Weaponizing tourism

The first punitive action Beijing took against Taiwan occurred in the first half of 2016, with reports that the quota on the number of Chinese tourists allowed to visit Taiwan would be cut by nearly half. Speaking to media, sources in the tourism industry revealed that the reduction was to be implemented in three stages: in the first one, implemented two months prior to the May 20 inauguration, the number of tourists was reportedly to be cut from 150,000 monthly to 100,000; from July, the total number of monthly visitors allowed would drop to 75,000; and to 37,500 starting in October. By October, Chinese tour groups were down 40 percent, although during the same period the number of independent travelers from China, a small fraction of the total, had risen by about 13 percent. For the whole of 2016, Chinese group tours to Taiwan were down about 30 percent, while total Chinese arrivals were down 16 percent year on year, according to statistics from the Tourism Bureau.

With the reductions, Beijing had weaponized tourism, something it had already done in the past when municipalities in Taiwan needed to be punished. For example, in 2009, Chinese travel agents threatened a boycott of Kaohsiung after a visit by the Tibetan spiritual leader the Dalai Lama, whom Beijing accuses of fostering separatism. The Chinese side did the same in protest over the screening at a film festival of a documentary about Rebiya Kadeer, an exiled Uighur leader also accused of separatism, this time in Xinjiang. The move resulted in hundreds of hotel cancellations by Chinese tourists and economic losses for the hotel industry in the port city.

After the 2016 elections, weaponized tourism no longer aimed to punish single municipalities governed by DPP politicians: the goal was now to inflict pain on the industry and foster discontent with the Tsai administration, which Beijing hoped would lead to pressure on the government to give in to Beijing's demands and recognize the "1992 consensus."

Approximately 10.44 million tourists visited Taiwan in 2015, with Chinese nationals accounting for more than 4.1 million, a historical high. The tourism industry accounted for approximately 4 percent of Taiwan's GDP in 2015. Amid the pressure, tour operators estimated the drop would result in monthly losses of NT$2.04 billion. Certain sectors of Taiwan's industry had become largely reliant on Chinese tourism, and it was those that Beijing targeted for mobilization. Thousands of them protested in September 2016, demanding the Tsai administration provide more government assistance and adopt measures to revive tourist arrivals from China.

If Beijing hoped the protests would turn into a headache for President Tsai, however, it would be disappointed (Horton 2017). The protests fizzled and failed to gain public sympathy. Meanwhile, new efforts by the Taiwanese authorities to bolster the tourism industry through diversification paid dividends. Despite the Chinese boycott, the total number of tourists who visited Taiwan in 2016 reached a new record of 10.69 million; 1.9 million Japanese nationals visited that year, accounting for 17.7 percent of the total, while 880,000 South Koreans did so, a 35 percent increase.

28 The illusion is broken

As the Tsai government reached out to Southeast Asia and made revisions to visa requirements, the number of tourists from ASEAN countries rose 16 percent in 2016. Tourism from Thailand alone was up 57 percent in 2016.

Rather than 2016 being a fluke, and despite Beijing's efforts to hurt Taiwan's tourism industry, total tourist arrivals rose again in 2017, to 10.739 million, up 0.46 percent from the previous year. According to Tourism Bureau statistics, China accounted for 2.73 million, or 25.44 percent, of the total, down 22.19 percent, while 1.69 million, or 15.76 percent (up 4.78 percent) came from Hong Kong and Macau. Southeast Asia brought in 2.14 million visitors, or 19.9 percent of the total and up 29.22 percent year-on-year. Arrivals from the Philippines rose 69 percent between 2016 and 2017. Vietnamese tourist figures nearly doubled, from 196,636 in 2016 to 383,329 in 2017. Japan accounted for 1.9 million, or 17.68 percent of the total, up 0.17 percent; and 1.05 million South Koreans, or 9.82 percent of the total, up 19.26 percent, visited Taiwan in 2017 (Taiwan Tourism Bureau 2018). The total number of arrivals again rose slightly in 2018 to 11,066,707, with China (−1.35 percent), Hong Kong/Macau (−2.27 percent), Japan (+3.7 percent), South Korea (−3.34 percent) and Southeast Asian countries (2.43 million, up 13.71 percent from 2017) accounting for a large share of total arrivals.

Beijing's attempt to undermine Taiwan's tourism industry and to "weaponize" the sector to pressure President Tsai did not yield the expected dividends for Beijing. Not only did the attempt not generate the hoped-for political pressure, it moreover compelled the government to redouble its efforts to reduce Taiwan's dependence on Chinese tourists and to diversify the market, something it should have done many years ago. This first test highlighted Taiwan's resilience and its ability to adapt to new challenges.

China has also weaponized tourism outside Taiwan, such as Palau, a small diplomatic ally of Taiwan in the Pacific, and the Vatican, which also recognizes Taiwan diplomatically (Callick 2017; Tanaka 2018). According to a notice by the China National Tourism Administration (CNTA), travel agencies that continue to promote tours to those destinations would be severely punished. The CNTA website currently lists 127 countries and regions that are "approved" for Chinese tour groups. None of Taiwan's official diplomatic allies are on the list. Besides being dragged into the cross-Strait issue, Palau has also gained importance in the U.S.' strategy in the Asia Pacific, providing access to airfields in the second island chain at a time when China has been expanding its military presence in the area (Clark 2017). And in July 2019, Chinese authorities banned individual travel to Taiwan "in light of current relations between the two sides of the Taiwan Strait" (Miao 2019). The measure raised doubts about the ability of residents from 47 major Chinese cities that since 2011 had been able to apply to visit Taiwan as individual travelers.

Beijing ends the "diplomatic truce"

Beijing then began poaching Taiwan's official diplomatic allies again. Its first move occurred two months prior to Tsai's inauguration, when it established relations with the Gambia, which had cut ties with Taiwan in November 2013. At the time, with the "diplomatic truce" still in force, Beijing had refused to establish official diplomatic relations with the impoverished African state. But with Tsai set to enter office, Beijing no longer had a reason for keeping Banjul at arm's length.

On 20 December 2016, São Tomé and Príncipe announced it was cutting ties with Taiwan and establishing diplomatic relations with the PRC. Prior to the 2016 elections, the small African nation of 201,000 people and a GDP of US$676 million in 2017 had sent a letter to DPP headquarters requesting US$210 million in financial assistance, threatening to cut ties with Taipei if the future government did not pay up. Extortion, a theme that would occur again and again as small allies played Taipei against Beijing, was something that the new government made clear it would not give into. So São Tomé and Príncipe switched to Beijing's camp.

Panama followed suit on 13 June 2017. The move came, as China had become one of the three largest users of the Panama Canal. In May the previous year, Landbridge Group (China) (嵐橋集團) had acquired Margarita Island Port, the largest port facility in Panama. As part of the US$900 million deal to control Panama's Margarita Island Port, Chinese groups had vowed heavy investments to upgrade port facilities and build a deepwater port capable of docking larger ships (Núñez 2017). Chinese state-controlled firms, including COSCO Shipping Corp (中國遠洋), have also been eying opportunities to develop land around the Panama Canal. The Panama Canal Authority was expected to open a tender to develop as much as 1,200 hectares of land around the canal by the end of 2017. According to sources in the diplomatic community, the manner in which Panama cut ties with Taipei was "disgraceful," "unnecessarily rude," and clearly meant to humiliate its former ally. For Beijing, gaining greater access to the Panama Canal was also part of its strategy to expand its influence into markets in Central and South America at a time of diminished inattention by Washington.

Then the Dominican Republic severed ties with Taipei on 1 May 2018, ending 77 years of relations between the Caribbean island and the ROC. This was followed by Burkina Faso on May 24, leaving Taiwan with a single official diplomatic ally in Africa, Swaziland.

On 21 August 2018, Taipei announced it was severing ties with El Salvador after the government there had, according to Taipei, made a request for an "astronomical sum" in financial assistance for the Port of La Union project as well as money to help its government win the next election. According to the Ministry of Foreign Affairs, Taipei had been aware that El Salvador had been in talks with Beijing on the possibility of establishing diplomatic ties since June 2018. No sooner had Taipei made the announcement than Beijing confirmed it was establishing diplomatic ties with El Salvador.

Then, within a week in September 2019, the Solomon Islands and Kiribati, two island-nations in the South Pacific, announced they were considering switching recognition to the PRC, prompting Taipei to preemptively end relations. Those developments also had important ramifications for the U.S.' security posture in the Indo-Pacific given the Solomon Island's ability to host a deepwater port that could

30 The illusion is broken

accommodate large-displacement vessels from the PLAN. Despite its denials, Beijing and the PLA Navy are known to have expressed interest in gaining access to the Solomon Islands as part of its expansionist strategy into the Pacific.

By then, Taiwan was left with only 15 official diplomatic allies, most of them small developing countries.[1] Upon severing ties, Taipei would close its embassies and recall its staff. In many cases, this would also affect ongoing assistance programs. In some cases, as with El Salvador, de-recognition would also come with a request by the former ally on its young people studying in Taiwan to relocate to China – a request that many would only begrudgingly abide by.

In all cases, Beijing invariably forced its new diplomatic allies to recognize the "one China" principle as a precondition for the diplomatic switch, and would advertise the deference to this principle so as to reaffirm its sovereignty claims over Taiwan. This was part of China's psychological warfare against the Taiwanese, intended to increase their sense of isolation and to amplify the notion that the international community is siding with Beijing in the dispute. This was meant to reinforce the sense of "historical inevitability." The poaching of Taiwan's allies was also meant to interfere in the 2020 elections by creating pressure on the Tsai administration to recognize the "1992 consensus" and "one China," and to favor candidates who hew to Beijing's line. Following the developments with the Solomon Islands in September 2019, a Beijing mouthpiece warned that if President Tsai was re-elected in 2020, China would grab all of the nation's remaining official diplomatic allies (Zheng 2019).

As with the weaponization of tourism, the actual impact of Beijing's diplomatic success was rather limited. Although Beijing has successfully used the attractiveness of its large economy and promises of largesse (which have not always materialized) to impoverished countries in need of infrastructure investment, for the Taiwanese the loss of official diplomatic allies has not substantially undermined morale. In many cases, the reaction on the street was "good riddance," stemming no doubt from the realization that Taiwan's former diplomatic friends were, in many cases, parasitical (by this I mean the governments involved, and not the people, who more often than not had no say in the decisions made by their officials). As more and more small, money-hungry states joined Beijing's camp, Taiwanese also came to realize that Taiwan had no interest in competing with China for allies. In fact, it could not afford to do so. Furthermore, there was agreement that the money saved from no longer having to give money to keep those relationships going could be put to more productive uses, such as in deepening Taiwan's unofficial relations with allied democracies that are interested in interactions with Taiwan that are more mutually beneficial (more on this in Chapter 7).

Not everybody agrees with this assessment. The Taiwanese diplomatic corps, for one, has a long institutional attachment to official diplomatic relations. This is in large part due to the prestige that is associated with working at an actual embassy, the title of ambassador rather than mere representative, and all the protocolar courtesies that come with such posts abroad (the same emotions apply to foreign diplomats posted to Taiwan). Another reason why some observers have felt more alarmed by the loss of official diplomatic allies is that however small they may be, the have a vote at the United Nations and can therefore support Taiwan at the UN General Assembly. However true that may be, such votes have not succeeded in ensuring Taiwan's participation at UN multilateral agencies, mostly because the center of gravity simply lies somewhere else – in Beijing's economic weight and growing influence, and, failing that, its veto power. As with other things, Taiwan has a much greater prospect of being able to play a role in the international community if it receives support from a coalition of sizable democratic allies like the U.S., Japan, India, Germany, the UK, Australia, France, Canada, and others.

Thus, in this author's opinion, the value of official diplomatic allies, and the necessity of keeping them on Taiwan's side, is actually limited. Taiwan has weathered the loss of seven allies since 2016, and arguably it can afford to lose more. I would even propose that Taiwan could lose all of its remaining official diplomatic allies and its existence as a modern nation-state would not be overly compromised as a result, provided it maintains – and expands – its constructive unofficial relationships with major economies and modern democracies. What keeps Taiwan free and healthy today aren't its official diplomatic allies; rather, its security rests on strong trade with major economies and security guarantees from states with a sizable military and a stake in stability in the Asia-Pacific. As with tourism, Beijing's assault on Taiwan's diplomatic allies could have the inadvertent effect of compelling the Taiwanese to identify who their real friends are and to do what is necessary to develop those relationships.

We should also note that the severance of official diplomatic ties between two countries does not mean that the relationship ceases altogether. Upon de-recognition, diplomats from both sides will negotiate new arrangements and, in due time, will re-establish a diplomatic representation, albeit an unofficial one, in their respective countries. Trade, cultural exchanges, and other engagements will eventually resume.

Another unexpected consequence of Beijing's poaching of Taiwan's official diplomatic allies was the reaction of the United States to El Salvador's move. Describing this development as an attack on the "status quo," the U.S. State Department said it was "deeply disappointed" and was reviewing its relationship with El Salvador as a result. A State Department official added that Beijing's efforts to "unilaterally alter the status quo with Taiwan" were harmful and "undermine the framework that has enabled peace, stability, and development for decades" (Associated Press 2018). Jean Manes, the U.S. ambassador to the South American country, said the move "is worrisome for many reasons" and "without doubt this will impact our relationship with the government." For his part, Florida Senator Marco Rubio threatened to block funding for El Salvador (Crabtree 2018). U.S. officials also expressed worries that Port of La Union – the very same commercial port in the country's east for which the government was asking billions of dollars in harbor development funding from Taipei – could be turned into a military base for China (Lo). The U.S. reacted similarly to the diplomatic switches in September 2019, with the Japanese government issuing an unprecedented note of concern at the developments and their implications for the region.

32 The illusion is broken

More worrying are efforts by Beijing since 2016 to undermine Taiwan's unofficial relations with other countries. In some cases, the effort has sought to erode terminology that may suggest statehood for Taiwan. On other occasions, the pressure has had a more concrete impact on Taiwan's ability to entertain ties with unofficial allies. In January 2017, the Nigerian government ordered that Taiwan's representative in the country move out of the capital, and demanded the name of the office be changed and its personnel reduced. In June the same year, the Nigerian government sent 25 police officers to seal off the office and remove the officials. Taiwan's representative office, now a mere "trade office," later relocated to Lagos (Liu and Hou 2018). "Republic of China (Taiwan)" was removed from its name. Also due to Chinese pressure, four other countries that have no formal diplomatic relations with Taiwan – Bahrain, Jordan, the United Arab Emirates, and Ecuador – requested in 2017 that Taiwanese representative offices in their countries be closed.

Beijing has often lodged protests with foreign governments for hosting Taiwanese delegations, even if those did not involve the participation of senior government officials. To give just one example, in July 2018 Beijing protested with New Delhi over a parliamentary visit to India. As in this case, Beijing often tries to reinterpret what is "permissible" within a country's "one China" policy or to substitute that agreement with the "one China" principle. "We hope that India would understand and respect China's core concerns and stick to the 'one China' principle and prudently deal with Taiwan-related issues and maintain sound and steady development of India-China relations," a Chinese foreign ministry spokesman said after the visit. On Taiwan's plans to upgrade its office with India, with which Taipei has unofficial diplomatic ties, the Chinese MOFA lamented, "We are always opposed to any forms of official contacts and exchanges between countries that have diplomatic ties with China and Taiwan [simultaneously] and we are also opposed to the establishment of any official institutions."

On some occasions, such pressure has succeeded in forcing the targeted government to cancel visits and exchanges with Taiwanese delegations, especially when the government in question is trying to repair or improve relations with Beijing. In other words, Taiwan's ability to engage unofficial partners often is contingent on the state of relations between Beijing and the country in question.

In February 2017, Cambodian president Hun Sen, a close ally of Beijing, publicly announced a ban on all displays of the ROC flag in the country and reiterated his country's staunch support for the "one China" policy. "I request to people here: Please don't raise the Taiwanese flag whenever you are gathering, even at the hotel during Taiwanese national holidays. It is not allowed," he told a gathering of the Cambodian-Chinese Association (Soumy 2017).

As mentioned in the previous chapter, in April 2016 Kenya deported Taiwanese suspected of telecom from to China despite efforts by Taiwanese officials to ensure they were returned to Taiwan to face trial. Other countries, including the Philippines, Cambodia, and Turkey, have deported Taiwanese to China in recent years, while pressure has been put on others, such as Thailand, to do so. In many cases, Taiwanese had collaborated with Chinese nationals in scam operations, which often targeted people in China. Beijing has argued that Taiwanese courts have been derelict in properly sentencing Taiwanese who have preyed on Chinese citizens, and there is some validity to that statement. However, the forced extraditions to China also come with their own sets of problems, chief among them the high likelihood that Taiwanese suspects will not receive a fair trial. The forced repatriations, furthermore, erode Taiwan's international space and contribute to the perception that Taiwanese nationals are subject to Chinese laws. One terrifying scenario resulting from this would be the forced extradition of Taiwanese accused by Beijing of breaking its National Security Law of 2015. As Beijing becomes increasingly extraterritorial in the application of its laws, Taiwanese nationals accused of, say, supporting "separatism" could be arrested in a third country and sent to China to face trial. Such risks are especially high in countries worldwide that do not enjoy rule of law or democratic rule, and which are highly dependent on Chinese financial aid.

It is not, however, only undemocratic countries that have given in to pressure from Beijing to send Taiwanese fraud suspects to China, regardless of the risks that, once there, they would not be able to get fair legal representation or a fair trial. In May 2018, Spain, considered a mature democracy, deported two Taiwanese fraud suspects to China. At this writing, Spain has sent 218 Taiwanese suspects to China (Ruwitch 2019).

Incidents such as the October 2015 abduction of Gui Minhai (桂民海), a Chinese-born bookseller of Swedish nationality, in Thailand and transfer to China, where he was put under extralegal detention, have highlighted the ineffectiveness – and sometimes reluctance – of democratic countries to protect their own.[2] The Gui case also makes it clear that in Beijing's eyes, regardless of whether they hold a passport from another country, people of Chinese descent are subject to China's domestic laws wherever they are. Another case which comes to mind is that of Dolkun Isa (多里坤·艾沙), an exiled Uighur leader whom Beijing accuses of being a terrorist. Isa, a German national since 2006, had been placed under an Interpol "red notice" – an international wanted alert. Beijing, which frequently asked European countries to arrest Isa, never provided evidence of the crimes it says he committed. Interpol lifted the wanted alert in February 2018 (Blanchard 2018).

For Taiwan, the two cases above cannot but bring to mind the circumstances under which one of its own, Lee Ming-che (李明哲), was captured in China for the crime of subversion. Lee, a human rights activist, disappeared in March while traveling to China. After months in detention, he went on trial at the Yueyang City Intermediate People's Court in Hunan Province (湖南岳陽中級人民法院) in September the same year for "attacking the Chinese government: and attempting to promote multiparty democracy on the group messaging application WeChat." He had also allegedly brought books about multiparty democracy to distribute to his contacts in China. Calls by Lee's family and the Taiwanese government were to no avail. For many, Lee's fate – he was sentenced to five years imprisonment in November – was a "warning shot" to other Taiwanese who sought to promote democracy in China (Chen 2017). The incident had a freezing effect on the willingness of Taiwanese NGO workers to conduct their work in China, which had

34 The illusion is broken

already become more problematic after China passed new laws in April 2016 barring foreign-funded NGOs from operating in China. There is much irony in this – Beijing claims Taiwan is part of China, but Taiwanese NGOs are subject to the restrictions on foreign nongovernmental entities. Human rights organizations in Taiwan and overseas decried the trial as unfair and said they believed Lee's confession had been extracted under duress.

Besides highlighting the increased risks of Taiwanese nationals traveling to China, Lee's arrest also caused a storm in Taiwan, where members of his family and civic groups accused the Tsai administration of passivity. While the anger is understandable, the accusations that the Tsai government could have done more to secure Lee's release are, in my judgment, unfair. There was only so much that the Tsai government could have done, given that Beijing wanted to make an example of Lee and absolutely resents foreign interference in its affairs. Furthermore, much of what the government did, first to learn about Lee's circumstances and then to secure his release, had to occur behind closed doors and under less than optimal conditions, given the "deep freeze" in cross-Strait relations. Although public expressions of outrage on the part of the Tsai administration may have been cathartic for his supporters and members of his family, it is difficult to imagine how this would have helped his situation. In fact, it could have made matters worse for Lee, not to mention that an emotional outburst could have had consequences for other aspects of relations across the Taiwan Strait, something that the president had to keep into consideration. The Tsai government in the end provided assistance to Lee's wife, Lee Ching-yu (李淨瑜), and two Straits Exchange Foundation officials accompanied her when she went to Hunan Province to attend her husband's sentencing in late November. The claim that the Tsai administration did nothing was invidious; and, in some case, it was little more than something to jump upon by groups that already had an unfavorable view of President Tsai. For most in the NGO community, however, the criticism was more the result of a lack of awareness of the functioning of government, and impatience over the slow progress made in the case.

If there was reason to be angry, it would have to be over the powerlessness of the Tsai government to affect the outcome. But as the Gui case proved, in the current atmosphere foreign governments have very limited ability to influence, let alone overturn, the decisions made by Chinese law enforcement agencies and its judiciary.

Another incident known to this author, which has not been revealed to the public, involved a young female Taiwanese who in December 2016 was held incommunicado for hours at the airport in Hong Kong before being sent back to Taiwan. Her "crime" was to have a sticker on her passport that read "Republic of Taiwan." This, along with the growing frequency with which Taiwanese nationals are denied visas to Hong Kong, is clear evidence that under "one country, two systems" the SAR has lost control over its immigration, which is increasingly dictated by the central government in Beijing. So much for preserving the territory's social and economic way of life after Retrocession!

Related to Beijing's attempts to deny Taiwan the diplomatic access it needs to maintain its sovereignty is its ongoing pressure on international multilateral organizations requiring statehood to block Taiwan's participation. Once again, Beijing has used this as a pressure point to force the Tsai administration into submitting to the "1992 consensus" and "one China," the logic being that, when the Ma administration agreed to those, Taiwan was able to gain "meaningful participation" – with Beijing's "permission," at various UN-affiliated agencies. Since 2016, Beijing has successfully blocked every attempt by Taiwan to participate, often as an observer, in meetings at agencies including Interpol, the World Health Assembly (WHA), and the International Civil Aviation Organization (ICAO).

What is especially frustrating for Taiwan is that Taipei's annual bids to participate in those organization's annual meetings have failed despite the support it has received both from its official diplomatic allies at the UN, and from a number of unofficial partners within the international community, among them the U.S. The idea that Beijing, which in recent years has succeeded in placing its nationals at the head of those organizations, has been given the power to "permit" who gets to participate in the meetings, is worrying. Among other things, this demonstrates an abdication by the international community, and the UN, to China's political posturing; it signals weakness and certainly gives the impression that the multilateral system, which has existed since the end of World War II, has ceded space to revisionist powers like China.

Every year in making its case for participation, Taipei has argued that the global system cannot afford to create unnecessary blind spots, and that deadly pathogens, wanted criminals, and aviation safety do not respect political borders. In other words, Taipei and its allies maintain that denying Taiwan the ability to meaningfully participate in those organizations is a threat to all – not just to Taiwan, but as the Severe Acute Respiratory Syndrome (SARS) outbreak in 2003 made clear, to the rest of the world, as viruses can travel from one capital to another in a manner of hours. Taiwan's inability to join those important organizations can result in delays, lack of access, and the inability of global partners to share information that is necessary to prevent a local outbreak from turning into a pandemic, catching a terrorist before he or she commits a crime that can affect thousands of people, or collaborating in a search-and-rescue operation after an air disaster in, say, the East China Sea. For the Taiwanese themselves, it means that their safety and their country's ability to access the expertise, information, and assistance it needs in times of emergency, is contingent on Beijing's approval. In some scenarios, the resulting delays can make a difference between life and death.

Due to Beijing's insistence on the Tsai administration bending to its demand on the "1992 consensus," China has therefore succeeded in hijacking institutions whose mandate it is to make the world safer for all of us.

When needed, Taiwan has found ways to work around its exclusion from such organizations. For example, during the 2017 Summer Universiade in Taipei, Taiwanese law-enforcement agencies were able to circumvent their inability to access Interpol's I-24/7 (I-24/7全球警察通訊系統) and Stolen and Lost Travel Documents (SLTD) database due to Taiwan's non-membership in the global organization (Liberty Times 2016) (before he disappeared during a visit to China and confessing

36 The illusion is broken

to bribery in a Chinese court in June 2019, the head of Interpol was Meng Hong-wei [孟宏偉], China's vice minister of public security) (Guardian 2019). Given the always existing potential for a terrorist attack against "soft targets" by groups like ISIS and al-Qaeda, Taiwan's law enforcement and intelligence agencies were responsible for the safety of the thousands of international participants – more than 11,000 representatives from 131 countries, including 7,639 athletes – who traveled to Taipei for the 12-day event. In the end, Taiwan cooperated with police and intelligence agencies from other countries to receive the information it needed. A similar model had been used during the World Games in Kaohsiung in 2009. Though pragmatic, this alternative was not optimal: as the "intelligence failure" that contributed to the 11 September 2001 terrorist attacks in the U.S. made clear, unnecessary layers in the sharing of information, not to mention the complexity of sharing classified material with agencies that are not formally "cleared" to receive it, can make the difference between preventing a deadly attack and terrorists being able to carry out their murderous activities.

As with other elements of its strategy, all of this is also meant to reinforce international perceptions that Taiwan is part of the PRC and that decisions pertaining to what Beijing claims as a province of China should pass through the central government in Beijing.

Erasing Taiwan

In academia, where few universities worldwide have programs that are dedicated to Taiwan as a subject of study in its own, China's efforts to undermine academic freedom have also contributed in some ways to abbreviate Taiwan's visibility. Using its economic clout and the desire by academic publishers to tap into the large Chinese market, Beijing has imposed conditions on the industry that have promoted censorship. Two incidents in recent years, in and of themselves unrelated to the controversy over the "1992 consensus," serve to illustrate this reality.

In 2017, Chinese authorities demanded that Cambridge University Press (CUP) remove 315 articles in its *China Quarterly*. Beijing also requested that as many as 1,000 e-books be taken off the CUP's Chinese websites. The issues covered in the articles targeted for deletion included the Tiananmen Square massacre, the Cultural Revolution, Tibet – and Taiwan. The U.S.-based Association for Asian Studies also confirmed that China had requested the censorship of around 100 articles in the *Journal of Asian Studies* – also published by CUP. After coming under severe criticism from academics, CUP reversed its decision to comply with China's demands.

Later that year, Germany-based Springer Nature, the world's largest academic book publisher, complied with China's demands and eventually removed as many as 1,000 articles in the *Journal of Chinese Political Science* and *International Politics*.

This type of censorship, not to mention the self-censorship that occurs in the academic world, where researchers and writers will oftentimes avoid focusing their research on subjects that are deemed unacceptable to the CCP for fear of losing the access or the visas that are needed for their research, has also had an eliding effect on Taiwan's visibility in academia. Still, despite the setbacks, there have also been some positive developments. In 2018, for example, the *International Journal of Taiwan Studies*, cosponsored by Academia Sinica in Taipei and the European Association of Taiwan Studies (EATS), was launched. Published by Brill, the publication aims to become a principal outlet for the dissemination of cutting-edge research on Taiwan. The Journal, and other such initiatives, proves that when groups of dedicated individuals come together and secure enough funding – always a challenge – they can find ways to counter Beijing's efforts to turn Taiwan into a non-entity.

Chinese embassies and consulates abroad have also taken the initiative in trying to prevent foreign universities from hosting Taiwanese cultural events. For example, the Chinese embassy in Spain in 2017 lodged a protest with the University of Salamanca's School of Social Sciences over the opening of a Taiwan Cultural Days event at the university. In its letter, the Chinese embassy lambasted the organizers of the event for causing "confusion and misunderstandings" about what it called "the Taiwan problem," such as referring to Taiwan as the "Republic of China (Taiwan)" and allegedly referring to former deputy foreign minister Simon Shen-yeaw Ko (柯森耀), Taiwan's representative to Spain, as "ambassador of Taiwan." Such references, the letter said, did not fall in line "with the Spanish government [which] has long followed the 'one China' principle." The letter also contained a not-so-veiled threat, stating that if the university, which has been included in China's recommended directory of the Ministry of Education of China, wanted to avoid "adverse effects" – e.g., the reduction of Chinese students – it should "cancel the remaining ["Taiwan Cultural Days"] scheduled events."

The dean of the university's School of Social Science subsequently ordered the last two days of the event cancelled, "due to circumstances not related to the School of Social Science."

In July 2018, the East Asian Olympic Committee (EAOC) revoked Taichung's right to host the first East Asian Youth Games scheduled for 2019, ostensibly due to pressure from Beijing. The announcement was made after the city had already invested NT$677 million in preparation for the games. Beijing blamed the outcome on "Taiwan separatists" and their referendum campaign to decide whether Taiwanese athletes should participate at the 2020 Tokyo Olympics under "Taiwan" rather than "Chinese Taipei." The "political interference," said An Fengshan, a TAO spokesman, was therefore entirely Taiwan's fault. The EAOC had granted Taiwan the right to host the games in 2014. It revoked that right due to "political factors" after an extraordinary meeting in Beijing, in which six of the eight members voted to kill the games in Taichung (Taiwan, an EAOC member, voted against, while Japan abstained).

Another area where Beijing has arguably scored more successes is in the private industry, where pressure has succeeded in convincing hotel chains, apparel stores and much of the airline industry to remove all references on their websites and online apps that may suggest statehood for Taiwan. Under threat of penalty for violating domestic laws such as the Cyber Security Law (網絡安全法), which came into force on 1 June 2017, and other advertising regulations, private firms with a

38 The illusion is broken

strong dependence on the Chinese market began giving in to the demands, often by referring to Taiwan as "Taiwan, Province of China," "Taiwan, CN," or other such designations. Prohibitions in the Cyber Security Law include using the Internet to "endanger national security, advocate terrorism or extremism, [or] propagate ethnic hatred and discrimination," to "overthrow the socialist system," to "fabricat[e] or spread false information to disturb [the] economic order" and "to incite separatism or damage national unity."

Among the first international brands to do so were the Marriott hotel chain, Zara, Medtronic, and Mercedes. In January 2018, Shanghai authorities shut down the Marriott website for a week after angry netizens threatened a boycott for listing Taiwan, Tibet, Hong Kong, and Macau as separate nations in a customer questionnaire.

Besides acceding to Beijing's demands, many of the companies went out of their way to demonstrate their adherence to "one China" and issued "sincere apologies" on their social media for "failing" to respect China's "territorial integrity." In many cases, the text read as if it had been scripted by the CCP, which, like the "confessions" of Chinese rights activists, it may very well have been. For example, after coming under fire, Marriott wrote, "We absolutely will not support any separatist organization that will undermine China's sovereignty and territorial integrity. We apologize for any act that may give rise to misunderstandings."

In May 2018, again after Chinese netizens first raised the issue on social media Weibo, apparel chain The Gap came under attack over a T-shirt, sold at one of its branch stores in Canada, which showed an "incomplete" map of China in front. The shirt in question was "missing" south Tibet, the South China Sea, and Taiwan. Soon afterward, the company issued a statement on its own Weibo account, which read, "Gap Inc. respects the sovereignty and territorial integrity of China. We've learned that a Gap brand T-shirt sold in some overseas markets failed to reflect the correct map of China. We sincerely apologize for this unintentional error." The company added that the products had been pulled from the Chinese market and destroyed. In late August 2018, it was Swedish furniture store Ikea's turn to become the target of angry Chinese netizens, who accused it of violating "one China" (TVBS 2018). The same month, grocery chain T&T Supermarket in Canada was the target of such attacks after a Chinese student in Canada discovered the store was showing an "incomplete" map of China – that is, without Taiwan. The student posted his complaint on Weibo, and in a script that is becoming far too common, the anger against the retailer mounted.

Overseas Taiwanese have also been targeted by the Chinese in recent years, often with threats of boycotts of their businesses for supporting "separatist" activities. According to a Taiwanese diplomat posted overseas, Taiwanese businesspeople have become reluctant to sponsor Taiwan-related activities in their host country due to fears of reprisals by China, which in some cases can have a detrimental impact on their business operations.

In January 2018, the Civil Aviation Administration of China (CAAC, 中國民用航空局) ordered all foreign airlines operating routes to China to conduct a "comprehensive review" of all their corporate websites and apps to ensure they complied with Chinese domestic laws. That same week, the CAAC (2018) reportedly summoned the representatives of 25 foreign airlines operating in China and demanded their companies remove all references to Taiwan as a country, as well as its national flag, from their websites immediately. Over the next few months, and despite strong protests from Taipei, most airlines complied with the regulations and Taiwan's visibility was consequently eroded. Taiwan was now listed as "Taipei, CN," "Taiwan, China," or other such designations. Air India, for its part, renamed Taiwan as "Chinese Taipei."

While raising awareness about the controversy, threats of boycotts, online petitions, and editorials in major newspapers did not succeed in swaying private firms, which understandably feared for their operations in China. Throughout all this, most governments also showed reluctance to involve themselves in the dispute, stating that government should refrain from interfering in the decisions of private companies. This, however, was an abdication of government responsibility and a refusal to confront China on an issue that was much larger than a simple pressure campaign on private companies. This was a clear example of authoritarian China dictating what we say in our own backyards. In other words, this was an external assault on our own freedoms of expression.

As this author observed in the *Globe and Mail* after Air Canada began referring to Taiwan as "Taipei, CN," and once it had become clear that Ottawa would not play a constructive role in the incident:

> Democracy, liberty and freedom should be areas of no-compromise in our negotiations with Chinese authorities. When we yield to Beijing's preposterous demands, the way Air Canada did on how it refers to Taiwan, we display our weakness and our willingness to compromise what we believe in. A revisionist regime that seeks to undermine and alter the international system can only see such weakness as an invitation to demand more – and in doing so, we sow the seeds of our own misfortune.
>
> *(Cole 2018a)*

Later on, writing in Canada's *Hill Times*, I observed that:

> The reputational damage has already been done, with many Taiwanese and supporters of the island nation's right to exist blaming not only Air Canada executives for the concession, but Canada as a whole and Prime Minister Justin Trudeau in particular.
>
> The contrast between the United States and Australia, where officials spoke up against the kind of harassment by Beijing that led to Air Canada's decision, and Ottawa, which has chosen to remain silent and to hide between the supposedly inviolable barrier that separates government and the private sector, has dealt Canada's image a serious blow.
>
> It has reinforced the perception, held by many already, that Trudeau's Ottawa has no moral fibre when it comes to dealing with China, and that it

40 The illusion is broken

will do anything to get to the free trade agreement with China it has coveted for so long. We've allowed ourselves to be berated, on our own soil, by Chinese emissaries who resent a free press; we've allowed our media environment to self-censor on important human rights issues in China that will affect the entire international system for years to come. And now we're allowing the most persistent autocratic system that probably has ever existed to redefine, for us, reality and the world we inhabit.

(Cole 2018b)

What became clear was that on their own, private firms had every incentive to comply with Chinese demands. Without assurances from their governments, or official guidance on the "one China" policy that Beijing was insisting upon, companies tended to comply in the full with Chinese demands and changed all references to Taiwan regardless of where, or the language in which, their websites were accessed. Conversely, in cases where governments provided some support to the airlines (Washington called the whole thing "Orwellian nonsense"), company executives either took more time before making a decision, which compelled Beijing to extend the deadline for compliance, or came up with arrangements that, while satisfying Beijing, also ensured some dignity for Taiwan and did not constitute a complete abdication of our values. The best example was probably that set by Japan Airlines (JAL) and All-Nippon Airways (ANA) (Kitamura 2018), which configured their websites such that references to Taiwan as part of China would only appear if a user selected his region as "China" or if one was physically in China when accessing the site. Besides appeasing Beijing and protecting the companies' interests, what these measures did was to let the Chinese live in their Orwellian bubble if they wanted, while at the same time protecting the rest of us from censorship. Later on, United would also show creativity in its response to Beijing's demands by using currencies rather than countries in its drop-down menu.

On this issue, there was little that the Taiwanese government could do. Despite threatened boycotts by Taiwanese consumers and Taiwan supporters abroad, the sheer size of the Chinese market meant that the impact of reduction in bookings would have at best a marginal impact on the companies' bottom lines. Later on, Taipei announced it was considering taking action against airlines that had given in to Beijing's demands, measures that, again, would only have limited impact due to the market imbalance and which could moreover have a negative impact on the willingness of foreign airlines to service routes to Taiwan. One recommendation I had made was to wait and see what kind of punitive measures, if any, Beijing would take against airlines that refused to comply with its demands and then to consider the possibility of taking China to international arbitration at the WTO for creating an unfair trade environment (ChinaFile 2018). Admittedly, such a response comported real risks for the airlines involved and furthermore would only have had a chance to succeed if governments became involved and coordinated their response. Absent this, airlines would be unfairly exposed.

What was certain in all this was that if governments did not, in concert, push back on China's assault on how we represent our world, Beijing would only but recognize weakness and escalate its demands. Having encountered little opposition in its coercion of airlines and other companies in the private sector, Beijing would understandably see this as an invitation to make additional demands on matters that have little to do with Taiwan. Unless we shut that door, Beijing will only ask for more; and the more we give in, the more we allow an authoritarian regime to dictate the very fabric of our reality.

In all of this, the lack of awareness about what a country's "one China" policy entails, what is and isn't permissible within the scope of that policy, has also compounded the problem. Time and again in his interactions with foreign government officials, this author has been struck by the lack of knowledge about the "one China" policy, which in most cases "takes note of" or "acknowledges" Beijing's contention that there is only one China and that Taiwan is part of China. Even some representatives to Taiwan, when asked to state what their country's "one China" policy is, are at a loss. In some instances, this blind spot has misled government officials and encouraged risk-avoidance. "Better not to deal with Taiwan," the belief goes, "lest this cause headaches with the Chinese embassy or consulate." Not to mention the potential effects on their career progression prospects. I have seen this in the reluctance of export control officers, who somehow had convinced themselves that their country's "one China" policy meant they could not sell any defense articles to Taiwan, and in decisions by officials to remove pictures showing someone waving Taiwan's national flag from an internal government report – reports that, unless they are leaked, should not ever be seen by the Chinese. Needless to say, if government officials do not understand their own "one China" policy, we can hardly fault the private sector for yielding to Beijing's threatening posture when it asks them to respect "one China".

Thus, in concert with its friends overseas, Taipei should redouble its efforts to educate government officials, the private sector, the media, and the public about their own country's "one China" policy – not to be confused with Beijing's "one China" principle – so as to reassure them that it is entirely possible to collaborate with Taiwan. In many ways, a country's "one China" policy is a construct meant to appease Beijing ideologically. But in practice, despite some very real limitations, it allows for a high amount of flexibility, even for the existence – which governments cannot state explicitly – of "one Taiwan" and "one China." Education, therefore, is key. Without it, we allow Beijing to dictate how we govern ourselves.

Chou Tzu-yu, the Taiwanese teenage artist who was victimized on election day in 2016, wasn't the only Taiwanese artist to get dragged into the cross-Strait dispute during that period. Often in response to online campaign by ultranationalist Chinese netizens – including, in some instances, the Communist Youth League of China (中國共產主義青年團) – several Taiwanese singers, actors, producers, and film directors were singled out by China for "crimes" such as supporting Taiwanese independence or the Sunflower Movement back in 2014. Chinese netizens would invariably unearth "evidence" from the Internet to prove their case against the

42 The illusion is broken

targeted members of the artistic community. Some Hong Kong artists also became casualties of that campaign.

There was nothing entirely new about this. Rumors of a "blacklist" of Taiwanese artists began circulating as early as in 2004. But there is no doubt that after 2016, the number of performers targeted increased by leaps and bounds.

In June that year, the League launched an online campaign targeting actress-turned-director Vicki Zhao (趙薇) for her decision to cast Leon Dai (戴立忍), a Taiwanese actor, as the lead actor in the movie she was working on at the time, titled "No Other Love" (沒有別的愛). Chinese netizens used footage from an interview Dai had given to the Falun Gong-funded NTDTV (新唐人電視台) as "evidence" of his political beliefs. That same year, Taiwanese director Wu Nien-chen (吳念真) also had to postpone his "Human Condition 3" (人間條件3) theater tour in China due to "political sensitivities." By late 2016, a "blacklist" issued by China's Ministry of Culture reportedly contained the names of 55 artists from Taiwan, Hong Kong, and Japan who were banned from performing in China due to their political beliefs (Apple Daily 2016a). Songs by targeted singers were removed from popular streaming services in China, including the ones owned by Chinese Internet giants Alibaba, Tencent, Baidu, and Netease. U.S. pop star Katy Perry was also banned from performing in China following a performance in Taipei in 2015 during which she displayed the Nationalist flag and wore a sunflower dress, which Chinese nationalists presumably interpreted as support for the previous year's Sunflower Movement.

Then, in July, members of the Taiwanese artistic community heard that the Chinese government was asking performing artists from Taiwan and Hong Kong to sign a declaration vowing not to participate in various "separatist" activities to "split the country." Provided they signed the list, prior involvement in such "separatist" activities would be "forgiven" (Apple Daily 2016b).

Later on, Chinese netizens began attacking Taiwanese artists by forcing them to state publicly that they are "Chinese" rather than Taiwanese. After facing such pressure, actress Vivian Sung (宋芸樺), who in an interview had once stated that Taiwan was her favorite country, Sung said she was "proud to be Chinese." The statement, which did not contain the same spontaneity as her initial comment about her favorite country, then added,

> I am a Chinese girl born in the 1990s. Taiwan is my hometown, China is my home country. I am deeply sorry for my mindlessness during the interview. I owe my opportunity to work in my home country of China to people's fondness of me in recent years.

Like forced confessions, it was clear that the U-turn had been made under duress and to ensure that her career in China did not suffer.

Many other – though not all – artists would capitulate in this fashion to protect their ability to tap into the lucrative market.

And that is exactly what the Chinese ultranationalists had decided to attack them on: Taiwanese "separatists" who seek to "split the motherland" (apparently now simply identifying as Taiwanese was enough to be accused of "separatism") had no right to enrich themselves in China. It was the age-old tactic, the lure of the Chinese market, where fortunes were supposedly made. Many fell for it. Not all became rich. Some Taiwanese artists tried their luck there, only to return to Taiwan a few years later, their lack of success attributed to their being "too Taiwanese." But the lure, like some powerful gravitational force, is one that, for many, is hard to ignore.

Although "admissions," such as that made by Sung, sparked angry reactions in Taiwan, most saw the pressure on artists as infantile, forced confessions that in no way were to be believed, and that, in the end, did not undermine Taiwan's sovereignty.

Information warfare

Another element of China's punitive strategy has been the ramped up campaign of disinformation, known in the vernacular as "fake news," targeting Taiwan. Without asking, Beijing has already received the assistance of pan-blue media in Taiwan, which since President Tsai assumed office have on several occasions used false or misleading reports to undermine the legitimacy of her administration. This long-standing practice – part of the "normal" battling for electoral purposes – has been a blemish on Taiwan's democracy. An oversaturated media environment, added to irresponsible practices in traditional media and extreme polarization, has contributed to this state of affairs. Incessant news reports alleging facts from almost inevitably "unnamed sources" have severely undermined the legitimacy of mass media while creating doubt among the public about the veracity of the information they consume. Polarization, meanwhile, ensures that domestic disinformation reinforces preconceived ideas about the government, and therefore no amount of corrections or official rebuttals will completely resolve the matter. While generating disinformation requires very little resources and energy – a reporter and a complicit editor can simply make it up – the amount of time and energy that is required for government to respond to false accusations can drain government resources. When, as has occurred on some occasions (for example, during President Tsai's stopover in Los Angeles and Taiwan's split with El Salvador in August 2018), as many as five pieces of disinformation are circulated in blue media, government officials can spend a large part of their days resolving those alone, meaning that they cannot fully concentrate their energies doing their actual work.

As discussed in Chapter 9, media polarization has been a key element in Taiwan's blue-versus-green divide, which among other things has weakened Taiwan's ability to resist pressure from China. Although such polarization and fabrication is certainly not limited to Taiwan and is as old as news itself, domestic polarization, media irresponsibility, and the emergence of social media has created a perfect storm for Beijing to exacerbate the information crisis that has beset Taiwan's news environment.

The CCP has banked on complicit media in the blue camp to act as "repeater stations" for its own disinformation targeting Taiwan, and has benefited from poor

44 The illusion is broken

fact-checking and corroboration practices in Taiwan's media in general to ensure that "false news" will enter Taiwan's media bloodstream. To do so, Beijing has relied on dozens of microblogging sites in China and in Taiwan, as well as WeChat and popular "content farms" (also known as "content mills"), to bombard its target with disinformation aimed at undermining support for the Tsai government. Several "red media" websites involved in such activities, many of them shut down in 2019, were operated by a businessman based in Taichung who is known to have attended the Strait Forum (海峽論壇) in Xiamen (Huang 2019). Content farms in particular, where users are paid by the authorities to create false information, have been effective in penetrating the news environment in Taiwan, where disinformation has been broadcast by both traditional media and online platforms like Facebook, as well as popular messaging apps like Line and China's WeChat (Weixin QQ). Many sites have directly targeted President Tsai, while others have propagated ultraconservative views on same-sex marriage or sought to undermine belief in Taiwan's future among young people by constantly referring to Taiwan as a "ghost island." One Facebook disinformation group is called "Ghost Island News."

Swarming and online bullying by live and troll social media accounts has also become a problem since 2016 and has tended to intensify around elections. Many of those accounts seem to belong to ethnic Chinese located in Malaysia and have attacked critics of politicians in Taiwan who are understood to be Beijing's favorites. Such accounts have also been used to spread and replicate disinformation first originated on content farms and Facebook pages.

In May 2019, Want Want Group (旺旺集團) chairman Tsai Eng-meng (蔡衍明), his son, Want Want China Times Media Group chairman Tsai Shao-chung (蔡紹中), and Want Want China Times Media Group vice chairman and former Taichung Mayor Jason Hu (胡志強) headed a Taiwanese delegation comprising more than 70 individuals from print, TV, radio, online, and new media to attend the 4th "Cross-Strait Media People Summit" (兩岸媒體人峰會) in Beijing. Among the Chinese officials who met with the delegation was Wang Yang (汪洋), a member of the Standing Committee of the Political Bureau of the Chinese Communist Party Central Committee and chairman of the National Committee of the Chinese People's Political Consultative Conference (CPPCC, 中國人民政治協商會議). Besides signing bilateral agreements, the delegates were also told that it was their responsibility to use their various outlets to promote "peaceful reunification," the so-called "1992 consensus" and the "one country, two systems" formula (Cole 2019a). The first cross-Strait media forum was held in Beijing on 6–7 November 2015. At the time, there were 34 representatives from Taiwan (Weiwenku 2017).

Earlier in 2019, it was also revealed that Want Want China Holdings (中國旺旺控股有限公司) has received as much as NT$15.26 billion (US$495 million) in subsidies from China since 2007. The media group denies that such injections have had any influence on its editorial line. Facing allegations that it is receiving editorial guidance from Beijing, the group filed a number of lawsuits throughout 2019, including one against the *Financial Times*' Kathrin Hille (RSF 2019).

It is also believed that PTT Board, a popular bulletin board among young Taiwanese hosted by National Taiwan University, has also been infiltrated by pro-Beijing elements. There, too, the frequency of references to Taiwan as a "ghost island" without a future has increased. Unsurprisingly, this coincided with the TAO's announcement of its "31 incentives" program to attract young and talented Taiwanese to go to China for work or study.

Among other issues, pension reform has been the object of a disinformation campaign with suspected ties to China. It is believed that such efforts were meant to alienate retired public servants and members of military from President Tsai by claiming that the administration aimed to adopt "draconian" reforms that would leave them penniless (Chung 2017). Among other things, the disinformation may have aimed to galvanize public protests against the government, which already had brought deep-blue and pro-unification elements together onto the streets. Disinformation has also been used by the PLA to spread fear of Chinese military intrusions into Taiwan's airspace (and the helplessness of the Taiwanese military to prevent such intrusions), as occurred when the PLA Air Force posted pictures on its social media showing Chinese bombers purportedly flying close to Taiwan's Jade Mountain.

Based on recent research by a small group of young Taiwanese Internet experts, which at this writing has yet to be published but has been seen by the author, Taiwan may be targeted by as many as 2,500 items of disinformation *every day*. Experts are now also trying to trace back the geographical origin of that disinformation. Tellingly, the volume of the disinformation analyzed by this group has tended to plummet during China's Golden Week seven-day holiday, a clear indication that elements based in China are behind this campaign.

Furthermore, recent analysis has shown that Beijing has hired a number of Taiwanese to generate disinformation on its behalf. The principal reason for this is the realization that, despite sharing a language, Taiwanese use of the Chinese language is idiosyncratic and contains expressions and characters that are not used in China, and vice versa. By using Taiwanese to generate false content, the CCP has thereby increased the legitimacy of the information, which could be doubted if a Taiwanese reader identified telltale Chinese expressions in the information he or she receives.

Although disinformation, computational propaganda, and cyber warfare now occurs in different parts of China, the primary base for CCP influence operations against Taiwan remains the Eastern Theater Command's (formerly Nanjing Military Region) 311 Base (61716 unit). Located in Fuzhou City, Fujian Province, 311 Base has been in operation since the 1950s, when it broadcasted propaganda via the "Voice of the Taiwan Strait" (VTS) radio station. Since 2008 or so, it has added social media, publishing, businesses, and other sectors to its psychological arsenal. Also known as the "Public Opinion, Psychological Operations, and Legal Warfare Base," (輿論戰心理戰法律戰基地) 311 Base works in cooperation with suspected united front agencies including the Association for Promotion of Chinese Culture (CAPCC, 中華文化發展促進會), the China Association for Friendly International Contact (CAIFC, 中國國際友好聯絡會), the China-U.S. Exchange

46 The illusion is broken

Foundation (CUSEF, 中美交流基金會), the Center for Peace and Development Studies (CPDS), the External Propaganda Bureau (EPB) and the China Energy Fund Committee (CEFC, 中華能源基金委員會) (Raska 2015).

As the end-of-year municipal elections approached in 2018, Taiwanese authorities were bracing themselves for an increase in the disinformation aimed at Taiwanese voters to affect the outcome and favor candidates who are deemed more palatable to Beijing. Among those who ostensibly benefited from disinformation aimed at the DPP and disproportionate coverage in Beijing-leaning media were Han Kuo-yu (韓國瑜), who was seeking (and won) election in Kaohsiung on the KMT ticket, as well as Taipei Mayor Ko Wen-je (柯文哲), who was seeking (and won) re-election against candidates from both the DPP and KMT. Ko, who formed a new political party, the Taiwan People's Party (臺灣民眾黨), on 6 August 2019, appears to have become a favorite of Beijing, with CCTV broadcasting features on him and boosting the idea that a Ko bid for the presidency could be imminent. Beijing's support seems to have increased following remarks by Ko to the effect that Taiwan and China are part of the same family. Ko's tech-savvy and vociferous army of online supporters has also upped the ante in recent months by shifting its tone to one of belligerence (and occasional threats of physical violence) against his detractors, something that had not been observed in the lead-up to the 2014 elections that brought him to power, when he collaborated with the DPP. The Ko camp has also resorted to legal action against his critics, many of them commentators on popular TV talk shows.

Having lost all hopes of finding allies in the DPP and KMT who can deliver on unification, the CCP could feasibly begin to assist, through its united front activities, independent candidates who may prove more malleable and controllable by Beijing, or marginals within existing parties. It will be interesting to watch whether small pro-unification parties in Taiwan and CCP proxies show their support for such candidates in the coming years.

Fears that the CCP could attempt to use disinformation (and other measures) to affect the outcome of elections are not unfounded. As Grayling (2017) observes in his book *Democracy and its Crisis*, manipulators are seeking to pervert the aims of representative democracy and exacerbate the distortions that democracy has suffered over time. As we have seen, Taiwan's democratic firewall has been one of the largest impediments to Beijing's successfully annexing Taiwan without use of force. Thus, absent a military intervention to resolve the issue, Beijing may have calculated that distorting Taiwan's democracy – by using democracy against it – is the solution. "The tragic paradox of the electoral route to authoritarianism," Steven Levitsky and Daniel Ziblatt (2018) write in *How Democracies Die*, "is that democracy's assassins use the very institutions of democracy – gradually, subtly, and even legally – to kill it."

Chinese "academics" attending trilaterals and conferences sponsored in whole or in part by PRC organizations with ties to the United Front Work Department have also used disinformation to mislead foreign scholars, who became unwitting collaborators in the disinformation campaign against Taiwan. In one instance, they succeeded in convincing top U.S. academics during an event in New York City that President Tsai's upcoming address at the Double Ten ceremony would contain new elements which could be seen as a "test" by Beijing and thus determine the future direction of cross-Strait relations. In reality, President Tsai had no intention of saying anything particularly new, nor did Beijing expect that she would. When President Tsai's address "failed" to provide anything new, analysts regarded her speech as a missed opportunity to reach out to Beijing.

Understanding the challenges posed by disinformation, Taiwanese NGOs have developed online apps that can help users verify whether information contained in a bit of news is indeed credible or false. Laudable though those efforts may be, such apps will only be salutatory if news consumers use them, and if the result of that query can reach enough ears and eyes to persuade large enough a segment of the population that the item in question is true or false. Saturated as we are with information, and given the passive means by which most people today access the news – it comes at us via Facebook, Twitter, and other social media, filtered by algorithms we are not even aware of, rather than us seeking it as we did in the past by accessing trusted news sites – it is unlikely that many people will take the time to check with an app to verify a bit of information.

Media themselves will have to become more responsible with the information they broadcast, while publications and sites that propagate disinformation will have to be selected out by market forces. Recently, Taiwan and partners in the international community have begun collaborating on media literacy projects that seek to identify means and mechanisms of disinformation and establish means, through watchdogs and education, by which the effectiveness of disinformation can be reduced. The impact of such collaboration remains to be seen; moreover, we should keep in mind that the agents of disinformation will be adaptive and often one step ahead of those who seek to check their nefarious activities.

United front work

Chapter 5 of *Convenient* spent a good amount of time listing the various organizations involved in united front work and political warfare against Taiwan. Since then, a report by the National Endowment for Democracy (NED) in the United Sates has come up with a new term to describe some of those activities. That term is "sharp power." According to NED, "authoritarian influence is not principally about attraction or even persuasion; instead, it centers on distraction and manipulation." It continues: "In the new competition that is under way between autocratic and democratic states, the repressive regimes' 'sharp power' techniques should be seen as the tip of their dagger – or indeed as their syringe."

Some of the key organizations involved in "sharp power" against Taiwan were mentioned in the earlier section on disinformation – CAPCC, CAIFC, CEFC, and so on, as well as media organizations, co-opted officials and pro-Beijing elements in the business community. Many, many more such agencies, some acting semi-independently while others under direct orders of the Chinese military-intelligence

48 The illusion is broken

apparatus, are involved in this campaign. The full list of participants in these activities, or a complete description of how they engage in political warfare, is beyond the scope of this book. In fact, it is probably impossible to provide a complete picture of such activities.

What is certain is that such activities, and the united front, now play a reinvigorated role in Xi Jinping's China. Besides elevating the United Front Work Department, Xi has reportedly added as many as 40,000 cadres to the body, with a special focus on operations abroad "to fight the bloody battle against our enemies ... with a strong determination to take our place in the world" (Griffiths 2018).

Despite the disparate nature of many of the organizations and individuals involved in China's "sharp power" activities, the general direction and tone is set by the CCP itself. Atop all this sits the aforementioned Chinese People's Political Consultative Congress, which is where all the relevant actors inside and outside the CCP – party elders, intelligence officers, diplomats, propagandists, soldiers and political commissars, united front workers, academics, and businesspeople – come together and where the strategic aims of political warfare and propaganda are developed.[3] Below the CPPCC Standing Committee, nine special committees bring together important national figures inside and outside the CCP. One of those committees is the Hong Kong, Macao, and Taiwan Affairs Committee (港澳台僑委員會). Honorary memberships are used primarily for Taiwanese businesspeople working in China (also known as *taishang*). Although Taiwanese regulations prohibit Taiwanese nationals from serving in any official state or CCP-related organizations, honorary membership has been used to circumvent those rules. As Mattis has noted, Taiwanese business associations with close links to Beijing, the Association of Taiwan Investment Enterprises on the Mainland (全國台灣同胞投資企業聯誼會) chief among them, have lobbied to drop these prohibitions.

In March 2017, then-CPPCC Chairman Yu Zhengsheng (俞正聲) unveiled a new guiding principle for united front work against Taiwan, shifting the emphasis from "three middles and the youth" (三中一青) – residents of central and southern Taiwan, middle- and low-income families, and small- and medium-sized enterprises – in early 2015 to "one generation and one stratum" (一代一線) – the young generation and the grassroots – in a bid to influence what is regarded as the "naturally independence-leaning" generation. This new emphasis has been reflected in various activities targeting young Taiwan since 2016, including the "31 incentives" (discussed later in this chapter) and a variety of cultural events. One such event, which caused much controversy, was the "Sing! China: Shanghai-Taipei Music Festival" (2017《中國新歌聲》上海·台北音樂節), which was scheduled to be held at National Taiwan University (NTU) on 24 September 2017. Organized by the Taipei City Government in conjunction with the Shanghai City Cross-Strait Cultural Exchange Promotion Association (上海市海峽兩岸交流促進會), the Shanghai Cultural Association (上海文化聯誼會), Shanghai Canxing Trading Co., Ltd. (上海燦星文化傳媒股份有限公司), and Shanghai Voice of Dream Media Co. (夢響強音文化傳播) (*China Review News* 2017), the event was eventually cancelled after protests by students and pro-independence advocates, though shows on other campuses were held as planned earlier in the week, as well as in 2015 and 2016.

Ostensibly cultural, the event was anything but: among other things, the Shanghai City Cross-Strait Exchange Promotion Association clearly states on its website that it is dedicated to the "peaceful unification of the motherland." Li Wenhui (李文輝), the "honorary chairman" of the association who came to Taiwan for the musical event, is the TAO's director of the Shanghai Municipal People's Government. Li's application for a visa to visit Taiwan after Lunar New Year in 2018 was turned down, presumably due to "inappropriate behavior" during one of his many visits to Taiwan (local reports alleged Li visited Taiwan about every two weeks) (Chung 2018).

Although the potential for recruitment or "brainwashing" during such "cultural" events is minimal, such activities serve to reinforce certain memes espoused by the CCP and on occasion their holding will come after local Taiwanese authorities agreed to name changes to comply with Beijing's preferences. For example, promotional material for the aforementioned Sing! China festival saw "National Taiwan University" changed to "Taipei City Taiwan University." More troubling is the high likelihood that CCP united front work agents use such visits to establish networks while in Taiwan. In other words, rather than the event itself, it is the extra activities that such individuals may engage in outside public scrutiny that poses a problem. Since the second term of the Ma administration, TAO officials had a tendency to go off-reserve when in Taiwan, bypassing central government figures and, sometimes off-schedule, meeting with locals. The risks of co-optation during such contact are relatively high and worthy of attention.

The Sing! China controversy also dragged other elements into the fray – members of the pro-CCP China Unification Promotion Party (CUPP), who engaged in physical clashes with students who were protesting the event. Among the assailants was Chang Wei (張瑋), the second son of CUPP founder Chang An-le (張安樂). Five others were charged over the physical clashes, including one of the protesters. On 30 July 2018, the Taipei District Court sentenced Chang Wei to 40 days in jail for assault, a sentence that could be changed to a fine.

Earlier that year, the young Chang had been involved in another altercation, this time at Taiwan Taoyuan International Airport, where he and other pro-CCP activists attempted to disrupt the arrival in Taiwan of pro-democracy activists in Hong Kong, among them lawmakers Edward Yiu (姚松炎), Nathan Law (羅冠聰) and Eddie Chu (朱凱迪), and activist Joshua Wong (黃之鋒), who had been invited to Taiwan to participate in a forum. Prior to their departure for Taiwan, the lawmakers and activists had also been threatened by pro-Beijing groups at the airport in Hong Kong, suggesting coordination between pro-Beijing elements in Taiwan and HKSAR. Reports also indicated that the individuals involved in the altercation at Taiwan Taoyuan International Airport belonged to both the Bamboo Union, which is close to the CUPP, and the Four Seas Gang, another triad that in recent years had tended to avoid involving itself in politics in order to focus more on its business interests.

50 The illusion is broken

Once on Taiwan's most-wanted list, Chang An-le returned to Taiwan in June 2013 after spending more than a decade in exile in China, where he is believed to have been recruited. During his exile in China, Chang reportedly built a close relationship with the "princelings" aristocracy and began to involve himself in cross-Strait issues. The former head of the Bamboo Union, who spent a decade in a U.S. federal prison in the 1980s for drug trafficking, became the perfect example of the "symbiotic relationship" that can develop between criminals and the CCP, something we have seen time and again in Hong Kong. Among his closest associations in China, which Chang claims was facilitated by an elder cousin who had stayed behind after 1949, was Hu Shiying (胡石英), the son of former CCP propaganda chief and vehement anti-reformist Hu Qiaomu (胡喬木) and reportedly a member of President Xi Jinping's "close circle."

Since his return to Taiwan in 2013, where he was detained for a few hours before being released, Chang has become a strong advocate for unification and the "one country, two systems" formula. On several occasions, he and his followers have engaged in physical clashes with activists and on 1 April 2014, attempted to evict Sunflower activists from the Legislative Yuan. Had it not been for a strong police cordon, a violent scene would most assuredly have ensued.

Starting in 2016, Chang's CUPP has also lent its support to other protest groups, including the deep-blue (and violence-prone) Blue Sky Alliance (藍天行動聯盟) and the "800 Heroes" (八百壯士) – groups opposed to President Tsai's pension reform – the very same protests that, as discussed earlier, were in part being fueled by disinformation. Those protests were also marked by violence, in one instance *between* CUPP and Blue Sky Alliance members when the latter complained about the presence of too many People's Republic of China (PRC) flags at the site. This particular incident was proof, yet again, of the limit to which deep-blue and anti-DPP groups will go when collaborating with pro-CCP elements. After all, the Blue Sky Alliance counts among its members many retired officers from the ROC military – the very military that fought the CCP in the Chinese Civil War.

The CUPP's resorting to violence has caused safety concerns among activists and politicians, fears that have been exacerbated by the Bamboo Union's access to firearms. In May 2018, a large cache of firearms – the largest in a decade, according to the authorities – was seized in Taiwan originating from the Philippines. A total of 109 firearms, including Bushmaster XM15-E25s, Spike's Tactical ST-15s, and a Striker-12 shotgun, as well as 12,378 rounds of ammunition, were found in Keelung. One officer said of the arms cache, "You could set up an army with those!" Commenting on the matter, Minister of the Interior Yeh Jiunn-rong (葉俊榮) said that if the guns had flown into the market, "the consequences would have been disastrous." The individuals arrested in the case were from the Bamboo Union. Some of them fled to Singapore but were eventually sent back to Taiwan.

The high incidence of violence at CUPP protests is not altogether surprising, given that many of its members during protests tend to be drawn from local gangs. While no serious act of violence has been committed, there are fears of possible escalation, especially if their targets begin to respond in kind. A tit-for-tat war between groups of civilians could quickly spiral out of control and destabilize society. Such a scenario could then, as we saw in Crimea, for example, serve as justification for Beijing to step in – this time to protect Chinese compatriots against attacks by Taiwanese "separatists." Violence could also be part of Beijing's efforts to "Lebanonize" Taiwan, an idea which was floated in a *Global Times* editorial in 2016. Such a strategy would seek to undermine state institutions and exacerbate political/ethnic divisions until the state loses its coherence, at which time Taiwan would be ripe for the taking by the CCP. One of the key pro-Beijing organizations in Taiwan involved in such destabilizing activities is the Concentric Patriot Association of the ROC (CPAROC, 中華愛國同心會), which has a long history of collaboration with the CUPP and of violent actions against society. Members of the CPAROC, as well as immigrant spouses from China, were also behind a controversy surrounding an illegal shrine to the CCP erected in Changhua County, which was demolished in September 2018 (Yan 2018). The same day, a spokesperson for the State Council's Taiwan Affairs Office accused the Tsai government of "persecuting" the pro-unification camp in Taiwan (TAO 2018a), rhetoric that, as in Crimea, could suggest future intentions of intervention to "protect" Chinese compatriots.

Although it has fielded candidates in local elections, the CUPP's main aim isn't electoral, where its political beliefs will almost certainly ensure its defeat. The CUPP plays the electoral game, what with the campaign offices (it has chapters in Taipei, Miaoli, Pingtung, Yunlin, Chiayi, and Tainan), trucks, blazons, and so on, to legitimize itself in the eyes of the public. Its principal role, however, is to penetrate Taiwanese society and use its funding to exert influence in a way that would undermine the political coherence of the state. In other words, in line with the CPPCC's "one generation and one stratum," the CUPP is targeting grassroots organizations and seeking to fill the vacuum left by the KMT's current travails. At the center of this activity are the CUPP-affiliated "Tainan Cross-Strait Exchange Promotion Association" (台南市兩岸交流協會) and the "Cross-Strait Taiwan Guangdong Exchange Association" (台粵交流協會會), which in recent years have seen a "steady stream" of Chinese officials on visits to Taiwan.

The CUPP has been increasing its influence with local temples (already seen as conduits for CCP political warfare), gangs, and businesses. It also presents itself as a

> go-between for China through village and ward chiefs, university students and young entrepreneurs, while setting up agricultural exchanges with China for representatives of Taiwanese farmers' associations and agricultural production and marketing groups.
>
> *(Commonwealth Magazine 2018)*

At a time when the CCP has lost faith in the ability of the KMT to facilitate unification, the CUPP is now an agent by which Beijing can seek to bypass Taiwan's state institutions and deal directly with the grassroots, with co-opted locals acting as agents. Like the CCP before and during the civil war in China, where it became "all things to all men" and created temporary alliances to manipulate local politics

52 The illusion is broken

(Westad 2003), the CUPP is offering itself as an agent for change, a provider of services to the poor, something that crime syndicates the world over have often done, usually at the expense of the central government. Another example that comes to mind is the Lebanese Hezbollah, which filled a vacuum in southern Lebanon in times of instability and, over time, became a political force to be reckoned with.

Interestingly, in January 2018, Mayor Ko attended a launch event for a book on Chiang Ching-kuo (蔣經國) published by Wu Jianguo (吳建國) at which Chang An-le was also present (*China Review News* 2018). Wu, a former president of National Kaohsiung University of Applied Sciences, moved to Shanghai several years ago. In an interview with the *People's Daily* (2006) in March 2006, Wu stated his goal of using culture to promote unification. Wu also told this author that he acts as an "adviser" to Mayor Ko, which sources in the Taipei City Government have confirmed, although they maintain that he does so in an unofficial capacity[5].

Despite the tendency among many Taiwanese to regard Chang and his followers as buffoons who should be left to their own designs, the CUPP should not be underestimated. Indeed, the protests they have organized over the years have been – occasional violence aside – rather laughable affairs. But that is a facade. Behind this lies something that should be taken much more seriously. Disagree with his politics or not, Chang An-le is no imbecile.

In August 2018, the CUPP's office in Taipei as well as Chang An-le's residence were raided by prosecutors. Prosecutors said they had gathered evidence of illegal activities that contravene the National Security Act (國家安全法), the Political Donations Act (政治獻金法), and the Organized Crime Prevention Act (組織犯罪防制條例). Among other things, the authorities were trying to determine whether the CUPP was illegally trying to influence the November elections, possibly using illegal funding from the CCP (Chang maintains that all the money comes from his business operations in China). Other CUPP officials were summoned for questioning.

The raid was evidence that the Taiwanese government was finally willing to act against the CUPP, which inexplicably had been allowed to operate normally since Chang's return to Taiwan in 2013. While permitting the existence of pro-unification parties such as the CUPP and New Party is a sign of political pluralism in Taiwan's democracy, their legitimacy and legality are nevertheless contingent on the parties respecting the rules of the game, something that, when it came to the CUPP, was very much in doubt.

The New Party (新黨), an ally of the CUPP, itself came under scrutiny in 2018 when a number of members were accused of colluding with a Chinese spy ring in Taiwan known as "Star Fire Secret Unit" led by Zhou Hongxu (周泓旭). In September 2017, Zhou, a Chinese student, was convicted of espionage and breaching the National Security Act, and was sentenced to 14 months (he was released in May 2018 after a successful appeal, though he was barred from leaving the country). In December 2017, New Party spokesman Wang Ping-chung (王炳忠), along with youth wing executives Ho Han-ting (侯漢廷) and Lin Ming-cheng (林明正), as well as a party accountant surnamed Tseng (曾), also became the objects of attention by prosecutors in the case, and Wang was eventually named a defendant. Wang's father, Wang Chin-pu (王進步), was also summoned for questioning.

Documents seized in the investigation against Wang Ping-chung showed he had been working with Chinese officials in 2013, before he had even met Zhou. In fact, Wang's troubling ties appear to have come to the attention of the national security apparatus when Ma Ying-jeou was still in office. Information seized in the raid showed the TAO had promised to provide Wang and Zhou as much as NT$16 million annually for their operations in Taiwan. Prosecutors said they had collected evidence that Wang had received money transfers from Chinese sources, and a note from him saying that he would "work under the guidance and assistance of the CCP to help the forces working to achieve unification across the Taiwan Strait."

No longer a viable political force in Taiwan's electoral politics, the New Party in recent years has reinvented itself as a CCP ally, much like the CUPP. Its chairman, Yok Mu-ming (郁慕明), has made several visits to Beijing since 2016, where he has had various interactions with members of the CCP, including Xi Jinping as well as then–CPPCC chairman Yu Zhengsheng and then–TAO chief Zhang Zhijun (張志軍). In late 2017, his party announced it intended to open a "liaison office" in China.

New Party and CUPP members have also interacted with overseas Chinese organizations that are suspected of being involved in united front work. On 2 December 2017, for example, Yok, as well as Wang Ping-chung and CUPP chairman Chang Fu-tang (張馥堂), attended a "Cross-Strait Development Forum" (兩岸和平發展論壇) in New York City hosted by the 全美中國和平統一促進聯合會 and co-sponsored by the New York chapter of the China Council for the Promotion of Peaceful National Unification (CCPPR, 紐約中國和平統一促進會) and the 美東華人社團聯合總會, with involvement by the US-China Cultural Exchange Society (美國美中文化交流促進會). Li Kexin (李克新), minister at the Chinese embassy in Washington, D.C., was also present.[4] Soon after their return from the forum, Wang and other New Party members were brought in for questioning by Taiwanese prosecutors.

Other smaller proxies of the CCP in Taiwan, including the Taiwan Red Party (TRP, 中國台灣紅黨 － 紅黨), have surfaced since Tsai assumed office in 2016. One of the more than 300 registered political parties in Taiwan, the TRP was launched in Taichung on 25 March 2017. In its declaration, the party states that it aims to "integrate the majority of Taiwanese farmers and fishermen" (「統合廣大農漁工」). Historically, those have been areas of KMT influence. In April 2019, the TRP co-sponsored an event in Taichung titled "2019 Peaceful Integration and Development Forum" (2019和平統一融合發展論壇) under the slogan "Promote the 1992 Consensus, Support Peace, Support Unification" (「宣揚九二共識、支持和平、支持統一」). The United Front Work Department-linked China Council for the Promotion of Peaceful Reunification (Taiwan) (CPPRC, 中國和平統一促進會 (台灣)), the China Peace Development Association (中華和平發展促進會), and the Taichung City Cross-Strait Business and Trade Association (台中市兩岸商務經貿協會) were also involved in hosting the event (Cole 2019b), which was eventually cancelled.

54 The illusion is broken

Also in April 2019, it was revealed that the TRP had been actively recruiting young Taiwanese to attend a Communist Party school in China since at least May 2017, two months after the party's registration. The first advertisement for the party school was seen on the Taiwanese Chinese Heart (台灣人中國心) Facebook page. The school in question was the Fujian Provincial Communist Party School – Taiwan Social Elite Class (中共黨校福建省委黨校台灣社會菁英班). Various pro-unification Face-book forums and social media apps provided the same cell phone number in Taiwan as the one used in the advertisements for the aforementioned "2019 Peaceful Integra-tion and Development Forum" in Taichung. Among the qualifications for admission stated in the ad are "support for 'one China'" and self-identification as a Chinese citizen. According to the ad, classes provide training on subjects such as Chinese law, Chinese economic theory, institutions, the Belt and Road Initiative, special eco-nomic zones, implementation, and practical experience sharing. Faculty comes from think tanks affiliated with the central leadership in Beijing (Cole 2019c). The online advertisement stated that the party school serves as an incubator of the central (Chi-nese) government, adding that the certificate can be used anywhere in the "Chinese mainland." According to journalist Melissa Chan (2012), "China's ruling Communist Party's 80 million members attend special [Party] schools to learn party ideology at facilities that serve as a training ground for the next generation of Chinese leaders."

As developments in Australia, New Zealand and elsewhere in recent years have made clear, the CCP relies on a constellation of associations and councils world-wide to orchestrate its "sharp power" and united front campaign. The telltale "pro-motion of peaceful national unification" is usually a sign that the association has some ties with the United Front Work Department back in China. Many of those organizations also perform their operations with some level of coordination from the nearest Chinese embassy or consulate. Chambers of commerce have also played a role in facilitating these operations. Naming all the organizations involved, and detailing the extent to which they are part of Beijing's united front apparatus is a challenge even for intelligence agencies. Not all of their operations are targeted at Taiwan; in many cases, their united front work efforts instead aim to shape the local environment to benefit China's growing aspirations.

Nevertheless, united front work units worldwide will, at some point or another, become involved in activities that seek to isolate Taiwan, erode support for it by local governments, and promote the inevitability of "national reunification." In some instances, this has also involved the co-optation of officials and academics. And exposing those corrosive operations comports certain risks for academics and journalists, as this author himself has experienced. As China's "sharp power" and assault on global democratic institutions become the subject of greater attention, its agents have become more willing to take legal action to silence its critics. For decades, the CCP has used threats and intimidation to silence investigative jour-nalists and academics inside China, often by shutting down entire publications or arresting individuals. More recently, gangsters with suspected ties to the CCP have resorted to violence to intimidate editors and journalists in Hong Kong. In some cases, the attacks resulted in serious injuries and created a hostile environment for the few Beijing critics who continue to operate in HKSAR media (in August 2018 the HK Foreign Correspondents Club also found itself in hot water for inviting Andy Chan Ho-tin [陳浩天] of the Hong Kong National Party to address the club) (Quackenbush 2018).

In recent years, China has become more extraterritorial in its efforts to intimidate critics. In a bid to silence those who risk exposing its illegal activities on foreign soil, where Beijing has benefited from lack of knowledge about its institutions and guiding ideology, the CCP and its affiliates have taken "lawfare" – the threat or use of legal action – abroad. This author was sued by the aforementioned CEFC in 2016; the Taipei District Court eventually ruled in the defendant's favor in February 2018. The plaintiff, Patrick Ho (何志平), the former Hong Kong home secretary who was secretary-general of the CEFC think tank in Hong Kong, was arrested in New York City for allegedly leading a multimillion-dollar bribery scheme in Africa on behalf of CEFC Shanghai, "with some deals supposedly arranged in the halls of the United Nations." In the indictment, U.S. officials said that Ho, who described himself as a "civil diplomat," along with former Senegalese top diplomat Cheikh Gadio, "had sent huge bribes to high-level officials in Chad and Uganda to secure business advantages for the Chinese energy company" (AFP 2017). According to the *South China Morning Post*, "The two men allegedly offered a US\$2 million bribe to Chadian President Idriss Deby (伊德里斯·德比) in exchange for 'valuable oil rights,' and another US\$500,000 to Uganda's Foreign Affairs Minister Sam Kutesa [薩姆·庫泰薩]." The business advantages included the acquisition of oil fields in Chad from CPC Corp, Taiwan (台灣中油), a deal that had been brokered, reportedly without proper review, when Ma Ying-jeou was still in office (Yang 2017). Among the claims that I had made in my article was the high likelihood that CEFC would use its fortunes to co-opt and corrupt officials in the pursuance of its activities. Patrick Ho, whose requests for home arrest have been turned down because he is a flight risk, was the plaintiff in my case back in Taiwan.

In March 2018, news emerged that Ye Jianming, the chairman of the energy company in Shanghai, was under investigation in China "on suspicion of violation of laws." Mr. Ye has not appeared in public since, and it is rumored that he may be under arrest. Among other things, it was demonstrated that CEFC "was in talks with Chinese shadow lenders for short-term loans with annual rates of as much as 36 percent to make up its cash shortfall" as it sought to generate cash for the acquisition of various assets worldwide (Chen and Wu 2018). Within month, the multi-billion-dollar energy company, which earlier had been on the brink of acquiring a highly publicized US\$9.1 billion stake in Russia's oil giant Rosneft, was brought to its knees. Ye was forced to step down, and much of CEFC's operations, including its substantial presence in the Czech Republic, where Ye had become adviser to the Czech President, Miloš Zeman, were taken over by state-run CITIC (中國中信集團). The Hong Kong–based think tank, meanwhile, was expected to cease operations, and Andrew Lo (路祥安), Ho's deputy at the organization and a former close aide to ex-Hong Kong leader Tung Chee-hwa (董建華), suddenly died of a "bad case of flu" in February 2018. Later in 2018, U.S. prosecutors accused

56 The illusion is broken

Ho of brokering arms transactions with Libya, Qatar, and South Sudan via an unnamed intermediary. Prosecutors also alleged that Ho had offered US$50,000 as well as a free trip to Hong Kong to John Ashe, the head of the U.N. General Assembly between 2013–2014, in exchange for cooperation after Ashe stepped down from the position (Lum 2018). At this writing, UN Secretary-General António Guterres has refused to call for an internal investigation.

One investigative journalist in the Czech Republic was also threatened with legal action for exposing CEFC's activities in his country. According to most analysts, CEFC had been using the Czech Republic as a springboard to expand its influence in other parts of Europe as part of Beijing's Belt and Road and 16 + 1 initiative. In many ways, CEFC had managed to make inroads in the Czech Republic in large part due to the weaknesses in its democratic institutions.

Ye may also have become victim of his own successes and self-appointed role as Chinese global man of influence. In his early 40s, the mysterious Ye had a tendency to portray himself as a philosopher cum geo-strategist. And his think tank, CEFC, was actively engaged in influence operations abroad, including the promotion of the "China model" as an alternative to liberal-democracy, China's claims to the South China Sea, the abandonment of Taiwan, and psychological warfare against Japan over its past crimes (comfort women, militarization, etc.), among other things. Thus, Ye may have come to be seen as a threat to Xi Jinping, who does not countenance the emergence of independent forces which one day could challenge him, as Bo Xilai (薄熙來) discovered to his detriment in 2013. Ye may have facilitated his own downfall by engaging in dubious financial practices to build his global empire; Ho's arrest in New York City had drawn too much attention to Chinese corruption, and this risked tarnishing the image of the Belt and Road Initiative; Ye, therefore, had to go, to be made of an example of. As with his other potential contenders, Xi had something – economic crimes – on Ye to target him for corruption.

As China continues to expand its presence overseas, particularly via its Belt and Road Initiative, a greater number of journalists and whistleblowers are bound to go public with information that the CCP and its proxies would rather remained hidden. Unfortunately, many of the countries targeted do not enjoy rule of law or robust democratic institutions. Consequently, Beijing's ability to coerce and silence its critics in those countries will be much more stronger than it was in my case, operating as I was, a Western national, in democratic Taiwan. Since my own bruising experience, I have campaigned for a global alliance to bring succor, guidance and financial support to members of the press who are thus targeted by China in their countries, especially as there are signs that Beijing has already developed close working relationships with the top law firms in most of the countries that fall under its Belt and Road Initiative.

China's 31 incentives and other sweeteners

Not all of China's active measures against Taiwan since 2016 have been overtly punitive. In February 2018, for example, the TAO unveiled a list of 31 "incentives" to attract young Taiwanese to relocate to China to work (TAO 2018b). The strategy, which involved 12 incentives related to business and 19 to social and employment issues, was the latest in a long list of efforts over the years to win the hearts and minds of the Taiwanese while increasing the economic interdependence between the two sides of the Taiwan Strait. It was very much in line with the "one generation and one stratum" (一代一線) strategy unveiled by then–CPPCC Chairman Yu Zhengsheng in March 2017.

On 3 August 2018, the State Council also announced that residents of Taiwan no longer needed work permits to work in China.

Among other things, the new measures, which some described as "unprecedented benefits," aimed to facilitate market access and competition for Taiwanese enterprises in China. Taiwanese would be allowed to invest in Chinese state-owned enterprises, and participate in public biddings and innovation programs. Chinese institutions were also expected to offer cooperation to strengthen the market position of Taiwanese firms operating in China and enable them to offer more services.

Meanwhile, highly educated Taiwanese were to see a loosening of regulations to study, initiate start-ups, or join the Chinese labor market in areas where doing so had been difficult to in the past. Taiwanese were to get better access to China's cultural industries, while restrictions on Taiwanese capital investment and technical participation in Chinese filmmaking would be relaxed. High-skilled professionals and technical personnel from 134 listed professions were invited to work in China, with all administrative restrictions annulled. Taiwanese patents brought to China were to be protected by Chinese law.

Taiwanese academics and universities would also be invited to participate in China's grant programs for research funding and become eligible for state subsides much as their Chinese counterparts.

As with everything else, Beijing was not extending this offer out of kindness. Instead, the 31 incentives were part of a program aimed at hollowing out Taiwan by creating a "brain drain," which even without the lure of China has become a matter of national security for Taiwan as it tries to reconfigure its economy for the 21st century (see Chapter 9). The 31 incentives were also part of an effort to capture knowledge and talent that China needs to build its economy for the future. And of course, it was implemented with the hope that young Taiwanese who agree to work or study in China would, over time, allow their exposure to transform their political convictions by eroding their self-identification as Taiwanese.

In other words, the 31 incentives were predicated on the same old notions of economic determinism that Beijing has tried in the past, not only over Taiwan but also in Tibet and Xinjiang. Although the promise of material gain could succeed in attracting young Taiwanese, history has shown that such dynamics rarely translate into political gain. Young Taiwanese will make the pragmatic decision of working in China if the opportunities are there, as they will if career prospects exist elsewhere. However, experience has shown that exposure to life in China has not generated the political effects expected by Beijing. Moreover, given that the 31 incentives, like other programs before it, are mainly utilitarian, there is a high likelihood that, after a few years, Taiwanese who responded positively to the measures will become disillusioned and choose to return home. That is because no matter what Chinese authorities say, Taiwanese and other "minorities" will eventually always be treated differently in China. Young Taiwanese whose have grown accustomed to living in a free and democratic environment will become all the more aware of the differences that exist between Taiwan and China after they spend a few years across the Taiwan Strait. For them, the reality of life in China is no longer an abstract; it is lived experience. While some will choose to stay behind, many will eventually decide to return to Taiwan or seek their fortunes elsewhere.

We can therefore predict, with a certain amount of certainty, that the 31 incentives, like other iterations before it, will not lead to a major shift in support for unification or self-identification as Chinese among the Taiwanese targeted by the program. The greatest threat to Taiwan stemming from this incentive package instead lies in its ability to deny Taiwan the brain trust, especially in the high-tech sector, it needs to build itself for the 21st century. Thus, Taiwan's greatest enemy in all this is its own stagnant economy and the glass ceiling that hovers above many young and ambitious Taiwanese who have come to question whether Taiwan can provide the environment they need to prosper and to start a family. As long as this problem has not been resolved, and as long as China's economy continues to grow, the lure of China will remain a national security issue for Taiwan.

In March 2018, the Executive Yuan unveiled a plan to counter China's 31 incentives. Consisting of four major policy directions, the plan aimed to attract and retain talent in Taiwan by building a quality education and work environment, maintain Taiwan's advantages in the global supply chain, deepen capital markets, and strengthen the cultural audiovisual industry (EY 2018). Whether that will be enough to stem to exodus remains to be seen.

At a more local level, Beijing has also sought to widen the divide between the central government in Taipei and outlying communities, chief among them the outlying island of Kinmen, which lies a few kilometers off the coast of China. The issue began in 2015 when, facing a possible water shortage, Kinmen's water authority signed a 30-year water purchasing agreement with Fujian Province. A 17 km water main connecting reservoirs on both sides was completed in 2018 at a cost of NT$1.35 billion and is expected to provide about 30 percent of Kinmen's total water supply. Under the agreement, Kinmen will import an average of 34,000 tons of water daily from Fujian at a cost of NT$9.86 per cubic meter of water.

Completion of the water main led to a dispute between the Kinmen authorities and the Mainland Affairs Council (MAC) in Taipei in July 2018 over a dedication ceremony. On one side, the Kinmen government said its main priority was to meet the rights and needs of Kinmen residents, while the MAC insisted on a downgraded ceremony due to Beijing's efforts to isolate Taiwan on the international stage. In a rare instance of insubordination, the Kinmen government refused to abide by the central government's directive and asked the MAC to reconsider its position. In the end, a smaller ceremony was held, but MAC officials did not participate.

Kinmen County Commissioner Chen Fu-hai (陳福海) was elected in the 29 November 2014, elections as an independent candidate. Besides the water project, he has raised the possibility of a wider "three new links" policy to incorporate an electricity link and a bridge to China. The growing dependence of Kinmen on China, not only for water, but eventually for electricity, risks exposing the outlying island to possible blackmail by Beijing, which for political purposes could threaten to turn off water or electricity provisions for the residents of Kinmen. In other words, Kinmen could eventually be held hostage, its ability to function contingent on Beijing's goodwill. This could eventually lead to a further erosion of ties between the government in Taipei and Kinmen, and a possible first step in the dismantlement of the territory controlled by Taiwan.

Military

The above has provided a list, by no means exhaustive, of the mostly coercive strategies adopted by Beijing since President Tsai's inauguration in May 2016, which in many instances constituted more of a continuation of earlier strategies than a clear shift in approach. While that strategy was expected to intensify in the lead up to the 2020 elections, with new elements added before this book hits the bookstores, the aims remain the same: to overwhelm Taiwan, break its morale, foster a sense of inevitability, isolate it internationally, increase the costs of resistance, and erode belief in and support for Taiwan's government and democratic institutions. Through these, Beijing hopes to sufficiently undermine morale in Taiwan so that its people will capitulate and sue for peace, which would inevitably occur on Beijing's terms. Whether that campaign will succeed in achieving all those objectives remains to be seen. As an insurance policy, Beijing has retained to option of using force to resolve the "Taiwan question" once and for all. In this role, the PLA serves two functions – to exacerbate the psychological campaign waged against Taiwan, and, if called upon as a last resort, to actively annex Taiwan by force of arms.

The geopolitical context and rationale for growing Chinese military activity near and around Taiwan will be discussed in greater detail in Chapter 4. The aim here is to analyze what role PLA activities since 2016 have played in Beijing's punitive strategy.

One of the objectives of increased military activity around Taiwan was the collection of intelligence. Among other things, this allowed the PLA to better understand Taiwan's Command, Control, Communications, Computers, Intelligence, Surveillance and Reconnaissance (C4ISR) architecture and response times whenever the Taiwanese Air Force had to scramble aircraft to intercept PLA Air Force (PLAAF, 中國人民解放軍空軍) jets flying close to Taiwan's Air Defense Identification Zone (ADIZ, 防空識別區). PLA Navy (PLAN, 中國人民解放軍海軍) vessels, meanwhile, no doubt used their transits in the Taiwan Strait, in the Strait of Miyako (宮古海峽), and the Bashi Channel (巴士海峽), as well as passages behind Taiwan in the West Pacific, to gather hydrographic data about the environment around Taiwan, all with a view to increasing the PLA's situational awareness

60 The illusion is broken

should Beijing one day call upon it to annex Taiwan by force. In other words, more frequent PLA activity served the purpose of familiarizing Chinese pilots and naval service members with a terrain they could be asked one day to conquer.

Just as important, the high frequency of military exercises and transits near and around Taiwan was an instrument of psychological warfare, one of the many rungs in Beijing's strategy to scare the Taiwanese into submission. The idea was to create a sense of encirclement and to do so often enough that a PLA military presence became a new normal for the Taiwanese, a fact of life that the leadership in Taipei could do little to counter. It was quantitative – more sorties in larger numbers – just as it was qualitative: the PLA military platforms making the transits were increasingly modern and well armed, which was meant to contrast with the aging Taiwanese military. Both were intended to showcase China's growing force projection capabilities.

One aircraft that made repeated transits was the PLAAF's Xian H–6K, a Chinese derivate of Soviet Tupolev Tu–16 bomber. The H–6K carries up to six YJ–12 anti-ship missiles or a similar number of CJ–10 land-attack cruise missiles. The *Liaoning*, China's first aircraft carrier, also made highly publicized transits in the Taiwan Strait to further accentuate the fact of a Chinese military presence near Taiwan (this is all fine and well in peacetime; however, in actual war, the last thing the Chinese would want to do is to place its aircraft carrier within reach of Taiwan's anti-ship missiles).

Beijing's unilateral activation in late 2017 of three additional east-west routes connecting M503 with China and opening the M503 route for northbound traffic in violation of a 2015 agreement with Taipei also served to tighten the noose around Taiwan. M503 is close to Taiwanese Air Force training areas, while two of the three new routes – W122 and W123 – pass by Taiwan's forward-deployed defenses on the outlying islands of Kinmen and Matsu.

On 31 March 2019, after several passages by PLA aircraft and vessels in recent months, the PLA upped the ante when two J–11 fighter aircraft penetrated the median line in the Taiwan Strait and remained on the Taiwan side for as many as 10 minutes, forcing Taiwan to dispatch interceptors, before retreating to the Chinese side (Westcott 2019). The intrusion – the first deliberate one since 1999 – also appeared to have a high level of coordination with the Central Military Commission, overseen by Xi Jinping, with civilian traffic ceasing altogether along the M503 line, which is managed by the Shanghai Flight Information Zone, hours prior to the incident (Chen 2019). The move also appeared to be in retaliation for the recent transits by U.S. Navy vessels in the Taiwan Strait, whose frequency had increased since 2018.

In its 2017 *National Defense Report*, Taiwan's Ministry of National Defense (MND) said it had identified a total of 23 PLA exercises between September 2016 and December 2017; those were in addition to PLAAF activity forcing Taiwanese combat air patrols (CAP). At least 10 exercises were held between the end of the CCP's 19th National Congress in October 2017 and the end of December that year.

Acknowledging the psychological warfare elements of the growing frequency of PLA exercises, in December 2017 Taiwan's MND announced that it would no longer publicize them unless there was something "unusual" about them.

As mentioned earlier, the PLAAF also used its official Weibo account to propagate disinformation about alleged intrusions near Taiwan, putting Jade Mountain well within sight. Meanwhile, Beijing also counted on so-called military experts who are often quoted in the media to exacerbate the psychological pressure on Taiwan. One of the most vocal hawks doing this service to the PLA is Song Zhongping (宋忠平), a military commentator for Hong Kong-based Phoenix TV who often writes opinion pieces for the CCP-mouthpiece *Global Times*. Oftentimes, before exercises are held, Song would publish remarks that were meant to create a sense of crisis, as he did when the PLA held live-fire drills off Quanzhou (泉州), Fujian Province, in April 2018. Song's comments would then usually be picked up by other Chinese media, including the *SCMP*, which would serve to legitimize his opinions. Often, the same comments would then be quoted by foreign media. All of this would amplify the pressure on Taiwan, often by blowing out of proportion military drills that, rather than being unprecedented and overly threatening to Taiwan, were instead routine and small-scale. Magically, small drills would become "stern warnings," and local exercises in waters near a coastal area of China would turn into "large-scale exercises in the Taiwan Strait." Interestingly, after such remarks were made in the media, officials from the State Council's TAO would repeat the same claims, which suggests a certain level of coordination between hawkish military commentators and the state apparatus in Beijing.

Psychological attacks against Taiwan are also aimed at support for its armed forces. In this, Taiwanese media often are willing actors: playing up mishaps and accidents, giving airtime to clueless actresses and public figures who from the comfort of their living room mock the services, and reinforcing the notion that Taiwan's defense apparatus is completely penetrated by Chinese intelligence. Taiwan's military indeed faces serious challenges in terms of personnel, recruitment, acquisitions, training, funding, aging platforms and high levels of cannibalism for parts; and it is quite true that it is a target of Chinese espionage. But those are problems facing any military – including the PLA, where corruption remains endemic and where the effects of China's one child policy will soon be felt (a question that is rarely asked is how many Chinese parents would be willing to sacrifice their only son in a military adventure against non-threatening Taiwan, especially if, in the inevitable "fog of war," things did not go as planned).

This campaign has succeeded in convincing some foreign analysts that Taiwan isn't worth the trouble defending, that Taiwan itself is not serious about its national defense. Why, some would ask, should Americans sacrifice their sons and daughters defending this distant place, notwithstanding the fact that it is a democracy and a longstanding U.S. ally, if the Taiwanese are not willing to do what is necessary to defend themselves? A lack of understanding about what Taiwan has been doing to improve its national defense, an at best vague notion of Taiwan's importance to regional stability in Asia and role as a first line of defense against authoritarian encroachment, is understandable. After all, for most people outside Asia, Taiwan is not on their minds and rarely makes the news. Why it matters to them is something that needs to be better explained; otherwise, we cannot expect them to sacrifice national treasure, let alone loved ones, in its defense. Add to this mix propaganda suggesting that the Taiwanese do not take defense seriously, or that their national security apparatus has been altogether compromised by China, and it becomes difficult to argue *against* abandonment. People in government and the security sector understand the importance of Taiwan; but those are small numbers, insufficient to influence public overall public opinion.

A recent poll by the Pew Research Center (2018) showed that even as American perceptions of China become more negative amid a trade war, tensions between Taiwan and China ranked last in a list of eight concerns. Only 22 percent saw the Taiwan–China dispute as "very serious" and 41 percent as "somewhat serious," compared with 62 percent who saw the large amount of American debt held by China as "very serious," followed by cyber attacks (58 percent), China's impact on the global environment (51 percent), loss of U.S. jobs to China (51 percent), China's policies on human rights (49 percent), the U.S. trade deficit with China (48 percent), and territorial disputes between China and its neighbors (34 percent). If it is to improve its chances of being seen as an integral part of how the U.S. should respond to China, Taiwan will need to do a much better job in countering Chinese propaganda suggesting abandonment and positioning itself in the imagination of ordinary people in the United States and elsewhere (more on this in Chapter 9).

The potential for military action against Taiwan remains a serious concern, and a possibility that Taiwanese from all walks of life should prepare against. Still, and despite all the saber rattling that has intensified since 2016, the military option remains a last resort for Beijing. The ultimate reason why the CCP expends so much time, money, and resources waging a psychological war against Taiwan is that it would rather not have to rely on the military option, as doing so would comport serious risks to China's global position, not to mention the potential for domestic discontent should an operation become more costly than the Chinese are willing to bear, something that would be much likelier if the U.S. intervened in the conflict on Taiwan's side. As the U.S. Department of Defense noted in its 2017 annual report to Congress (2017) on the Chinese military:

> Large-scale amphibious invasion is one of the most complicated and difficult military operations. Success depends upon air and sea superiority, the rapid buildup and sustainment of supplies onshore, and uninterrupted support. An attempt to invade Taiwan would strain China's armed forces and invite international intervention. These stresses, combined with China's combat force attrition and the complexity of urban warfare and counterinsurgency (assuming a successful landing and breakout), make an amphibious invasion of Taiwan a significant political and military risk. Taiwan's investments to harden infrastructure and strengthen defensive capabilities could also decrease China's ability to achieve its objectives.

The unique geography of Taiwan, weather conditions in the Taiwan Strait, and the limited number of beaches around Taiwan that would be suitable for an amphibious invasion – sites that the Taiwanese military has had decades to study and build up defenses in preparation for such a scenario – mean that PLA planners would face a large number of formidable problems that, as a military analyst recently observed, "have no easy solutions." As Ian Easton (2017) notes:

> Taiwan's 770-mile-long coastline is remarkably unsuited for amphibious operations. Nearly 75 percent of the island is covered in mountains, and the rest is either heavily urbanized or rough terrain. Taiwan's east coast is principally made up of cliffs, blades of mountain rock slicing straight down from the central mountain range into the Pacific's dark depths. It would be a dangerous place to land in force. There are three small coastal flats, but they are ringed with East Asia's tallest mountains and connected to the rest of the island by roads and rail lines that pass though long tunnels and gorges. The ROC military has plans in place for quickly demolishing these vulnerable transportation channels. Any attacker that landed on the beaches here would almost certainly find him encircled by a wall of rock that could not be climbed over or passed under.

Conditions along the west coast, Easton writes, are more forgiving and contain "workable landing beaches that could be captured to facilitate [an] invasion." However, "few of them are large enough to support landing operations by major units and all are enveloped by some kind of unfavorable terrain" and, in the few places where it is uninhabited, the coastline features "sprawling mudflats" which form "a natural barrier to landing operations."

The idea that the PLA could win a war over the Taiwan Strait in a matter of days, with casualties on the Chinese side in the two or three digits, therefore, is pure propaganda – the PLA generals, and the Central Military Commission, now under the direct control of Xi Jinping, know it.

Part of the propaganda that has accompanied PLA modernization in recent years, and more so since Xi came to power, is the notion that China will attack Taiwan by 2020. That fixed date has been misrepresented in the media: what Xi has ordered is for the PLA to have the *capability* to launch an attack against Taiwan by the beginning of the third decade of the 21st century – not an attack itself. One thing that every security analyst and political scientist knows is that the decision to use force isn't contingent on capability alone; *intent* is also necessary. Moreover, as recent research into the Chinese military suggests, key figures within the PLA system are themselves aware that they do not at present have the wherewithal to ensure a successful invasion of Taiwan, though those gaps are being reduced gradually. In the meantime, China bristles its feathers like a peacock to intimidate its opponents and suggest inevitability for the Taiwanese. Taiwan needs to see clearly between what constitutes psychological warfare and real signals of intent to use force.

64 The illusion is broken

So far, the psychological warfare campaign against it has not caused panic among the Taiwanese, who have reacted pragmatically to the noise. At the same time, they do not want to lull themselves into a false sense of security based on the notion that the Chinese will never attack. The day could come when Beijing does feel it has accumulated enough power and shaped the environment in its favor enough that it calculates it can win a quick, high-intensity war against Taiwan. Such a day would become much closer if U.S. guarantees of security were removed, hence the need to tighten the relationship with the U.S. by doing what is necessary.

Another scenario in which a PLA attack against Taiwan would become more likely would be when discontent and instability in China threatened the CCP's ability to remain in power, at which point the leadership could decide to use an external distraction to boost its legitimacy and redirect anger at an external opponent. In such a situation, the rational calculations that in the past had militated against embarking on military adventurism could change, and an "irrational" leadership could adopt policies that hitherto would have seemed ill-advised, if not suicidal. Even here, however, I am not convinced that Taiwan would be the most inviting target for the externalization of a domestic crisis: the risks of failure and potential costs would be too high, which, if the attack failed, could instead of saving an embattled CCP increase the discontent against it. Therefore, other, weaker targets within the region would be likelier options for a CCP struggling to remain in charge. If Taiwan had to be attacked under such an externalization scenario, outlying islands, or Taiping Island (太平島) in the South China Sea would be likelier targets.

Still, we cannot discount an attack on Taiwan entirely. Even if it is the least likely scenario for the next few years, the possibility of military action still exists. And there could come a day when hawkish (and less rational) forces within the CCP and the PLA, players who are even more impatient than Xi Jinping, could force his hand or push him aside. Thus far Xi seems to have the situation under control, but that equilibrium is a formidable task and predicting the future stability of the CCP, and that of Chinese society (see Chapter 4), is always challenging, in large part due to the fact that the information we need to make such assessments often is inaccessible.

This chapter has sought to provide an overview of the many ways in which Beijing has sought to punish Taiwan since the election of Tsai Ing-wen in January 2016. It is by no means an exhaustive list, and no doubt more incidents will be added to that list by the time this book comes to print. More official diplomatic allies could be lured, and more international firms may be pressured by Beijing to remove references to Taiwan. Nevertheless, this section provides sufficient examples to demonstrate the CCP's modus operandi and the rigid ideology that buttresses these activities.

Despite the exponential growth in Beijing's pressure against Taiwan, China has so far not succeeded in breaking the resistance of the democratically elected leader of this country, and the majority of Taiwanese have not been swayed by the sticks and carrots (mostly sticks) pointed at them since 2016. The ongoing impermeability of Taiwan is a clear reminder of its resilience – the solidifying civic identity and democratic practices that, together, have denied the CCP the object of its desire.

Still, despite the Tsai administration's overall success in weathering the storm, some elements within Taiwanese society – here and overseas – have grown impatient with Tsai, whom they accuse of being too soft in her response to China's belligerence. It is to this political force that we turn in the next chapter.

Notes

1 To put things in context: the combined GDP in 2017 of the seven diplomatic allies that have ended relations with Taiwan since 2016 is approximately US$374.5 billion, or one third of Taiwan's US$1.18 trillion.
2 See Gui Minhai, Pen America. https://pen.org/advocacy-case/gui-minhai/
3 With thanks to Peter Mattis for his conceptualization of the role and aims of the CPPCC.
4 See: 2017年全美中國和平統一促進會年會暨海峽兩岸和平發展論壇: YouTube, www.youtube.com/watch?v=3Nw8D9GSloU and www.youtube.com/watch?v=oxADVlR5JrI
5 Wu was also involved in the lawsuit by the aforementioned CEFC against the author.

References

Agence France-presse (AFP) (2017) "Former Hong Kong Home Secretary Patrick Ho Arrested in US Over Alleged Africa Bribery Scheme," *SCMP/AFP*, 21 November. www.scmp.com/news/hong-kong/law-crime/article/2120784/us-arrests-former-hong-kong-home-secretary-patrick-ho.

Apple Daily (2016a) "強國55人黑名單流出 杜汶澤何韻詩黃耀明林夕有份," 30 December. https://hk.news.appledaily.com/china/realtime/article/20161230/56109922.

Apple Daily (2016b) "【不斷更新】戴立忍風波延燒　台星被迫簽署 「不分裂國家」聲明," 26 July. https://tw.appledaily.com/new/realtime/20160726/915843/.

Associated Press (2018) "China, US in Clash Over El Salvador Dropping Taiwan," 22 August. https://apnews.com/ef950ee0280e45e6b5f59dd7e28ebad0.

Blanchard, Ben (2018) "China Upset as Interpol Removes Wanted Alert for Exiled Uighur Leader," *Reuters*, 24 February. www.reuters.com/article/us-china-xinjiang/china-upset-as-interpol-removes-wanted-alert-for-exiled-uighur-leader-idUSKCN1G80FK.

Callick, Rowan (2017) "China Bans Vatican Tours by Its Citizens," *The Australian*, 23 November. www.theaustralian.com.au/news/world/china-bans-vatican-tours-by-its-citizens/news-story/b2b70b70c5bfc5aa6979302f2adfd7fc.

Chan, Melissa (2012) "Inside a Chinese Communist Party School," *China Digital Times*, 25 January. https://chinadigitaltimes.net/2012/01/inside-a-chinese-communist-party-school/.

Chen, Aizhu and Kane Wu (2018) "CEFC Senior Staff Banned from Overseas Travel Amid Chairman Probe: Sources," *Reuters*, 20 April. www.reuters.com/article/us-cefc-probe-travel-ban/cefc-senior-staff-banned-from-overseas-travel-amid-chairman-probe-sources-idUSKBN1HR1U7.

Chen, Jia-wen (2019) "海峽中線無法律效力　「強制驅離」知易行難," *United Daily News*, 1 April. https://udn.com/news/story/10930/3731798.

Chen, Wei-han (2017) "Lee Ming-che Sentenced to Five Years," *Taipei Times*, 29 November. www.taipeitimes.com/News/front/archives/2017/11/29/2003683108.

ChinaFile Conversation (2018) "Do American Companies Need to Take a Stance on Taiwan?" 11 May. www.chinafile.com/conversation/do-american-companies-need-take-stance-taiwan.

China Review News (2017) "兩岸音樂交流大狂歡　24日台大登場," 18 September. http://hk.crntt.com/crn-webapp/touch/detail.jsp?coluid=3&kindid=0&docid=104815055.

China Review News (2018) "新書發表會　馬英九與柯文哲王不見王," 12 January. http://hk.crntt.com/crn-webapp/touch/detail.jsp?coluid=255&kindid=0&docid=104939592.

Chung, Li-hua (2018) "上海台辦主任李文輝來台遭拒 陸委會：爭議多," *Liberty Times*, 22 February. http://news.ltn.com.tw/news/politics/breakingnews/2346899.

Chung, Li-hua and Hsu Guo-zhen (2017) "國安單位：反年改陳抗 有中國勢力介入," *Liberty Times*, 28 July. http://news.ltn.com.tw/news/focus/paper/1119633.

Civil Aviation Administration of China (CAAC) (2018) "民航局約談達美航空相關負責人：要求其立即整改、公開道歉：中國民用航空局 – 新聞中心 – 民航要聞," 12 January. www.caac.gov.cn/PHONE/XWZX/MHYW/201801/t20180112_48569.html (link has since been taken down).

Clark, Colin (2017) "'Indispensable' Palau Deal At Risk; Will China Get Access?" *Breaking Defense*, 27 June. https://breakingdefense.com/2017/06/indispensable-palau-deal-at-risk-will-china-get-access/.

Cole, J. Michael (2018a) "Air Canada's Kowtowing to China Sends a Dangerous Signal," *Globe and Mail*, 17 May. www.theglobeandmail.com/opinion/article-air-canadas-kowtowing-to-china-sends-a-dangerous-signal/.

Cole, J. Michael (2018b) "Ottawa Can't Shirk Responsibility in China-Taiwan Air Canada Controversy," *Hill Times*, 23 May. www.hilltimes.com/2018/05/23/ottawa-cant-shirk-responsibility-china-taiwan-air-canada-controversy/144702.

Cole, J. Michael (2019a) "More Than 70 Participants from Taiwanese Media Industry Attend 4th Cross-Strait Media Summit in Beijing," *Taiwan Sentinel*, 11 May. https://sentinel.tw/more-than-70-participants-from-taiwanese-media-industry-attend-4th-cross-strait-media-summit-in-beijing/.

Cole, J. Michael (2019b) "The Battle Between Taiwan's Democratic Ideals and China's Subversive Proxies: Where Do We Draw the Line?" *Taiwan Sentinel*, 11 April. https://sentinel.tw/battle-taiwans-democracy-versus-ufw/.

Cole, J. Michael (2019c) "Organizers of Aborted Pro-Unification Rally Recruiting Taiwanese for Communist Party School," *Taiwan Sentinel*, 13 April. https://sentinel.tw/recruiting-tw-ccp-party-school/.

Commonwealth Magazine (2018) "United Front Target Taiwan's Grass Roots: Gangs, Temples, Business," 22 August. https://english.cw.com.tw/article/article.action?id=2083.

Crabtree, Susan (2018) "Rubio Vows to Cut Off Aid to El Salvador Following China Policy Change," *Washington Free Beacon*, 22 August. https://freebeacon.com/national-security/rubio-vows-cut-off-aid-el-salvador-following-china-policy-change/.

Easton, Ian (2017) *The Chinese Invasion Threat: Taiwan's Defense and American Strategy in Asia*, Arlington: Project 2049 Institute, pp. 143–149.

Executive Yuan (EY) (2018) "政院：四大面向及八大強臺策略　務實因應中國大陸對臺31項措施," www.ey.gov.tw/Page/9277F759E41CCD91/70ea5798-56c6-4fbc-ba06-730ac87264df

Grayling, A. C. (2017) *Democracy and Its Crisis*, London: Oneworld, p. 148.

Griffiths, James (2018) "China Ready to Fight 'Bloody Battle' Against Enemies, Xi Says in Speech," *CNN*, 20 March. https://edition.cnn.com/2018/03/19/asia/china-xi-jinping-speech-npc-intl/index.html.

The Guardian (2019) "Former Interpol Chief Meng Hongwei Confesses to Bribery in Chinese Trial," 20 June 20. www.theguardian.com/world/2019/jun/20/former-interpol-chief-meng-hongwei-put-on-trial-for-bribery-in-china.

Horton, Chris (2017) "China's Attempt to Punish Taiwan by Throttling Tourism Has Seriously Backfired," *Quartz*, 10 February. https://qz.com/907429/chinas-attempt-to-punish-taiwan-by-throttling-tourism-has-seriously-backfired/.

Huang, Yan-cheng (2019) "【陸委會「抹紅」發威】兩岸海峽論壇在即　高雄、台中、雲林不去了," *UpMedia*, 8 August. www.upmedia.mg/news_info.php?SerialNo=64870.

Kitamura, Toshifumi (2018) "JAL, ANA Change 'Taiwan' to 'China Taiwan' on Websites," *Japan Today*, 19 June. https://japantoday.com/category/business/japan-airlines-change-%27taiwan%27-to-%27china-taiwan%27-on-websites.

Levitsky, Steven and Daniel Ziblatt (2018) *How Democracies Die: What History Reveals About Our Future*, London: Viking, p. 8.

Liberty Times (2016) "國際刑警組織大會　外交部證實台灣無法參加," 5 November. http://news.ltn.com.tw/news/politics/breakingnews/1877348.

Liu Kuan-lin and Elaine Hou (2018) "Taiwan's Office in Nigeria Drops 'Republic of China' from Name," *Focus Taiwan*, 5 January. http://focustaiwan.tw/news/aipl/201801050009.aspx.

Lo, Kinling (2018) "China's New Alliance Stirs US Worries Over Possible 'Military Base' in El Salvador," *South China Morning Post*, 22 August. www.scmp.com/news/china/diplomacy-defence/article/2160731/chinas-new-alliance-stirs-us-worries-over-military-base.

Lum, Alvin (2018) "Former Hong Kong Minister Patrick Ho Accused of Being Illegal Arms Dealer by US Prosecutors as They Turn up Heat Ahead of New York Bribery Trial," *South China Morning Post*, 3 October. www.scmp.com/news/hong-kong/law-and-crime/article/2166847/former-hong-kong-minister-patrick-ho-accused-being.

Miao Zong-han, Wang Shu-fen, Yeh Su-ping and Joseph Yeh (2019) "China Bans Individual Travelers from Visiting Taiwan," *Focus Taiwan*, 31 July. http://focustaiwan.tw/news/acs/201907310013.aspx.

Monaco, Nicholas J. (2017) "Computational Propaganda in Taiwan: Where Digital Democracy Meets Automated Autocracy," Google Jigsaw Working Paper No. 2017.2. Computational Propaganda Research Project, University of Oxford. http://comprop.oii.ox.ac.uk/wp-content/uploads/sites/89/2017/06/Comprop-Taiwan-2.pdf.

Núñez, Odalis (2017) "Inicia construcción del Puerto de Contenedores Panamá-Colón," *Telemetro*, 7 June 7. www.telemetro.com/nacionales/Inicia-construccion-Puerto-Contenedores-Panama-Colon_0_1033397385.html.

People's Daily (2006) "吳建國：欲做兩岸"文化統一"的倡導者," 14 March. http://tw.people.com.cn/BIG5/14814/14891/4200180.html.

Pew Research Center, Global Attitudes and Trends (2018) "As Trade Tensions Rise, Fewer Americans See China Favorably," 28 August. www.pewglobal.org/2018/08/28/as-trade-tensions-rise-fewer-americans-see-china-favorably/.

Quackenbush, Casey (2018) "In Defiance of China, a Pro-Independence Activist Speaks at Hong Kong's Foreign Correspondents Club," *Time*, 14 August. http://time.com/5365243/hong-kong-china-andy-chan-foreign-correspondents-club-fcc/.

Raska, Michael (2015) "Hybrid Warfare with Chinese Characteristics," *RSIS*, 2 December. www.rsis.edu.sg/rsis-publication/rsis/co15262-hybrid-warfare-with-chinese-characteristics/#.W4Oa52VCJBw.

Reporters Without Borders (RSF) (2019) "Taiwan: Abusive Libel Suit Against Financial Times Correspondent," 24 July. https://rsf.org/en/news/taiwan-abusive-libel-suit-against-financial-times-correspondent.

Ruwitch, John (2019) "Spain Deports 94 Taiwanese to Beijing for Telecom Fraud," *Reuters*, 7 June. www.reuters.com/article/us-china-taiwan-spain-spain-deports-94-taiwanese-to-beijing-for-telecom-fraud-idUSKCN1T80IP.

Soumy, Phan (2017) "Hun Sen Bans Taiwan Flag from Cambodia," *Cambodia Daily*, 6 February. www.cambodiadaily.com/news/hun-sen-bans-taiwan-flag-from-cambodia-124609/.

State Council Taiwan Affairs Office (TAO) (2018a) "國台辦新聞發布會輯錄：國務院台灣事務辦公室," 26 September. www.gwytb.gov.cn/xwfbh/201809/t20180926_12095513.htm.

State Council Taiwan Affairs Office (2018b) "關於印發《關於促進兩岸經濟文化交流合作的若干措施》的通知," 28 February. http://www.gwytb.gov.cn/wyly/201802/t20180228_11928139.htm.

Taiwan Tourism Bureau (2018) "Visitor Statistics for December 2017," 23 February. http://admin.taiwan.net.tw/statistics/release_d_en.aspx?no=7&d=7330.

Tanaka, Takayuki (2018) "Taiwan Relations Unchanged Despite Chinese Pressure: Palau President," *Nikkei Asian Review*, 18 May. https://asia.nikkei.com/Politics/International-Relations/Taiwan-relations-unchanged-despite-Chinese-pressure-Palau-president.

TVBS (2018) "台灣與中國並列！IKEA這張圖讓網友氣炸：把店全關了," 28 August. https://news.tvbs.com.tw/world/981924.

U.S. Department of Defense (2017) "Annual Report to Congress: Military and Security Developments Involving the People's Republic of China 2017," p. 77.

Weiwenku (2017) "'兩岸媒體人北京峰會圖片展'精彩揭幕," 24 November. www.weiwenku.org/d/103889332.

Westad, Odd Arne (2003) *Decisive Encounters: The Chinese Civil War, 1946–1950*, Stanford: Stanford University Press, p. 9.

Westcott, Ben (2019) "Taiwan Scrambles Jets to Confront Chinese Fighters After Rare Incursion," *CNN*, 1 April. https://edition.cnn.com/2019/04/01/asia/china-japan-taiwan-jets-intl/index.html.

Yan, Hong-jun and Chen Guan-bei (2018) "五星共產寺開拆 魏明仁撤退," *Liberty Times*, 27 September. http://news.ltn.com.tw/news/focus/paper/1235119.

Yang, Jia-hsin (2017) "誣指顛覆台灣華信跨海告寇謐將," *China Times*, 26 June. www.chinatimes.com/newspapers/20170626000334-260108.

Zheng, Sarah (2019) "Re-Elect President Tsai Ing-wen in 2020 and Taiwan Will Lose All Its Allies, Beijing Warns," *South China Morning Post*, 17 September. www.scmp.com/news/china/diplomacy/article/3027673/re-elect-president-tsai-ing-wen-2020-and-taiwan-will-lose-all.

3

TROUBLE IN THE GREEN CAMP

As the foregoing chapters have demonstrated, since her inauguration in May 2016, President Tsai Ing-wen has faced a difficult, and often hostile, cross-Strait environment. It is one that, furthermore, is unlikely to improve for the foreseeable future. Despite the incessant and escalating attacks on Taiwan's sovereignty by Beijing, President Tsai has remained consistent in the lines that she will not cross as well as in the flexibility that she has extended to the Chinese leadership from the outset. In other words, President Tsai has stuck to her commitment to maintaining the "status quo" in the Taiwan Strait; she continues to recognize the "historical fact" that in 1992 the two sides of the Taiwan Strait had held meetings; she has not dismantled the various agreements signed between Taipei and Beijing during the Ma Ying-jeou presidency; and she has governed under the "ROC constitutional order" and constitution. At the same time, she has refused to acknowledge the so-called "1992 consensus," which Beijing has made a precondition for talks, and does not subscribe to Beijing's "one China," instead calling upon its leadership to recognize that the existence of the ROC Taiwan is an indisputable fact.

By remaining firm on these issues, President Tsai has put the ball in Beijing's camp. And as we saw, China's reaction has been to punish Taiwan. In many ways, this turn of events is reminiscent of what occurred during the first term of the Chen Shui-bian administration, when early overtures by Taipei were also rejected by Beijing. This time around, however, the global context is markedly different, and where Beijing succeeded in tarnishing president Chen's reputation in the early 2000s, so far the CCP has failed in its efforts to bring down President Tsai's image internationally.

A number of reasons help explain this. That includes changing perceptions of China's rise since the beginning of the 21st century: the PRC's behavior since Xi Jinping came to power has negated the belief that China's rise would be "peaceful" and that the Asian giant would become a "responsible stakeholder" as defined by

70 The illusion is broken

the West. Also different is the fact that Taiwan's principal ally, the U.S., isn't currently embroiled in two messy wars in the South Asia and Middle East, as it was in the wake of the 11 September 2001 terrorist attacks. Admittedly, the U.S. still faces a number of external security challenges, including terrorism, an unfinished war in Afghanistan, North Korea, and possibly Iran. But this time, President Tsai and her advisers have arguably been more keenly aware of the international situation and adjusted their policies so as not to cause unnecessary alarm in Washington, D.C. (more on this in Chapter 5).

Performing that balancing act between Taipei, Beijing, and Washington, however, has come at a price for President Tsai. The preservation of Taiwan's image as a responsible actor in Asia (in contrast with the widely held belief that it was a "troublemaker" under Chen) has forced the Tsai administration to avoid doing certain things in response to Beijing's growing belligerence. And for a segment of Taiwanese society, this has been perceived as a sign of weakness.

President Tsai's troubles with that particular segment of the Taiwanese electorate began early on, with the appointment of a Cabinet that, in their eyes, was too "blue," comprising several officials who were products of a system that, for decades, had been dominated by the KMT. Many of them, furthermore, were *waishengren* and therefore could not, in their opinion, be fully trusted with doing what was right for the country. One of the early targets was David Lee (李大維), a career diplomat who served as foreign minister until he was replaced by Joseph Wu (吳釗燮) in February 2018 as part of a Cabinet reshuffle, which some analysts regarded as a concession to the deeper side of the "green" camp (Lee then went over to the National Security Council as secretary general). Indeed, President Tsai constituted a Cabinet (and a group of close advisers at the Presidential Office) that was largely male and autocratic; after a campaign in which she promised reform and to empower a newer generation of Taiwanese who had come of age during the Sunflower Movement, the contrast disappointed many who wanted immediate change. There are several reasons why she made those appointments – her "brain trust" was not unlimited, and some of her initial choices refused to enter government. In some cases, President Tsai made concessions, and a few of those were, I would argue, indeed of questionable wisdom.

Another consideration that no doubt weighed heavily in her decisions was the need to ensure continuity and stability. It is very likely that President Tsai and her advisers knew of the challenges that were to come in cross-Strait relations. Moreover, 2016 was also an election year in the U.S. and Taipei needed to send signals of reassurance that a new DPP administration would not destabilize the Asia Pacific and thereby add headaches to the future U.S. president. It is important here to point out the level of mistrust of the DPP – some of it warranted, some unfair – that still existed in many foreign capitals eight years after the Chen administration. In some cases, which I personally witnessed at meetings in foreign capitals, perceptions of the DPP bordered on resentment. It was clear that the DPP had an image problem abroad, one that the Tsai government would have to repair. And to her credit, she has done rather well on that front (see Chapter 7).

Lastly, President Tsai had won the 2016 elections by appealing to moderates and winning over swing voters who may otherwise have voted for the KMT candidate. President Tsai therefore needed to maintain the trust of that important group of voters. And from 20 May 2016 onward, she was president not only to the 6.89 million Taiwanese who voted for her on 16 January: she was answerable to the nation's entire 23 million souls.

As Beijing began luring official diplomatic allies and escalated its efforts to undermine Taiwan's visibility internationally, the pressure on President Tsai to retaliate in some way began to mount. It made sense to turn the other cheek for a while, but after months of growing hostility by Beijing and the arrest of Taiwanese activist Lee Ming-che by China, some people in the green camp had had enough. They wanted President Tsai to do something that would showcase Taiwan's determination. But for the most part, the Tsai government limited itself to official statements – at least publicly. Over time, the inaction led to accusations: President Tsai was too moderate, especially at a time when the KMT was weak and disorganized. Worse, she didn't represent Taiwan; her government was the same Republic of China, an illegitimate government in exile, as some of her more vocal critics alleged. Many focused on her government's unwillingness to change the name of certain institutions, such as the General Association of Chinese Culture (GACC, 中華文化總會), refusing to look past the name and to acknowledge that, since 2016, those institutions have promoted an altogether Taiwan-centric message that they most certainly would agree with.

"Not my president," some began to write, as if President Tsai somehow ruled over an entity that existed in a parallel universe.

As discussed earlier, President Tsai has equated Taiwan with the ROC, a proposition that does not meet everybody's approval in Taiwan. Many still have problems with the "national flag," which they see as an imposition and not the flag that ought to represent Taiwan within the international community. Others, for entirely legitimate reasons, still regard the ROC as a party-state that inflicted tremendous savagery on the Taiwanese people after World War II, starting with the 228 Massacre of 1947 (二二八事件) and followed by decades of White Terror (臺灣白色恐怖時期). All of this is perfectly understandable. However, that ROC no longer exists: little by little over the decades, it was absorbed and refashioned by the people it sought to control. From pressures both domestic and external, the KMT even was compelled to liberalize in the 1980s, the first, important step toward democratization. Today, democracy is the only game in town in Taiwan, and only outliers like the CUPP and the New Party genuinely believe that a non-democratic alternative is preferable. For every KMT member who sounds like an echo of the 1970s you will find 10, especially in the younger generations, who have embraced what makes Taiwan distinct today.

Admittedly, the official name, constitution, and many of the symbols harken back to that period, as still do a number of the institutions of governance today. But in everyday experience, in the values that keep this nation together and in what it is determinedly *not*, the ROC is Taiwan. This was arrived at not by shock, but rather through gradualism and evolution, a process that continues to this day.

72 The illusion is broken

What Taiwan's difficult international situation has caused, however, is to convince some members of the green camp that a shock is the only solution. To them, Taiwan will never be truly independent until it sheds its de facto independence under the official name of the ROC and achieves *de jure* independence through a referendum, as well as name rectification and a new constitution. In other words, for them, only a declaration of independence will ensure Taiwan's sovereignty and the dignity of its people. For them, the "status quo" isn't quite the same as having an independent status.

As Beijing stole more allies and successfully pressured international firms to stop referring to Taiwan as "Taiwan," the need to take action on formal independence became urgent. Others saw the theft of official diplomatic allies as doing a service to Taiwan: according to them, Taiwan would shed the mantle of the ROC on the day the ROC lost its last official diplomatic ally. Only then would a sovereign Taiwan emerge, phoenix-like, from the ashes of the ROC.

Taiwan has every right to seek formal independence, to change its official name and to write a constitution that reflects contemporary reality. Unfortunately, the aspirations of its people are challenged by a neighbor next door that denies them that fundamental right, and which threatens to use force should Taiwan act on that desire. The force disparity that exists between Taiwan and China, added to an international context that, largely due to economic reasons, continues to favor Beijing, means that a formal declaration of independence now would be suicidal. Not only would doing so likely trigger a devastating attack by China, it could also convince Washington that its action had "provoked" Beijing and therefore not obligate it, as per the TRA, to come to Taiwan's assistance. The risks, therefore, are simply too high, and no president should compromise the security of her citizens by engaging in such adventurism. The key here isn't justice or human rights; it is, rather, one of pragmatism, of being intelligent and strategic in how Taiwan can best ensure its survival and growth as an independent state.

We should note here that a good number of President Tsai's harshest critics and most vocal proponents of a formal declaration of independence often are Taiwanese who live overseas and who would not directly feel the repercussions of such policy decisions back in Taiwan. Many of them have also criticized Taiwanese in Taiwan for being too timid, even of having been "brainwashed" by the KMT. The same critics would, in 2019, accuse Tsai of lying about her PhD from the London School of Economics (LSE), a travesty of pernicious disinformation that lasted several months.

For now, this pragmatism calls for the maintenance of the "status quo" and the retention, however appalling to some, of the ROC as the official name of the country. Recognizing that the "status quo" is anything but static, and that it has shifted in Beijing's favor in recent years, calls for various corrective measures to be taken by Taipei and its allies worldwide. Some of those have been taken, and arguably many more should be implemented.

Besides the high risks of military intervention following a declaration of independence, there is no assurance that, in the current geopolitical environment, the international community would recognize a Republic of Taiwan. The same dynamics that have forced governments to adopt a "one China" policy would remain, and undoubtedly Beijing would continue to insist that diplomatic relations with the PRC remained zero-sum – in other words, that no government can entertain diplomatic relations with China if it has official ties with Taipei. A declaration of independence, therefore, though satisfactory for its proponents, would leave Taiwan just as isolated as it is today under its official ROC iteration. Clarity on its official name would perhaps, as some have argued, dispel the misperceptions and confusions caused by the name Republic of China, though even here such confusion as it is said to exist abroad has arguably been inflated by advocates of a declaration of *de jure* independence. (Does anyone really confuse the Republic of Korea and Democratic People's Republic of Korea, two societies that, like Taiwan and the PRC, have grown in measurably different directions over the years?)

Advocates of a declaration of independence also seem to operate under the belief that (assuming it does not spark a war in the Taiwan Strait), a newly born Republic of Taiwan would somehow be in a better position to govern itself. In other words, dispensing with the old nomenclature and symbols would magically give birth to a better government. The problem with this argument is that it assumes a complete overhaul of government institutions in Taiwan, nothing short of a revolution. However, as it already exists as a modern state, Taiwan could ill afford a complete overhaul of its institutions, as this would lead to chaos. It is also difficult to imagine that, after formal independence, the Taiwanese could fire the tens of thousands of employees in government institutions and replace them with other people. For one thing, Taiwan could not find tens of thousands of qualified individuals to take over the positions vacated by civil servants from the previous system. Consequently, even after a declaration of independence, government institutions in Taiwan would continue to functions as they did before; and what's more, the same people, with the same baggage, beliefs, and political views, would continue to ensure their functioning. It is therefore very difficult to imagine how *de jure* independence would change how the country is governed. Such change is, perforce, gradual; and gradual change toward a better Taiwan can occur even under existing institutions and under the official name of ROC.

That may be a difficult pill to swallow for those who cannot abide living in a country whose official name is the Republic of China, and for many of them that name and its associated symbols are constant reminders of a traumatic past. But that pill remains a necessary one. Under the current circumstances, Taiwan cannot afford to dispense with pragmatism. The risks of departing from that strategy are simply too high.

Thus far the people who have pressured the Tsai administration to lower the threshold on referenda so that one could be held on a declaration of independence remain a minority within the green camp. In excluding constitutional change from the issues for which referendum laws have been revised, President Tsai has signaled her refusal to bend to the pressure from that segment of the green camp, which in recent months has included former president Chen Shui-bian and his supporters.

74 The illusion is broken

And wisely so, arguably. Beijing's pressure on Taiwan has also aimed to cause a split within the "green" camp between the mainstream DPP supporters who agree with the administration's polity on cross-Strait relations and the "deep greens" that want the government to adopt a more "extremist" course of action. Needless to say, any shift toward the "deep green" end of the political spectrum is sure to cost the Tsai administration supporters among the swing and "light blue" Taiwanese who voted her into office in 2016. Widening the gap between the greens and blues would empower extremists on both sides and re-energize the divisions in Taiwanese society that has slowly started to heal (Cole 2018).

Listen to the discourse of extremists in the "blue" and "green" camps, and it is clear that their worldview isn't a desirable one for Taiwan: it is marked by intolerance, distrust, and a firm belief in nation-building along ethnic lines – in other words, a return to the unhealthy notions of ethnic Taiwanese versus *waishengren*. If such ideology were to gain ascendance again, the resulting divisions would only weaken Taiwan and play to Beijing's advantage. That, above all else, is why a Taiwanese president should avoid catering to the extremist base.

Lastly, yielding to the pressure from the "deep green" camp to adopt a more retaliatory stance against China would only give Beijing justification for intensifying its punishment. The unfortunate fate of the Taichung games is an example of how Beijing will punish any campaign to change the name under which Taiwanese athletes can compete at the Olympics (though the case could be made that even without such an initiative China could still have sought the cancellation of the games in Taiwan) (Chang 2018). However satisfying it would be for the "deep green" base to engage in a tit-for-tat war with Beijing, this is a campaign that Taiwan simply cannot hope to win, as size and numbers simply aren't on its side. What it can have is time; but for time to be in its favor, Taiwan has to be wise and patient. It needs to counter Chinese pressure asymmetrically. Allowing the "deep greens" to dictate policy would take Taiwan back to the period between 2004 and 2005, when the embattled Chen administration turned to that highly ideological base to secure support (Chu 2016). No good could come from this.

As such, even if this exposes her and other members of her government, like former premier Lai Ching-te (賴清德), once the darling of the deeper green camp who challenged her in the primary in 2019, to further criticism, President Tsai must maintain her moderate stance on cross-Strait relations. That isn't only with a view to the 2020 presidential elections, in which her continued moderation could indeed have cost her votes within the "deep green" camp; but even more importantly, to avoid eroding the fragile ties that bind Taiwanese society together. Taiwan's future lies with the moderates, those who have the ability to transcend color politics and so-called ethnicity. A responsible leader cannot allow extremists on either side of the political spectrum to hijack policy and thereby turn back the clock on a long, incomplete process of healing among the people of Taiwan.

On another front, "deep greens" have also pressured President Tsai to amend the Amnesty Act (赦免法) and issue a pardon to former president Chen Shui-bian, who was sentenced to 19 years in prison for crimes related to bribery and graft in 2010, but has been on medical parole since 2015 on condition that he would not involve himself in politics. Groups advocating for a pardon claim there were "irregularities" in his case and have accused the KMT government of incarcerating the firebrand for political reasons. For President Tsai, that pressure represents another potential trap: while pardoning the former president would appease the "deep green" camp, such a move would inevitably lead to charges of political interference in the judiciary and alienate a large segment of the "blue" camp. Not to mention that such a precedent could open the door for future pardons of politicians who were convicted of various charges, which would compromise the very foundations of the country's legal system. Already, in addition to the pressure for his pardon, Chen's involvement in politics and appearances at public events, ostensibly in violation of the conditions for his medical release, have put President Tsai in a tight spot by exposing her government to accusations that it has turned a blind his to Chen's "illegal" political activities (NOWNews 2018). Regardless of the merits of the case for Chen's pardon – and those are highly contested – Chen shui-bian and his followers have put Tsai in a very difficult position at a time when the president, her hands already full with a difficult domestic *and* external situation, cannot afford to be waging rear-battles within her own camp.

At times, dissatisfaction within the "deep green" side of the "green" camp has also been amplified by the perception within civil society that the Tsai administration has failed to fulfill the various promises it made during its election campaign. However, we should be careful not to equate civil society with the "green" camp. In fact, many activists are, by their very nature, critical of government institutions in general and therefore just as likely to regard the DPP with suspicion as they would the KMT. As we shall see in Chapter 8, their demands furthermore tend to focus on domestic issues rather than matters pertaining to Taiwan's strategic engagement or cross-Strait relations. Nevertheless, discontent in those circles has exacerbated perceptions within some segments of the "green" camp that President Tsai is weak, or that she is not to be trusted.

So far the segment of the "green" camp that has called for a departure from a moderate stance vis-à-vis China has been small enough that the Tsai administration could afford to ignore its more radical demands. It remains to be seen whether future punitive actions by Beijing, which are certainly expected in the lead-up to 2020, will further embolden, and perhaps increase the ranks of, that group. Whatever happens, the Tsai administration will need to weigh the risks of losing the "deep green" vote in the next elections against the risk of alienating swing and "light blue" voters. One advantage for President Tsai is that the "deep greens" have no viable alternative in elections at the national level – small parties such as the New Power Party (時代力量) have yet to emerge as a national force capable of contesting the presidency, and other candidates, from the KMT or even Ko Wen-je, they will not vote for. At its worst, then, President Tsai and the DPP would face the prospect of "deep green" voters deciding to stay home on election day, or voting for one of the marginal candidates who have since emerged but whose appeal is probably insubstantial.

76 The illusion is broken

Given all this, the Tsai administration arguably can afford to stick to a moderate course of action, although Beijing's intransigence, as well as unrest in Hong Kong during 2019, has given her greater room to maneuver and the necessary incentive to be more vocal in her opposition to Beijing. Momentum within the "green" camp toward a more radical policy will never be such that continuing to ignore the demands of the "deep greens" would be destabilizing for the party. Resisting that domestic pressure, meanwhile, will ensure a more hospitable international environment for Taiwan and allow it to build bridges with friends within the global community whose assistance has become indispensable for Taiwan's survival. It is to these that we turn in the next section of this book, which places cross-Strait relations since 2016 in a regional and global context.

References

Chang, Jing-ya (2018) "東亞青運會主辦權遭取消 胡志強：什麼事都怪別人也不對," *Liberty Times*, 24 July. http://news.ltn.com.tw/news/politics/breakingnews/2497883.

Chu, Yun-han, Larry Diamond and Kharis Templeman (2016) *Taiwan's Democracy Challenged: The Chen Shui-bian Years*, Yun-han Chu, ed, Boulder: Lynne Rienner, p. 16, 26.

Cole, J. Michael (2018) "China's Great Squeeze Strategy Against Tsai Ing-wen," *Taiwan Sentinel*, 25 July. https://sentinel.tw/chinas-great-squeeze-against-tsai-ing-wen/.

NOWNews (2018) "陳水扁為陳致中站台認定違規　中監：未來不核准類似活動," 24 March. www.nownews.com/news/20180324/2723083.

PART 2

The regional and global context

4
TAIWAN AND CHINA'S GREATER AMBITIONS

Geopolitics and ideology

Although Taiwan remains one of the "core" interests of the CCP and unification a key element of its ideology, it is important to understand that China's designs upon Taiwan do not occur in a vacuum: they are in fact part of a larger strategic context. Thus, despite the great importance the CCP places on Taiwan in its rhetoric, Taiwan is not an end in itself but rather one of several variables involved in China's grand strategy. Realizing this should help us understand that Beijing would not be satisfied with the incorporation of Taiwan; rather, annexation is simply one step – a necessary one at that – in China's *regional* and *strategic* aspirations, the key aim of which is to displace the U.S. as the hegemonic power in the Indo-Pacific. Once we understand this, it becomes clear that the argument, made by some analysts in recent years, that the conflict in the Taiwan Strait is a mere "family quarrel" and that the U.S. should "trade" or "abandon" Taiwan to appease Beijing, is based on a deeply flawed understanding of the CCP's grand strategy (Goldstein 2018). In fact, ceding Taiwan would empower and embolden Beijing, which could spell even greater trouble down the road for status quo powers in the region.

Part of Beijing's designs on Taiwan are explained by its sense that historical grievances – from the "century of humiliation" to the neutralization of the Taiwan Strait by the U.S. from the Korean War on – need to be redressed, and that China, after lying low for decades, now has the capacity to do so. Fixing history and regaining China's "rightful" place in the hierarchy of nations is one of the stated aims of the CCP, which has staked much of its legitimacy with the Chinese people on making that a reality.

Efforts to secure those longstanding objectives have intensified markedly with Xi Jinping at the helm. Marked by his characteristic brazenness and impatience, Xi's foreign policy largely explains rising apprehensions within the region as hopes of a "peaceful rise" fade, and why a number of countries have called upon the U.S. to deepen its engagement with the region, and why others, such as Japan and India,

80 The regional and global context

have begun to play a more proactive balancing role in the Indo-Pacific. Ironically, the banding together of several Asian countries in reaction to greater assertiveness on the part of China has exacerbated the one dynamic that, above all else, explains China's territorial expansion in recent years, and that is China's deep, unresolved sense of vulnerability and insecurity, which has persisted since the founding of the PRC in 1949. As Khan (2018) writes, "There is a curious paradox to Xi Jinping's PRC. The country is more powerful than it has been at any point since its founding, and yet it also feels more insecure than it has since 1968–1969, when a major war with the Soviet Union threatened." Turning to reactions within the region, he observes, "Those problems of strategic geography have become harder to deal with, principally because China's growing weight has led to greater resistance from its neighbors and competitors." Nathan and Scobell (2012) adopt a similar view, observing that, Taiwan is one of "the key pieces of a geographically deep, politically unstable hinterland that Beijing must control in order to assure the security of the Han heartland."

Rather than a signal of strength and self-confidence, China's growing assertiveness – the military expansion and muscle flexing, occupation and militarization of the South China Sea, and hectoring/co-optation of smaller countries – is the result of that insecurity. Ironically, the more territory China captures to resolve that insecurity issue, the more vulnerability vectors it adds, a trap that all imperial powers before it have fallen into. Imperialism has its own twisted logic, whereby a power needs to acquire more territory to assuage its fears, but then the new territory acquired itself becomes the object of perceived threats and therefore must in turn be defended through the acquisition of even more territory.

The South China Sea, which for all intents and purposes it has annexed, was long seen by Beijing as a strategic vulnerability that needed to be plugged. The same applies to the East China Sea, where in 2013 Beijing unilaterally declared an Air Identification Defense Zone (ADIZ) covering most of the area. These moves are intended to address vulnerabilities over military access and approach vectors for foreign powers (East China Sea) and fears of a possible embargo against China in the South China Sea, through which much of the world's goods and energy, necessary for China's economic survival, transits. Defending those captures in turn necessitates the neutralization of other vulnerabilities within and beyond the first island chain. All of this is intended to increase what is known as "strategic depth."

Located in the middle of that island-chain is Taiwan, whose continued existence as a sovereign state and alliance with the U.S. is seen as a threat both to the Chinese mainland *and* to its recent "acquisitions" in the region. In Beijing's view, capturing Taiwan would block off a major corridor through which U.S. forces could attack the Chinese mainland while giving it the ability to threaten U.S. forces based in Okinawa and elsewhere in Japan. Obviously China would not stop at Taiwan, however, as the island's annexation would create new vulnerabilities and needs to defend that new territory, especially given the likely alarm with which Tokyo and Washington would react to that development. Once China annexes Taiwan – and this is why I have long argued that proponents of Taiwan's "abandonment" by the

Taiwan and China's greater ambitions **81**

U.S. and the international community are wrong – the logic of vulnerability would compel Beijing to push outward and to secure control of, or limit its opponents' access to, the second island chain – the invisible line in the Pacific Ocean that links Japan, Guam, Palau all the way to Papua New Guinea (Erickson and Wuthnow 2016). As Bismarck once said, "he who seeks to buy the friendship of his enemy with concessions will never be rich enough," a truth that proponents of Taiwan's abandonment should well keep in mind.

Having acquired Taiwan, China could then use the island to greatly expand its PLA force projection, both naval and aerial. The potentially destabilizing effects that the annexation of Taiwan would have on the entire region, not to mention the increased risks of armed conflict resulting from contact with the PLA well beyond its traditional area of operations, cannot be underestimated. Among other things, the "loss" of Taiwan would dramatically increase Japan's sense of vulnerability, given Beijing's territorial claims to the Ryukyus, and likely prompt the leadership in Tokyo to embark on a dangerous arms race with Beijing.

Much of China's foreign policy under Xi, therefore, has become a "battle-ground," one that is characterized by both Chinese strength and vulnerability, where "contrary to superficial impressions, the urgency that sometimes gives China the appearance of a juggernaut is driven more by a sense of precariousness and self-doubt than by any clearly reason belief in its inevitable triumph" (French 2017). How the region, and the rest of the world, reacts to this new phenomenon will have direct consequences for Taiwan's ability to stand up to its large neighbor. According to Allison (2017), China's rise and challenge to U.S. primacy in Asia could create a "Thucydides trap" and thereby increase the risks of an armed clash between the two superpowers. Whether such an outcome is inevitable remains to be seen. What is certain, however, is that as long as Beijing feels insecure, Taiwan will remain a coveted object, with or without the CCP ideological add-ons. More than a mere "family quarrel," Taiwan is in fact an integral part of a region-wide struggle involving two hegemonic powers, a number of mid-sized countries, and several smaller ones.

China's strategy to annex Taiwan is also shaped by regional and global dynamics, including perceived weaknesses in the international system. Consequently, crises such as Russia's invasion and annexation of Crimea in 2014 and the international community's failure to prevent this violation of Ukraine's territorial integrity, sent signals that the CCP is sure to have noticed. The Chinese leadership has also learned lessons on how to mitigate the effects of the punitive measures, such as sanctions, that have been implemented in retaliation for external aggression by the Russian Federation. The same can be said of the failure by the international community to prevent China from annexing and militarizing the South China Sea, or for ignoring a ruling by the International Court. Other developments, such as the Korean Peninsula, could also create strategic opportunities that Beijing could seek to exploit. One scenario, which seems less likely now that the two Koreas are involved in dialogue, would involve a U.S. military attack against Pyongyang, a moment of distraction that Beijing could seize to launch a military attack against Taiwan. Given the historical baggage that comes with the Korean Peninsula and Taiwan – the

82 The regional and global context

neutralization of the Taiwan Strait during the Korean War – the CCP could regard a new round of U.S. hostilities against Beijing's Korean ally as the perfect occasion to get even with Washington and thereby erase the humiliation it suffered in the 1950s (Cole 2017). The possibility of U.S. military action seemed high in 2017 and faded with the June 2018 Kim Jong Un summit with Donald Trump in Singapore; however, the nature of that conflict being what it is, there is no guarantee that talks will lead anywhere, and in the months and years ahead it is entirely possible that tensions would return to such a level that the U.S. would once again contemplate preventive military strikes against Pyongyang to eradicate its nuclear program and effect regime change.

The Pacific hasn't been the only area where China has sought to shape the environment in its favor, however. Similar efforts have been launched with the strategic revival of the Silk Road, linking China to Europe through Central Asia, and across Eurasia, where China has been hard at work "diminishing or eliminating the physical obstacles to greater integration" (Macaes 2018). Aware that there is no assurance things will turn out in its favor in the Indo-Pacific, Beijing has therefore sought to expand its "strategic periphery" by looking inland to secure and develop alternative routes that would not be subject to a naval embargo, as could be the case in the Pacific. By embarking on these ambitious projects simultaneously, China is trying to reduce its strategic vulnerability; but as in the Asia-Pacific, the new Silk Road and Eurasian projects, what with the investments, acquisitions, pipelines, and military bases that are necessary to make this project a reality, will in turn serve to increase Chinese exposure and thereby fuel the desire to acquire and secure more real estate – the imperial trap again.

The theoretical framework for Beijing's greater assertiveness in the Asia-Pacific and elsewhere has underpinned the CCP's rhetoric. Given the shift from a more consensus-style of leadership within the CCP and the centrality of Xi Jinping Thought to China's policy, the language used in Xi's major addresses is therefore of particular importance, as this can give us clues as to the current and future course of China's foreign policy.

Addressing the 19th National Congress of the Communist Party of China on 18 October 2017, Xi observed that "Today, we are closer, more confident, and more capable than ever before of making the goal of national rejuvenation a reality." The centrality of the CCP in this rejuvenation, and the need to inevitably challenge the status quo, was evident.

> Realizing our great dream demands a great struggle. It is in the movement of contradictions that a society advances; where there is contradiction there is struggle. If our Party is to unite and lead the people to effectively respond to major challenges, withstand major risks, overcome major obstacles, and address major conflicts, it must undertake a great struggle with many new contemporary features.

He continued: "This great struggle, great project, great cause, and great dream are closely connected, flow seamlessly into each other, and are mutually reinforcing,"

Xi said. "Among them, the great new project of Party building plays the decisive role."

Turning to national security, Xi said:

> We must do more to safeguard China's sovereignty, security, and development interests, and staunchly oppose all attempts to split China or undermine its ethnic unity and social harmony and stability. We must do more to guard against all kinds of risks, and work determinedly to prevail over every political, economic, cultural, social, and natural difficulty and challenge.

To ensure national security, military reform has been a key endeavor since the 18th Party Congress. Addressing the progress made in the five years to the 19th Party Congress, Xi said:

> With a view to realizing the Chinese Dream and the dream of building a powerful military, we have developed a strategy for the military under new circumstances, and have made every effort to modernize national defense and the armed forces. We convened the Gutian military political work meeting to revive and pass on the proud traditions and fine conduct of our Party and our armed forces, and have seen a strong improvement in the political ecosystem of the people's forces. Historic breakthroughs have been made in reforming national defense and the armed forces: a new military structure has been established with the Central Military Commission exercising overall leadership, the theater commands responsible for military operations, and the services focusing on developing capabilities. This represents a revolutionary restructuring of the organization and the services of the people's armed forces. We have strengthened military training and war preparedness, and undertaken major missions related to the protection of maritime rights, countering terrorism, maintaining stability, disaster rescue and relief, international peacekeeping, escort services in the Gulf of Aden, and humanitarian assistance. We have stepped up weapons and equipment development, and made major progress in enhancing military preparedness. The people's armed forces have taken solid strides on the path of building a powerful military with Chinese characteristics.

And for the next five years:

> We have reached a new historical starting point in strengthening national defense and the armed forces. Confronted with profound changes in our national security environment and responding to the demands of the day for a strong country with a strong military, we must fully implement the Party's thinking on strengthening the military for the new era and the military strategy for new conditions, build a powerful and modernized army, navy, air force, rocket force, and strategic support force, develop strong and efficient joint operations commanding institutions for theater commands,

84 The regional and global context

and create a modern combat system with distinctive Chinese characteristics. Our armed forces must be up to shouldering the missions and tasks of the new era entrusted to them by the Party and the people [. . .]

A military is built to fight. Our military must regard combat capability as the criterion to meet in all its work and focus on how to win when it is called on. We will take solid steps to ensure military preparedness for all strategic directions, and make progress in combat readiness in both traditional and new security fields. We will develop new combat forces and support forces, conduct military training under combat conditions, strengthen the application of military strength, speed up development of intelligent military, and improve combat capabilities for joint operations based on the network information system and the ability to fight under multi-dimensional conditions. This will enable us to effectively shape our military posture, manage crises, and deter and win wars.

We should ensure that efforts to make our country prosperous and efforts to make our military strong go hand in hand. We will strengthen unified leadership, top-level design, reform, and innovation. We will speed up implementation of major projects, deepen reform of defense-related science, technology, and industry, achieve greater military-civilian integration, and build integrated national strategies and strategic capabilities. We will improve our national defense mobilization system, and build a strong, well-structured, and modern border defense, coastal defense, and air defense.

(Xi 2017)

In his address, Xi also spent a lot of time sending signals of reassurance about China's intentions and goals of achieving mutually beneficial economic terms that fully respect the interests and independence of its interlocutors. Those reassurances, however, have been undermined not only by China's recent behavior in the East and South China Sea, but also by the debt trap that has characterized much of its investments abroad and which further underscores the neocolonial nature of China's expansion. No world leader better explained the apprehensions caused by this than Malaysian Prime Minister Mahathir Mohamad, who told Premier Li Keqiang during a visit to Beijing in August 2018 that, "We do not want a situation where there is a new version of colonialism happening because poor countries are unable to compete with rich countries." The Malaysian leader made the remarks after Beijing failed to convince him to reverse his decision to cancel two China-funded projects – US$20 billion East Coast Rail Link (ECRL) and the US$2.3 billion Trans-Sabah Gas Pipeline (TSGP) – in his country. In what was regarded as a major setback for China's Belt and Road Initiative (BRI), Mahathir spoke for many other countries targeted by BRI when he stated that the investments were neither viable nor necessary, and often only served Beijing's strategic interests. Still, many countries in Africa and elsewhere have been lining up to secure infrastructure investment and loans from China; Xi Jinping and Li Keqiang have also engaged in proactive diplomacy with those countries. In October 2018, the government of

Sierra Leone also announced it was shuttering a US$400 million airport project that was to be financed by a loan from China. The project, which was negotiated by the previous government of Sierra Leone, would have been built by Chinese firms and also managed and maintained by China. In his announcement, President Julius Maada Bio said the airport was unnecessary and would have imposed an unfair cost on the people of his country (Schumacher 2018).

Fears have been growing that China has been using its growing overseas spending spree "to gain footholds in some of the world's most strategic places, and perhaps even deliberately luring vulnerable nations into debt traps to increase China's dominion as US influence fades in the developing world" (Dasgupta 2018). In recent cases, the debt trap has resulted in Beijing's cancelling debt that governments were unable to repay in return for China gaining control of infrastructure in those countries, including port facilities. This includes Sri Lanka, whose government, under an agreement signed in July 2017, handed over economic control of its deep sea Hambantota port to the partly state-owned China Merchants Port Holdings (CM Port, 招商局控股港口有限公司) on a 99-year lease, turning Sri Lanka, as one commentator put it, "into a modern day "semi-colony" (Mourdoukoutas 2018).

Other countries that could fall to China's "predatory economics" and "debt distress" strategy include the 11 island-nations in the Pacific, which have accumulated nearly US$1.3 billion in debt over the past decade (Greenfield and Barrett 2018). Four of them (down from six after the Solomon Islands and Kiribati switched recognition in September 2019) are official diplomatic allies of Taiwan, and are located in areas that are crucial to the integrity of the second island chain. Eight other countries, Djibouti, Tajikistan, Kyrgyzstan, Laos, the Maldives, Mongolia, Pakistan, and Montenegro, have been identified as being at risk from BRI debt (Fernholz 2018). It is also very important to emphasize how seriously Beijing has taken the BRI initiative. Besides sinking substantial sums of money into this project, the Chinese government has very closely studied the legal systems of every single country targeted by BRI. This author has had occasion to peruse the two leather-bound volumes, titled *Legal Environment Report of the "Belt and Road" Countries* (一帶一路 – 沿線國家法律環境國別報告), that have been produced by the All China Lawyers Association (中華全國律師協會) for this project. For each country, China contracted the most prominent law firms in the countries involved to provide a detailed analysis – in Chinese and English – of the legal environment Chinese investors will be facing. No doubt, part of this highly professional exercise was meant to identity the weaknesses and "grey zones" in each of the countries involved.

Beyond the territorial aspects of China's expansion is the battle that the CCP has been waging on ideological grounds: A global crisis in democracy, which deepened following the 2008–2009 financial crisis, and signs of a return to U.S. isolationism and protectionism under President Donald Trump have created, or so Beijing believes, a strategic opportunity for revisionist forces to challenge the U.S.-led liberal-democratic world order that has underpinned international relations

86 The regional and global context

since the conclusion of World War II. Thus, China has begun touting its "China model" of "meritocratic authoritarianism" as a more suitable form of governance than the "messy" democracy that it argues has undermined growth in many parts of the world. No Chinese intellectual has done more to publicize this outlook than venture capitalist Eric X. Li (李世默) (2012), who in an editorial in the *New York Times* in 2012 titled "Why China's Political Model Is Superior," wrote that:

> The West's current competition with China is therefore not a face-off between democracy and authoritarianism, but rather the clash of two fundamentally different political outlooks. The modern West sees democracy and human rights as the pinnacle of human development. It is a belief premised on an absolute faith.
>
> China is on a different path. Its leaders are prepared to allow greater popular participation in political decisions if and when it is conducive to economic development and favorable to the country's national interests, as they have done in the past 10 years.
>
> However, China's leaders would not hesitate to curtail those freedoms if the conditions and the needs of the nation changed . . .
>
> The fundamental difference between Washington's view and Beijing's is whether political rights are considered God-given and therefore absolute or whether they should be seen as privileges to be negotiated based on the needs and conditions of the nation.
>
> The West seems incapable of becoming less democratic even when its survival may depend on such a shift. In this sense, America today is similar to the old Soviet Union, which also viewed its political system as the ultimate end.
>
> History does not bode well for the American way. Indeed, faith-based ideological hubris may soon drive democracy over the cliff.

The flaws in Li's argument will be discussed later in this chapter. Suffice it to say here that the "China Model" has had traction in many parts of the world, and not just in developing countries which may seek to emulate China success to grow their economies while keeping tight controls on political freedoms.

President Trump's assault on globalization and free trade has also given Beijing the chance to position itself as the new champion of global trade and multilateralism; and in doing so, the opportunity to rewrite rules which Beijing has long argued had been imposed to unequally benefit the West. For a number of developing countries needing infrastructure investment but whose leaders are loath to abide by the transparency and accountability requirements that come with loans from organizations like the IMF and the World Bank, China has been a blessing, a source of much-needed funding with apparently no strings attached – though as we saw, the "debt trap" could have serious ramifications on the sovereignty of the nations involved. China's emergence as a global lender has helped strengthen undemocratic regimes, thus helping fuel the global democratic crisis, and bolstered corruption in the name of efficiency.

As with the territorial issues, Taiwan is at the intersection of the ideological battle that is now being waged between the liberal-democratic order and revisionist forces led by China and Russia. A product of the Westphalian definition of the state — which incarnates a deep contradiction for Beijing's civilizational view of statehood — Taiwan also serves as an example of an Asian society that can reconcile its Confucian roots with democratic practice. In fact, despite its many imperfections, Taiwan's democracy is arguably the most successful, and certainly the most permissive and vibrant, of all the democracies in East Asia. Besides peaceful alternations of power and regular free and fair elections, Taiwan has a highly active civil society and has become a leader in many aspects of the human rights canon, including the rights of LGBTQI individuals.

In addition to serving as a "firewall" against authoritarian encroachment, Taiwan's democracy, open society, and free press are also direct challenges to Beijing's offer of an alternative form of governance and international order. That is why much of its efforts against Taiwan in recent years have aimed to thwart Taiwan's democratic institutions and undermine popular support for this form of governance. Beijing has used psychological and political warfare ("sharp power"), propaganda, disinformation and corruption in Taiwan and elsewhere to discredit democracy and increase the appeal of the alternative systems it offers. Like Russia over Crimea, much of the CCP's disinformation has been part of "a calculated effort to undo logic and factuality" (Snyder 2018). Far too frequently, global media, whose human investment in Taiwan is rarely long-term, have internalized and propagated those memes.

Beijing has also ramped up its efforts to shape the international rules and institutions that govern cyberspace. "China's more visible efforts at writing the rules of the road for cyberspace have centered on the UN," Adam Segal (2018) wrote in a recent article for *Foreign Affairs*. Preferring a state-centric vision, Beijing hopes for a future model of Internet governance that prioritizes the state over the private sector and society, and has sought to "mobilize the votes of developing countries [at the UN], many of which would also like to control the Internet and the free flow of information." China's BRI has also given rise to a "digital Silk Road" where much of the digital infrastructure — fiber-optic cables, mobile networks, satellite relay stations, and data centers — is being developed by Chinese companies. Through its participation in the World Internet Conference, and its successes in having Tim Cook and Sundar Pichai, the CEOs of Apple and Google, respectively, echo Chinese officials' language on Internet openness despite Beijing's severe restrictions on free speech, China is also influencing the future of the Internet on a global scale and could undermine Internet freedom outside its borders. Its pressure on international airlines and companies throughout 2018 to change language on their Internet sites and apps is an early indication of the shape of things to come should its efforts go unopposed.

Eradicating the existence of Taiwan as a successful democratic state — either by force or gradual erosion through sustained pressure — would constitute a major victory for the CCP, one that, furthermore, could have repercussions for the appeal of

88 The regional and global context

democracy in other parts of the world. Thus the neutralization of Taiwan isn't simply about the acquisition of territory that is essential for Beijing's sense of security, but is also about removing a first-line combatant in the ideological battle that the CCP is now waging on the international community.

Taiwan has served as a source of inspiration for many countries across Southeast Asia and has provided much-needed assistance to civil society, NGOs and political parties involved in human rights and democracy promotion in that increasingly important part of the world. Democratic aspirations across Asia, and the rules of transparency and accountability that come with them, have stood in the way of China's ambitions there, as Mahathir's election in May 2018 and opposition to Chinese investment in Malaysia, make perfectly clear. Beijing had found it much easier to work with his predecessor, Najib Razak, whose government was notorious for its corruption and undemocratic practices. As with Taiwan, the democratic "firewall" makes it more difficult for authoritarian regimes to get what they want from other countries. In late September, the Maldives, a small country in the Indian Ocean that has been caught in a war of influence between China and India, voted out of office the Beijing-backed incumbent, Abdulla Yameen, a repressive autocrat who had taken his country closer to China during his five-year term. Ibrahim Mohamed Solih, of the democratic movement, promised to restore relations with India and to reduce his country's reliance on China (Safi 2018a). A series of infrastructure projects initiated by the Yameen government had been funded with loans from China estimated at US$1.3 billion, a debt equal to more than 25 percent of the archipelago's GDP that critics feared would result in undue influence from China on the country (Safi 2018b). Academic research demonstrates that there is no direct correlation between democracy and low corruption. By itself, the holding of regular elections – the minimum requirement for democracy – isn't sufficient to make corruption less rampant. Properly working institutions, accountability to the public, transparency, a civil society, and free press are also necessary. Conversely, absent these additional aspects of a mature democracy, high-level and systemic corruption is likelier, although it rarely gets reported (Heymann 1996).

In some cases, Taiwan's interactions with civil society and democrat parties in Southeast Asia have even compelled pro-Beijing regimes, such as Hun Sen's in Cambodia, to fabricate claims of political interference against Taiwan, which were then used by pro-CCP media in Hong Kong and Taiwan to attack Taiwan's democracy-promotion efforts as well as the DPP (Kijewski and Sokchea 2017). Taiwan has also been accused by Beijing and pro-CCP elements in Hong Kong of fomenting instability in the SAR by supporting pro-democracy and independence movements.

For Taiwan, being democratic is not, in and of itself, sufficient for it to expect assistance from the international community as it faces off against authoritarian China. Unfortunately, this often has been the automatic argument used by Taiwanese politicians and supporters of Taiwan to convince others that they should help it. Rather, the Taiwanese side needs to find ways to explain *why* preserving a free and democratic Taiwan is in their interest. In other words, proponents of Taiwan shouldn't count on altruism but rather on self-interest. Taiwan and its democracy matter to the international community because the island-nation is an integral part of a global battle, a line of defense against a model of authoritarian rule that is inimical to the values that define the liberal order. The disappearance of Taiwan as a free and democratic state probably wouldn't be directly felt in most countries worldwide, and in fact a large number of people outside Asia likely wouldn't even realize this had occurred. But that loss – a victory for anti-democratic forces – would embolden revisionists and encourage them to escalate their assault on the global rules and institutions that have been in place since the end of World War II. If the CCP and other authoritarian regimes do not encounter opposition – and Taiwan is at the front lines of that opposition – there could come a day when the same people who were ignorant of the extinction of democracy in Taiwan find themselves having to combat revisionism on their doorstep. In fact, the first signs that this is already happening are with us today, with Chinese netizens and agencies dictating, *in our own countries*, how we refer to Taiwan on company websites or which map of China is the "correct" one.

Another area in which the Taiwan Strait is directly connected to a larger sphere is in the realm of economic espionage in cyberspace. As with the other areas discussed above, namely territory and ideology, China is using cyber espionage as part of a strategy to build up its strength and to displace its opponents. As a 2018 report by the U.S. National Counterintelligence and Security Center (2018) noted, "China has expansive efforts in place to acquire U.S. technology to include sensitive trade secrets and proprietary information. It continues to use cyber espionage to support its strategic development goals – science and technology advancement, military modernization, and economic policy objectives" by using a "complex, multipronged technology development strategy that uses licit and illicit methods to achieve its goals."

Besides a direct targeting of Taiwanese firms, many of the strategies listed in the report could exploit Taiwan's key role in the global high-tech sector and close relationship with the U.S., making it both a victim and, potentially, an unwitting partner of China. These strategies include: non-traditional collectors (individuals for whom science or business is their primary profession to target and acquire U.S. technology), joint ventures, research partnerships, academic collaboration, science and technology investments, mergers and acquisitions, front companies, talent recruitment programs, intelligence services, and finally laws and regulations to disadvantage foreign companies and give an advantage to its own companies. According to the report, cyber espionage activities prioritize the energy/alternative energy industry, biotechnology, defense technology, environmental protection, high-end manufacturing, and information and communications technology. The report identifies 49 priority sectors and technologies targeted by cyber espionage, from advanced pressurized water reactor and high-temperature, gas-cooled nuclear power stations to smart grids, biopharmaceuticals to new vaccines and drugs, aerospace, radar and optical systems, energy-efficient systems, 3D printing, high-performance composite materials, space infrastructure and exploration

90 The regional and global context

technology, artificial intelligence, high-end computer chips and quantum computing, and communications.

Addressing this extraordinary threat will require the U.S. to collaborate not only with its private sector "to address science and technology gaps through cyber research and development as a way of mitigating the malicious activities of threat actors in cyberspace," but also with allies in the international community, including Taiwan, that are equally threatened by aggressive Chinese activity in this domain. In light of the interconnectivity of the global economic system and the vulnerabilities created by software supply chain operations, leaders in technology, in the private sector and in government, will have every interest in plugging potential gaps that could be exploited by countries like China. Therefore, as with territory and the battle of ideas, Taiwan, as a responsible and law-abiding member in the international community, will be an indispensable partner to the U.S. and other countries around the world as they react to the threat of cyber espionage.

We should also point out that all three areas are interconnected and mutually reinforcing; and that Taiwan moreover lies at the intersection of all three – building its national strength through rampant cyber espionage, China is in a better position to modernize its military, threaten its neighbors, confront the U.S. in Asia, and develop technologies and software which can be used to strengthen authoritarian controls in China and around the world. All three should provide opportunities for the Taiwanese government and civil society to reach out to and work with the international community. In doing so, Taiwan would further demonstrate why its independence and continued existence as a democracy are key assets for the global community.

Challenges to Xi and the fragility of authoritarian rule

China's greater assertiveness since 2013 is largely attributable to Xi Jinping, whose personality and worldview are characterized by impatience, a strong sense of historical destiny, and paranoia. For Xi, the Chinese Dream is now, not something that can be attained sometime in the future. His ruling style and consolidation of power have also fueled a sense of invulnerability. Much of Xi's potential opponents within the CCP, people like Bo Xilai (薄熙來) and domestic security chief Zhou Yongkang (周永康), have been swatted away like flies, many of them falling to an anti-corruption campaign that, according to Chinese reports, has been widely supported by the public. The anti-graft campaign has reached the upper echelons of the CCP and the PLA, including General Fang Fenghui (房峰輝), a former member of the Central Military Commission (CMC, 中央軍事委員會), which Xi now heads, and former chief of the CMC Joint Staff Department. Former generals Guo Boxiong (郭伯雄) and Xu Caihou (徐才厚), who had both served as vice chairmen of the CMC, have also been caught by the anti-corruption net, while former general Zhang Yang (張陽), who served alongside Fang, committed suicide in November 2017. According to Xinhua News Agency, "more than 100 PLA officers at or above the corps-level, including two former CMC vice chairmen, have been investigated and punished" since the 18th Party Congress in 2012. Writing in 2016, Cheng Li (李成) (2016) of the Brookings Institution in Washington put that figure at 160 senior officials, including civilian leaders at the vice-minister and vice-governor levels or above, and military officers with the rank of major-general or higher. According to Minxin Pei (裴敏欣) (2016), "collusive corruption" inside the PLA, "the ultimate guarantor of the CCP's survival," has reached "epidemic proportions." The same applies to the Ministry of State Security (MSS, 中華人民共和國國家安全部), while the very agencies in charge of discipline inspection have themselves been hit with corruption scandals. According to Pei, despite Xi's efforts to root out corruption, "the roots of crony capitalism in general, and collusive corruption in particular, run much deeper" and will continue to undermine state stability.

In many cases, the individuals who were probed and arrested had close relationships with Xi's predecessors, suggesting that factionalism has also had something to do with the fate of many of the cadres and "tigers" thus targeted.

Xi's impressive success in getting rid of potential challengers has also been accompanied by a tightening of ideological thought that has affected every sector of Chinese society and the emergence of a cult of personality the likes of which had not been seen since Mao Zedong. For example, "Xi Jinping Thought on Socialism with Chinese Characteristics for a New Era" (習近平新時代中國特色社會主義思想) was enshrined in the CCP's constitution in the fall of 2017 and in the PRC constitution in spring 2018.

Those excesses were compounded by the decision, made during the 19th Party Congress in October 2017, to remove the terms limits for a president. Introduced by Deng Xiaoping, the two-term limit had been intended as a mechanism to prevent the re-emergence of a Mao-styled supreme leader, whose unchecked powers and ambitions had led to the catastrophes of the Great Leap Forward and Cultural Revolution. Combined with the personality cult, the lifting of the term limits has created fears in some Chinese circles of a possible return to Maoist excesses, and contributed to some criticism of Xi in and outside China. As Wu notes, "post-Mao leaders have increasingly needed those congressional endorsements of their legitimacy and authority . . . which might indicate a positive connection weak leaders and the regularization of Congress elections" (Wu 2015). Although the jury is still out on whether Xi is a 21st century incarnation of Mao, what is certain is that he is a "strong leader," arguably the strongest since Mao. And like Mao, Xi does not seem to feel the need to legitimize his personal rule through that regularized and institutionalized exercise.

Xi's anti-graft campaign has also sparked discontent among the "second-generation reds" (the children of revolutionary-era Communist Party leaders) and "princelings" that, as entrepreneurs under Deng's reform and opening-up era, had accumulated tremendous wealth. A substantial number of princelings, which have been part of Xi's support bloc since 2012, were forced to step down after the 19th Party Congress under party rules that require people who have reached the age of 68 to retire from politics. Those developments may have created a circle of disgruntled former officials and party members who are now outside the system. Pension

92 The regional and global context

reform in the military has also fostered discontent among former members of the military, leading to unprecedented protests in the summer of 2018.

All of this has given rise to rumors of a feud which exploded during a meeting at the beach resort of Beidaihe (北戴河) in Hebei Province in August 2018, and much speculation about the stability of Xi's control of the CCP. According to most analysts, Xi has the situation well under control and we are a long way from seeing the emergence of anyone in a position to challenge his leadership. The lack of transparency in Chinese politics – which forces China hands to scrutinize state-run newspapers to count the number of times Xi is mentioned in leading articles and to see whether photos of the Chinese leader feature prominently on the front pages, hoping to unearth clues of possible internal battles at the CCP – makes assessments of regime stability an exercise in speculation. That being said, it can be argued that the tightening of controls across China, the crackdown on the Internet and civil society, the politicization by Xi of the anti-corruption campaign to bury his competitors, and the ideological drive which has penetrated government bodies, schools, the intelligence services, and the military, are all signals of a leader who is not altogether confident about his ability to keep things under control. It can also be argued that rather than being loved, Xi is feared as a leader, with the implication that signs of weakness could quickly be exploited and acted upon by his detractors.

It is also important to ask, as Li does in *Chinese Politics in the Xi Jinping Era*, whether, in his replacing collective leadership, Xi was "lucky enough to arrive at just the moment in history when his consolidation of power – to upset the inertia and possibly even prevent a split of the CCP leadership – was appealing to the Chinese public and most other Chinese leaders, especially those in the current PSC [Politburo Standing Committee, 中國共產黨中央政治局常務委員會]" or did so "more through 'hook and crook,' Machiavellian dealings, and the assembly of strong loyalist networks, thus returning the CCP to an era of strongman politics." The answer to that question will be an important factor determining Xi's ability to remain in power, as well as the nature of whoever replaces him, through party mechanisms or via a coup.

By making himself the objectification of and indispensable agent for the realization of the Chinese Dream, Xi has moved away from the rule-by-consensus that had characterized previous iterations of the regime. Consequently, as long as things seem to be moving in a positive direction for China, both domestically and externally, Xi's leadership should remain secure. However, should the situation deteriorate, Xi alone, as the pinnacle of power, will be blamed for mishandling the situation. His authoritarian tendencies and control of all the key positions within the party-state apparatus also make it likely that he is not receiving all the information he needs from his advisers to make the right decisions in addressing highly complex issues. Call this the sycophant-dictator trap. Lastly, the removal of the president's term limit has closed off a useful channel for discontent and negotiations over the composition of the future leadership, which meant that would-be successors in the CCP knew they only had to bide their time for a chance to reach the upper echelons of the party. With that possibility removed, less peaceful means of regime replacement, such as a coup, are now likelier, which is a key ingredient for instability. As Minzner (2018) observes, under Xi's authoritarian revival, "China is now steadily cannibalizing its own prior political institutionalization . . . once a source of stability for the Party-state."

All of this occurs at a time of extraordinary challenges for China, in both the domestic and external realms. Slowing economic growth, environmental deterioration, and a rapidly aging society that will impose severe strains on the social safety net, are just some of the issues that could soon haunt the CCP leadership. Externally, a deepening trade war with the U.S., which some people in China have already accused Xi of mishandling, as well as an increasingly difficult strategic environment – also blamed on Xi's overzealous foreign policy – could threaten to derail, or at the very least delay, the Chinese Dream.

While still performing relatively well, with a target 6.5 percent growth for 2018, China's economy is undeniably slowing down and is unlikely to return to the impressive growth it has experienced over the previous decade. Problems caused by financial excess and property bubbles continue to haunt the country's economic prospects, while the trade war with the U.S. will likely drag those numbers down, depending on its duration and the severity of the tariffs imposed by Washington. By the end of 2016, debt accounted for 277 percent of the nation's GDP. The CCP's efforts to reform the market, shift China's economy away from the export-reliant model, and to engineer slower, more self-sustaining growth, are in their early stages and success is not guaranteed, while stimulus spending becomes less and less effective the more it is used.

Environmental degradation, from air pollution to poisoned rivers, continues to pose a serious risk for Chinese society. By the half of the first decade of the 21st century, the economic costs of environmental degradation (primarily healthcare and loss of life) accounted for approximately 8 to 12 percent of GDP, and those are expected to rise as China's economic and industrial development continues apace (Economy 2010). Soil pollution alone is said to cost China 1.1 percent of GDP, and water pollution 2.1 percent. As many as 459 "cancer villages" are said to exist around China, many of them located close to highly polluted rivers. Lack of incentives, over-reliance on slogans and campaigns, as well as systemic corruption and continued overwhelming reliance on fossil fuels will also likely hinder success in that area, which in turn will increase healthcare costs and associated social problems.

Meanwhile, China is on its way to becoming one of the oldest societies in the world. By 2050, the median age will be 49 – nine years older than in the U.S. During that period, the number of men between the age of 20 and 25 will have dropped by half. Chronic disease, such as dementia and diabetes, are on the rise as the population ages. By 2040, China's median age and associated problems will be similar to those faced by countries like France and Germany and Japan today. However, China's GDP per capita will be significantly lower, and significantly less evenly distributed, than in those countries, which will compel the CCP leadership to make very difficult decisions in terms of how it allocates its budget. Depending on what Beijing decides – and that decision could have to be made as early as

94 The regional and global context

in the next decade – either military spending as a share of the total government budget (6.1 percent in 2017, or about 2 percent of GDP)[1] will have to drop, or, to avoid doing so, the CCP will have to "allow growing levels of poverty within an exploding elderly population" and possibly an even wider gap between the nation's wealthy and the poor (Haas 2012). An economic downturn, or even a slowing economy, will inevitably compound the problem. According to French, "the need to fund China's ballooning social security cost, beginning in the near future, will create monumental new burdens for the society that will radically undermine most of today's straight-line assumptions about the country's future wealth and power."

China's ability to address these extraordinary problems, meanwhile, is undermined by the lack of bureaucratic reform and controls imposed by the state on civil society. To adequately meet the domestic challenges, Ang writes, "the government must release and channel the immense creative potential of civil society, which would necessitate greater freedom of expression, more public participation, and less state intervention." However, if Xi remains inflexible in his desire to impose strict discipline on Chinese society – "in his eyes, necessary to contain the political threats to CCP rule" – then "he cannot expect the bureaucracy to innovate or accomplish as much as it has in the past" (Ang 2018). Similar political constraints have undermined efforts to deal with the threat from environmental pollution. As Economy writes,

> Beijing is sharply constraining the role of civil society by silencing authoritative voices or activists who challenge government policy, invoking national security overlay on environmental protection, embedding party committees within NGOs to supervise their activities, and limiting opportunities for cooperation with foreign counterparts.
>
> *(Economy 2018)*

The consequences of those deepened restrictions on NGOs, she writes, is "a community that is less independent and capable of holding the government accountable in the ways that helped launch the movement to clean the air in the late 2000s."

From all this, it is clear that Xi's paranoia, accompanied by his ideological drive and greater restrictions on religious groups, civil society and its ability to engage with foreign NGOs, are undermining, rather than reinforcing, the state. Those decisions, made purely for political reasons and to shield the CCP from critics within Chinese society and perceived threats from abroad, have reversed many of the institutionalized reforms, many in them only partly, since 2003. This decision, along with his populism and centralization of power, could come back to haunt him by providing his opponents, largely silent for the time being, with the ammunition they need to force him to step down.

Xi's political goals, upon which he has staked much of his legitimacy, also risk being undermined by the mounting problems discussed above. Or rather, the window of opportunity to accomplish his objectives, such as the annexation of Taiwan, may be narrowing fast. Thus, Xi could have concluded that he must realize the

Chinese Dream *before* he can turn to the issues at home, such as the economy, the environment, an aging society, and other matters. In other words, Xi may be conscious that he is running out of time. If that is the case, then this would help explain the otherwise seemingly self-defeating authoritarian revival, stricter ideological controls, populism, ultra-nationalism, militarism, and risk-taking abroad that have characterized China since his coming to power. It is, needless to say, one hell of a gamble. As French argues in *Everything Under the Heavens*, "Xi has made his dramatic break with the famous Deng Xiaoping strategy of biding one's time" and "has decided that china must seize whatever advantages it can now before its window of opportunity slams shut within the next ten or, at best, twenty years." This, he adds, "will make the immediate future a moment of maximum risk between the United States and China" – and for Taiwan, the annexation of which is at the very center of Xi's ambitions and legacy.

If French is right, and I believe he is, then 2018–2038 will be a period of particularly high risks for Taiwan. We have already seen projections of China using force against Taiwan between 2020–2022. As we discussed in the previous section, the likelihood that China will initiate major military operations against Taiwan is contingent on several factors, including the belief in Beijing that unification in some form can be accomplished without needing to use force, Taiwan's own deterrent capability, and the level of support Taiwan receives from its principal security guarantor, the U.S., as well as Japan and other players within the international community. The re-election of Tsai Ing-wen (or another DPP candidate) in 2020 and the promise of another four years of almost-zero progress on unification could convince Beijing that force is the only option, especially if the CCP believes that the window of opportunity to seize Taiwan by military means is, due to demographic trends and economics, closing fast. All of this means that we cannot take the relatively careful approach to external policy, or the "rational" decision-making, that characterized Xi's predecessors for granted. While I would argue that Xi still would rather not gamble his legacy on an unpredictable – and possibly devastating – military adventure across the Taiwan Strait, his break with precedent on several other matters, including the overturning of institutionalized reform, suggests that we are dealing with a new kind of leader. In many ways, Xi is the personification of *megalothymia*, which the political scientist Francis Fukuyama (2018) says "thrives on exceptionality: taking big risks, engaging in monumental struggles, seeking large effects, because all of these lead to recognition of oneself as superior to others." For Taiwan and its allies, making sure that the Chinese do not give in to the temptation to use force during that dangerous window of opportunity should be the main priority. Taiwan, therefore, must continue to buy time. Among other things, this means making greater investment in its deterrent capability, readiness and training, as well as more clearly defined "red lines" by the U.S. and Japan on what would trigger a U.S. intervention in the Taiwan Strait. Needless to say, the same logic applies to other parts of the world that also happen to be in Xi's crosshairs.

We also cannot count on the possibility, remote at this point, that any leader, who replaced Xi, should he encounter a serious challenge to his leadership and

96 The regional and global context

were deposed, would be in any way more patient or less nationalistic than his predecessor. In other words, it is too soon to tell whether Xi's assertiveness is an aberration or part of developing trends within Chinese society in general and the CCP in particular.

Note

1 China's official defense budget for 2017 was US$151.4 billion. SIPRI estimated it to be US$228.2 billion. See, "What Does China Really Spend on Its Military?" ChinaPower, Center for Strategic and International Studies. https://chinapower.csis.org/military-spending/. According to World Bank data, health expenditure in China accounted from 5.32% of GDP in 2015, the latest figures available.

References

Allison, Graham (2017) *Destined for War: Can America and China Escape Thucydides's Trap?* New York: Houghton Mifflin Harcourt.

Ang, Yuen (2018) "Autocracy with Chinese Characteristics," *Foreign Affairs*, May–June, pp. 39–46.

Cole, J. Michael (2017) "A U.S. Attack on North Korea: Could China Retaliate Against Taiwan?" *National Interest*, 27 December. https://nationalinterest.org/blog/the-buzz/us-attack-north-korea-could-china-retaliate-against-taiwan-23825.

Dasgupta, Saibal (2018) "Mahathir Fears New Colonialism, Cancels 2 Chinese Projects on Beijing Visit," *Times of India*, 21 August. https://timesofindia.indiatimes.com/world/china/mahathir-fears-new-colonialism-cancels-2-chinese-projects-on-beijing-visit/articleshow/65493634.cms.

Economy, Elizabeth (2010) *The River Runs Black: The Environmental Challenge to China's Future*, Ithaca: Cornell University Press, p. 91.

Economy, Elizabeth (2018) *The Third Revolution: Xi Jinping and the New Chinese State*, New York: Oxford University Press, p. 184.

Erickson, Andrew S. and Joel Wuthnow (2016) "Barriers, Springboards and Benchmarks: China Conceptualizes the Pacific 'Island Chains'," *China Quarterly*, January, pp. 1–22. www.dtic.mil/dtic/tr/fulltext/u2/1002513.pdf.

Fernholz, Tim (2018) "Eight Countries in Danger of Falling into China's 'Debt Trap'," *Quartz*, 8 March. https://qz.com/1223768/china-debt-trap-these-eight-countries-are-in-danger-of-debt-overloads-from-chinas-belt-and-road-plans/.

French, Howard W. (2017) *Everything Under the Heavens: How the Past Helps Shape China's Push for Global Power*, New York: Alfred A. Knopf, p. 270, 281–282.

Fukuyama, Francis (2018) *Identity: The Demand for Dignity and the Politics of Resentment*, New York: Farrar, Straus and Giroux, p. xiv.

Goldstein, Lyle J. (2018) "The United States Must Be Realistic on Taiwan," *National Interest*, 7 August. https://nationalinterest.org/feature/united-states-must-be-realistic-taiwan-28187.

Greenfield, Charlotte and Jonathan Barrett (2018) "Payment Due: Pacific Islands in the Red as Debts to China Mount," *Reuters*, 31 July. www.reuters.com/article/us-pacific-debt-china-insight/payment-due-pacific-islands-in-the-red-as-debts-to-china-mount-idUSKBN1KK2J4.

Haas, Mark L. (2012) "America's Golden Years? U.S. Security in an Aging World," in *Political Demography: How Population Changes Are Reshaping International Security and National Politics*, Jack A. Goldstone, Eric P. Kaufman and Monica Duffy Toft, eds, Oxford: Oxford University Press, p. 57.

Khan, Sulmaan Wasif (2018) *Haunted by Chaos China's Grand Strategy from Mao Zedong to Xi Jinping*, Cambridge: Harvard University Press, p. 7.

Kijewski, Leonie and Meas Sokchea (2017) "Fresh News 'Plot' Thickens as Site Publishes Allegations Taiwanese 'Extremist Group' Trained CNRP," *Phnom Penh Post*, 1 September. www.phnompenhpost.com/national/fresh-news-plot-thickens-site-publishes-allegations-taiwanese-extremist-group-trained-cnrp.

Li, Cheng (2016) *Chinese Politics in the Xi Jinping Era*, Washington: Brookings Institution Press, p. 3, 5.

Li, Eric X. (2012) "Why China's Political Model Is Superior," *New York Times*, 16 February. www.nytimes.com/2012/02/16/opinion/why-chinas-political-model-is-superior.html.

Macaes, Bruno (2018) *The Dawn of Eurasia: On the Trail of the New World Order*, London: Allen Lane, pp. 59–60.

Minzner, Carl (2018) *End of an Era: How China's Authoritarian Revival Is Undermining Its Rise*, New York: Oxford University Press, p. 34.

Mourdoukoutas, Panos (2018) "China Is Doing the Same Things to Sri Lanka That Great Britain Did to China After the Opium Wars," *Forbes*, 28 June. www.forbes.com/sites/panosmourdoukoutas/2018/06/28/china-is-doing-the-same-things-to-sri-lanka-great-britain-did-to-china-after-the-opium-wars/#584b0cfb7446.

Nathan, Andrew J. and Andrew Scobell (2012) *China's Search for Security*, New York: Columbia University Press, p. 196.

National Counterintelligence and Security Center (2018) "Foreign Economic Espionage in Cyberspace," www.dni.gov/files/NCSC/documents/news/20180724-economic-espionage-pub.pdf.

Pei, Minxin (2016) *China's Crony Capitalism: The Dynamics of Regime Decay*, Cambridge: Harvard University Press, pp. 156, 261–262.

Philip, B. Heymann (1996) "Democracy and Corruption," *Fordham International Law Journal*, Volume 20, Issue 2. https://dash.harvard.edu/bitstream/handle/1/12967838/Democracy%20and%20Corruption.pdf?sequence=1&isAllowed=y.

Safi, Michael (2018a) "Maldives Voters Throw Out China-Backed Strongman President," *The Guardian*, 24 September. www.theguardian.com/world/2018/sep/23/maldives-voters-throw-out-china-backed-strongman-president.

Safi, Michael (2018b) "Maldives Election: Fears China-Backed President Could Return Country to Dark Days," *The Guardian*, 21 September. www.theguardian.com/world/2018/sep/21/maldives-election-fears-china-backed-president-could-return-country-to-dark-days.

Schumacher, Elizabeth (2018) "Sierra Leone Nixes Controversial China-Funded Airport," *Deutsche Welle*, 10 October. www.dw.com/en/sierra-leone-nixes-controversial-china-funded-airport/a-45832726.

Segal, Adam (2018) "When China Rules the Web," *Foreign Affairs*, September–October, pp. 10–18.

Snyder, Timothy (2018) *The Road to Unfreedom: Russia, Europe, America*, New York: Tim Duggan, p. 151.

Wu, Guoguang (2015) *China's Party Congress: Power, Legitimacy, and Institutional Manipulation*, Cambridge: Cambridge University Press, p. 265.

Xi, Jinping (2017) "Secure a Decisive Victory in Building a Moderately Prosperous Society in All Respects and Strive for the Great Success of Socialism with Chinese Characteristics for a New Era," Delivered at the 19th National Congress of the Communist Party of China, 18 October. www.xinhuanet.com/english/download/Xi_Jinping's_report_at_19th_CPC_National_Congress.pdf. 習近平：決勝全面建成小康社會 奪取新時代中國特色社會主義偉大勝利-在中國共產黨第十九次全國代表大會上的報告：新華網, www.xinhuanet.com/politics/19cpcnc/2017-10/27/c_1121867529.htm.

5

U.S.–TAIWAN RAPPROCHEMENT

Since the end of World War II, no country has been as important to Taiwan as the United States, and this continues to be true today. Although uncertainty surrounded the future of the relationship following the transition of power from the KMT to the DPP in 2016 and, later that year, the election of Donald J. Trump as the 45th president of the U.S., there is no doubt that bilateral ties have deepened markedly over the past two years in a way that has been beneficial to Taiwan.

Part of this is attributable to the Tsai administration's policies, which have emphasized stability and predictability and put a premium on reassuring Washington. During both the final months of the Obama administration and the new Trump administration, Taipei successfully struck a balance between defending Taiwan's interests and reassuring Washington that Taiwan would not be a source of instability in the Taiwan Strait. Although President Tsai's olive branch to Beijing – the recognition of the "historical fact" that the two sides met in 1992, the ROC constitutional order, commitment to the "status quo" and so on – caused some discontent within the green camp in Taiwan, it also demonstrated to U.S. authorities that her government would not engage in adventurism that risked sparking armed conflict in the Taiwan Strait, which could compel the U.S. to intervene and get dragged into a war with China. Wisely, President Tsai also skirted the issue of a referendum on constitutional or name change, which not only would have given Beijing more ammunition to squeeze Taiwan but, as occurred in 2005 when the Chen administration began flirting with referenda, could have effected a chill in U.S.-Taiwan relations for the instability that such a move risked causing.

As a result of the Tsai administration's cautious and, in this author's view, wise approach to the triangular relationship, Beijing has been unable, as it was during the Chen Shui-bian years, to convince Washington and the international community that Taiwan, or the DPP, are the source of instability in the Taiwan Strait. In fact, while Beijing's punishing strategy against Taiwan since 2016 has had some (limited) effects on the island-nation, perceptions of this crackdown on Taiwan have been overwhelmingly negative, so much so that on the whole, it is Beijing, not Taipei, that is seen today as the irresponsible party in the Taiwan Strait; it is Beijing that is seen to be changing the "status quo," and it is Beijing – and Xi Jinping – that now has earned the sobriquet of "troublemaker."

This has been accompanied by the realization, in Washington and elsewhere, that tensions in the Taiwan Strait exist not because of the DPP or its pro-independence views, but rather due to the incompatibility of the two systems that exist in Taiwan and China. In other words, the conflict transcends political parties in Taiwan and would remain even if the KMT had won in 2016 or comes back to power in a future election. The chief cause of this, of course, is the civic nationalism that has developed in Taiwan over the years, epitomized by its people's embrace of democracy. We also should not underestimate the impact of developments in Hong Kong, where "one country, two systems" has opened the eyes of many analysts and officials who, in the past, would have been more amenable to the proposition that the same system was suitable for Taiwan and that the Taiwanese were irresponsible for turning this offer down. More and more, the reality of being ruled by the CCP – regardless of its promises to respect social systems and ways of life – is getting understood by the international community, and this has generated more understanding as to why the Taiwanese are opposed to "peaceful" annexation. Discoveries about Beijing's inhumane treatment of Uighur Muslims in Xinjiang, with reports of concentration camp-style conditions and mass re-education programs, have also played a role in convincing people around the world that Taiwan is wise to refuse being ruled by a party that is capable of such things against its own people.

Above all else, however, is the realization in Washington and across the U.S. establishment that longstanding U.S. policy toward China, which operated under the assumption that engagement would produce a China that is more like us – more liberal, if not democratic – has been an abject failure. Up until a few years ago, that view still had its proponents in U.S. government, academia, and the business community. Wait, champions of engagement would tell us. Give its economy sufficient time to create a middle class and, as the theory went, the CCP will have no choice but to embrace some form of democratization. While the world waited, it also turned a blind eye to human rights abuses, cyber espionage, and the mounting evidence that the Chinese model was mercantilist, rapacious, and unfair to foreign competitors. Several businesses, intent on making a fortune in China, were cheated out of their technology and intellectual property, but still they went, convinced that the horror stories would not apply to them. Meanwhile, many countries in the West allowed Chinese state-firms to acquire shares in, or to purchase outright, companies, or to bid for major projects in the telecommunications and other sectors, with little attention being paid to the potential national security risks associated with those transactions.

All of this is now changing, and one person, more than anyone else, is to blame for this state of affairs: Xi Jinping. Under him, it has become impossible to still argue that further engagement will cause a shift in the direction of Beijing's politics.

100 The regional and global context

Contrarily, Beijing has taken, and the CCP has made every effort to strengthen its ideological grip on Chinese society and whoever comes into contact with it. Under Xi, the social environment in China has become much more repressive than it had been under his predecessors; under his guard, the PLA has challenged the regional order and sent many of China's neighbors into a panic; and under him, the CCP has greatly intensified its efforts to rewrite the international order and to undermine institutions worldwide. For the former pro-Beijing voices in Washington and elsewhere, it is now evident that the largesse of the international community has only contributed to China building up its national strength so that it can now challenge the very order that permitted its re-emergence as a major player. All hopes that being nice could rein it in or loosen the grip that ideology still has on the CCP and Chinese society have been dashed. It was still possible to believe in a more palatable outcome when Hu Jintao was still in power; under Xi, anyone who still believes in that fantasy should be kept at a distance from policy-making circles.

The transformation in Washington circles has been nothing short of stunning. And as a result of this, more and more U.S. policy makers and academics have begun looking at Taiwan less as an appendage to China than as a partner in its own right. Although Taiwan will never be entirely separated from the context of China, the alternative that the island-nation has offered and its commitment to being a responsible stakeholder have contrasted sharply with the China that the international community struggles to conjugate with today. The shift in attitudes in the U.S. has been institutional: from the Executive branch to Congress, the Department of Defense to the State Department (the latter long seen as "pro-Beijing"), and throughout the think tank community, China is now perceived as an opponent, a challenger, and a threat to the liberal-democratic order. Fears caused by President Trump's supposedly "transactional" and unpredictable style have also compelled other parts of the U.S. government to be more vocal about Taiwan and the need to defend democracies, if only to provide a counter to a possible "deal" between Trump and Xi involving Taiwan.

Consequently, the closer ties that have existed between Taiwan and the U.S. since 2016 have not been solely the result of presidents Tsai or Trump. The context in which that bilateral relationship operates has itself changed dramatically and could only result in rapprochement between Taipei and Washington (*Apple Daily* 2018). Trump himself, a momentary aberration caused by an outlier who, as some see it, happened to find himself in the Oval Office, or the escalating trade war between the two giants in 2019, only partly account for this unprecedented rapprochement; rather, the closer ties are the results of trends and choices that China has made since 2012, and of Washington's responses to them. Instead of creating a world in which it would have been easier to make the case for unification, Beijing's behavior since Xi took over has given Taiwan, and the rest of the world, munitions aplenty to make the case for Taiwan's continued existence as an independent sovereignty. And for the U.S., the logic of a sovereign Taiwan goes well beyond Washington's responsibilities under the Taiwan Relations Act: China's belligerence and threat to the regional – and perhaps global – order has put a premium on supporting countries in Asia that are in the front lines of the clash of ideologies that is now upon us.

Much has been made of the famous 10-minute telephone conversation between President Tsai and president-elect Trump in December 2016. For many in Taiwan, the precedent-making congratulatory chat was a signal that prevailing U.S. policy on Taiwan was about to undergo a major transformation. Beijing, for its part, regarded this development with alarm and attributed this to Trump's inexperience. After the incident, Beijing officials redoubled their outreach efforts to Trump's team to ensure there would be no repeat of such "offenses" to the "one China" policy.

Whether the president-elect took the call from President Tsai due to his inexperience is debatable; what is more certain is that the people around him who made the call possible had ample foreign policy experience and understood that, for all the publicity it generated, the brief exchange of pleasantries was entirely symbolic: the just-elected leader of a democracy was talking on the phone with another elected leader. For Tsai, the call had a legitimizing effect as well, and served as a signal to Beijing that her relationship with the U.S., as head of the DPP, would be unlike that which had characterized Chen Shui-bian's. In other words, it signaled that the relationship had been repaired (Cole 2016a).

Symbolic though it may have been, the call also arguably marked the first in a long cycle of reactions by Beijing to any signs of rapprochement between Taipei and Washington – and every time, it was Taiwan, not the U.S., that suffered the consequences (Cole 2016b). From that moment on, Beijing made it a point to punish the weaker party in the triumvirate. Over time, this would compel people in Taipei and friends abroad to consider whether mere symbolic gains for Taiwan were meaningful enough to warrant whatever retaliatory action was sure to follow from Beijing. More and more, it became clear that a premium should be put on developments that helped bolster Taiwan's sovereignty – in other words real gains – than on symbolic gestures which, though pleasant and morale boosters, had little if any concrete impact on Taiwan's overall position vis-à-vis China and within the tough international environment.

For all its efforts to guide the incoming U.S. president in a direction more to its liking, Beijing was at first rewarded a little more than a week after he took President Tsai's call with Trump questioning whether the U.S. should continue to abide by its "one China" policy. The remark, made during an interview on "Fox News Sunday," threatened to overturn four decades of U.S. policy. Besides causing consternation in Beijing, Trump's comments also exacerbated fears that Taiwan could be used as a "bargaining chip" in other matters. "I fully understand the 'one China' policy," he said, "but I don't know why we have to be bound by a 'one China' policy unless we make a deal with China having to do with other things, including trade" (Bohan and Brunnstrom 2016). The following day, Beijing expressed "concerns" and later on stated that it would "never bargain with Washington over issues involving its national sovereignty or territorial integrity," which obviously was meant to include Taiwan. Weeks later, China retaliated with military aircraft and naval transits in the Taiwan Strait, which included the aircraft carrier *Liaoning*. After much to-ing

102 The regional and global context

and fro-ing, in a 9 February 2017 telephone conversation with Xi Jinping, Trump agreed to honor the "one China" policy (Feast 2017).

Although Trump did a complete 360-degree on the "one China" policy, ending up where he had begun, his threat to undo longstanding U.S. policy on Taiwan and China nevertheless provided an opportunity to explain to Americans, and to the rest of the world, what a country's "one China" policy entails. A surprising number of people, even some in government, tend to confuse their country's "one China" policy with Beijing's "one China" principle – and Beijing has done what it can to maintain that confusion. Far too often, journalists, officials, and academics forget that the "one China" policy is an agreement of sorts reached upon the establishment of official diplomatic relations with the PRC. In it, a state normally "acknowledges" or "takes notes" of Beijing's view that there is only "one China" and that Taiwan is part of China. What is often lost in that nuance is the fact that "acknowledging" and "taking note" are far from agreeing that Taiwan is part of China, let alone the PRC. Also lost on many is what is possible within the scope of a country's "one China" policy when it comes to engaging Taiwan. Unfortunately, Beijing has exploited this lack of knowledge to compel states into avoiding Taiwan, or to engage in risk-avoidance by limiting their interactions with Taipei.

Two months later, Trump held his first summit with Xi at his Mar-a-Lago estate in Florida, a meeting which, though light on the substance, nevertheless suggested that relations between China and the U.S. were back on an even keel after a bumpy start (Nakamura 2017). Some analysts even concluded that the summit was cause for guarded optimism that progress could be made on the South China Sea, North Korea, and Taiwan.

Less than six months after his groundbreaking telephone conversation with President Tsai, the Trump pendulum had swung from questioning the "one China" policy to reaffirming it (later on he would even praise Xi for his authoritarian rule and lifetime mandate) (Phillips 2018). In Taipei, fears that Taiwan could become part of some sort of transaction between Washington and Beijing – especially on North Korea, which by then it had become evident would be one of the Trump administration's top priorities – came back to the surface, although some, including me, argued that Trump could not go it alone and that other parts of the U.S. government would never countenance the unilateral abandonment of a longstanding ally in Asia.

For the next little while, despite the uncertainties and apprehensions, things were pretty much back to normal, and continuity, rather than shock treatment, features in the U.S.' relations with Taiwan and China.

There were, nevertheless, problems from the start. Chief among them was the long time it took, under Trump's first secretary of state, Rex Tillerson, to appoint officials to key positions at the State Department. One hundred days into his administration, nearly half of the positions at the State Department, including a number of ambassadorships, were still unfilled. In many cases, leftovers from the previous administration stayed behind in an "acting" capacity until new appointments were made. Compounding the problem was the Trump administration's decision to push out a number of top officials. By October 2017, more than six months into the new administration, more than 100 senior appointments across the U.S. government had yet to receive confirmation by Senate. One year into his presidency, eight out of 10 top posts at the State Department were still vacant (Faries and Rojanasakul 2018).

For several months, Foggy Bottom was in disarray. For U.S. officials posted overseas, including diplomats at the American Institute in Taiwan (AIT), the confusion back in Washington often was a source of frustration and undermined morale. In some cases, officials seeking guidance or a green light on certain initiatives involving Taiwan had to wait several weeks before they could hear back from senior officials in the capital; oftentimes, when hardworking AIT officials called back to State Department, the phone simply went unanswered.

Besides the hurdles caused by Tillerson's organizational chaos, democracy promotion also wasn't high on the new secretary's agenda – or the president's, for that matter. Given the premium that Taiwan puts on its role as a democracy, and its uses as an instrument of "soft power" with states and the nongovernmental community, the lack of interest in democracy promotion back in Washington limited Taiwan's ability to interact with foreign counterparts on that issue. In some cases, nonprofits had to step in to ensure that certain democracy-related events in which the State Department was expected to play a role could be held as planned.

Over time, and with the replacement of Tillerson with Mike Pompeo in March 2018, the situation appeared to have improved, and AIT officials were able to enjoy some normalcy in their interactions with Washington.

Often in the U.S.-Taiwan relationship, too much focus has been put on major arms sales to Taipei, and too little to other measures that contribute to the comprehensive strengthening of bilateral ties. Although arms packages, to which we will turn later in this chapter, have defensive and political significance, making headlines and often attracting the wrath of China, other, quieter forms of engagement have been going on which are helping Taiwan counter Beijing's efforts to isolate it internationally. One very promising initiative between the U.S. and Taiwan is known as the Global Cooperation and Training Framework (GCTF, 全球合作暨訓練架構). Since the launch of this initiative in 2015, a total of 16 rounds of GCTF workshops have been held in Taiwan, touching on matters including transnational crime and forensic science, enterovirus laboratory diagnosis, humanitarian assistance and disaster relief, e-commerce and combating disinformation through media literacy. As Christopher J. Marut said at the GCTF MOU signing ceremony in June 2015, the new framework

> will build upon [previous] successes and explore new ways to harness U.S. and Taiwan expertise and teamwork for the benefit of the regional and global communities. We launch this in recognition that the biggest challenges facing the world today will only be solved through encouraging different but complementary experiences, perspectives, and competencies. Taiwan is leading the way, from promotion of women's empowerment and entrepreneurship as a driver of economic development, to fostering a robust civil society

104 The regional and global context

as the vanguard of a vibrant democracy. Taiwan has much to share, and this framework will push the sharing process forward.

(AIT 2015)

The workshops are paid for by the Taiwanese government and provide an opportunity for experts from the U.S. and elsewhere to come to Taiwan and establish connections with their Taiwanese counterparts in various fields of expertise. Recently, some of the GCTF workshops have been enlarged to bring in experts and officials from other countries in the region, including Japan and Australia.

Other types of quiet engagement have taken the form of delegations of congressional members and their aides, congressionally mandated commissions, governors, academics, think tank analysts, defense experts, journalists, businesspeople, investors, and others to Taiwan, which as with GCTF provide opportunities for U.S. experts and officials to engage in direct communication with their counterparts in Taiwanese government, academia, and the private sector. In many but not all cases, Taiwan's MOFA plays a role in setting the agenda for the visitors. Since 2016, the volume and frequency of such delegations from the U.S. as well as other countries have increased exponentially, which attests to the greater interest that is being paid to Taiwan, for its own sake and as part of growing efforts to better understand the region. In early 2019, Taiwan also hosted the Regional Religious Freedom Forum, an event co-hosted by the U.S. State Department and Taiwan's MOFA, and co-organized by the Taiwan Foundation for Democracy at which the U.S. ambassador-at-large for International Religious Freedom, Sam Brownback, was present (Wen 2019). The event, which among others involved Uyghurs from Xinjiang, Chinese Christians and Tibetan Buddhists, drew loud complaints from the Chinese government but proceeded unhampered, despite protests outside by pro-Beijing groups such as the CUPP.

Another area in which closer U.S. engagement with the region could have some positive effects for Taiwan's external relations is the Indo-Pacific Strategy (IPS), which in many ways follows upon years of soul-searching about a U.S. "pivot" or "rebalancing" to Asia to balance against China's rise. Involving economics – as a response to China's Belt and Road Initiative – diplomacy and security aimed primarily at working more closely with ASEAN countries, the Trump administration's IPS also overlaps with Japan's "Free and Open Indo-Pacific," a broad strategy which was introduced by Japanese Prime Minister Abe Shinzo in 2016. Other countries, including India, Australia, and South Korea, have also begun laying out strategies to increase their interactions with countries in Southeast Asia.

Behind the IPS is "a geopolitical competition between free and repressive visions of world order . . . in the Indo-Pacific region." Jim Mattis, President Trump's secretary of defense at the time, also defined the IPS as the centerpiece of the administration, adding that Washington "cannot accept Chinese actions that impinge on the interests of the international community, undermining the rules-based order" (Akimoto 2018).

The core component of the IPS is a Quad of nations – the U.S., Japan, India, and Australia. The Quad itself remains very much a vague concept, and many analysts have argued that the success of the effort is contingent on inclusiveness rather than limiting itself to the four principal players. For Taiwan, the IPS also overlaps with the Tsai administration's New Southbound Policy, which aims to diversify Taiwan's economy in order to reduce reliance on China, as well as to engage Southeast Asia at the social and educational level. There is also recognition in Washington of a possible role for Taiwan in the IPS, inasmuch as it has aspirations that run in parallel with efforts by other countries. Speaking during a special briefing in April 2018, Alex N. Wong, Deputy Assistant Secretary, Bureau of East Asian and Pacific Affairs, told his audience in Washington:

> it's not just India that is pursuing greater engagement with East Asia and Southeast Asia. There are a number of crisscrossing strategies throughout the region. So if you look at India's Act East Policy, if you look at South Korea's New Southern Policy, if you look at Japan's own Free and Open Indo-Pacific Strategy, if you look at Australia's Foreign Policy White Paper, if you look at Taiwan's new Southbound Policy, these partners in the region are all seeking to increase political, security, and economic ties, particularly with the ASEAN states. And that's in our interest. If we can have these crosscutting relationships that form a very strong fabric devoted to a rules-based free and open order, that can only strengthen the prosperity of the region, strengthen the fabric of stability in the region, and that's something that we support.
>
> *(U.S. Department of State 2018)*

Given Taiwan's difficult position in the international system, its ability to play an active role in the IPS or the Quad – Taiwanese academics (mostly academics affiliated with the Institute for National Policy Research [INPR, 國策研究院]) were able to participate during a meeting of the Quad-Plus in Tokyo in 2018 – will always be contingent on member states' willingness to let it in and on Washington's leadership (more on this in Chapter 7).

While apprehensions about a possible Sino-U.S. "deal" involving Taiwan ebbed and flowed following the election of the "transactional" Donald Trump, the U.S. Department of Defense, led by Jim Mattis, remained steadfastly committed to the relationship with Taiwan. As one of the "adults" in the Trump administration, Mattis's consistent and vocal support for Taiwan provided welcomed reassurances. Speaking at the Shangri-La Dialogue in Singapore in June 2017, Mattis told an audience of defense experts, military and government officials:

> The Department of Defense remains steadfastly committed to working with Taiwan and with its democratic government to provide it the defense articles necessary, consistent with the obligations set out in the Taiwan Relations

106 The regional and global context

> Act, because we stand for the peaceful resolution of any issues in a manner acceptable to the people on both sides of the Taiwan Strait.
>
> *(DOD 2018a)*

Mattis's comments expectedly sparked anger among Chinese officials at the Dialogue. Senior PLA Colonel Zhao Xiaozhuo (趙小卓) lamented that the secretary of defense's comments would "encourage the independence-leaning movement in Taiwan, which will harm the peaceful development of the cross-strait relationship." Other Chinese delegates present, meanwhile, criticized Mattis's emphasis on the TRA and underscored Beijing's call for Washington to end arms sales to Taiwan, while pro-Beijing media reported on the matter with headlines that suggested that Mattis had somehow "outraged" the Chinese leadership (Chan 2017). Despite the criticism, the following year, Mattis repeated the message almost word-for-word, although he added a line about "unilateral efforts to alter the status quo," which clearly was aimed at recent bullying by China:

> The Department of Defense remains steadfastly committed to working with Taiwan to provide the defense articles and services necessary to maintain sufficient self-defense consistent with our obligation set out in our Taiwan Relations Act. We oppose all unilateral efforts to alter the status quo, and will continue to insist any resolution of differences accord with the will of the people on both sides of the Taiwan Strait.
>
> *(DOD 2018b)*

Congress, which has become more vocal on the need to provide assistance to Taiwan both due to Beijing's unilaterally altering the "status quo" in the Taiwan Strait and to balance against any possibility that President Trump could make a unilateral decision to abandon Taiwan as part of a "deal" with Beijing, has also scored a number of successes since 2016 with the passage of acts which could bring real benefits to Taiwan.

An important, yet often unnoticed, element to Congress's more proactive role in encouraging U.S. rapprochement with Taiwan is the fact that the bills in question have received bipartisan support. This is not only a reflection of the aforementioned changing attitudes in the U.S. toward China, but also marks a shift from past party behavior, in which Republicans generally were more supportive of Taiwan, and Democrats of China. Increasingly, as a result of the changing context and the realization that Beijing has been unilaterally altering the "status quo," both Republicans and Democrats are proving likelier to support closer engagement with Taiwan. And of course, the willingness of the president to sign those bills into law has also been an important factor.

Two bills in particular, the Taiwan Travel Act (H.R. 535, 台灣旅行法) and the National Defense Authorization Act (NDAA, 國防授權法) of 2018 and 2019, have resulted in conditions that are favorable to Taiwan. Passed unanimously by the House of Representatives on 9 January 2018, by the Senate on 28 February and signed into law by President Trump on 16 March the same year, the Taiwan Travel Act contains three provisions: (1) that officials at all levels of the U.S. government should be able to travel to Taiwan to meet their Taiwanese counterparts; (2) that senior Taiwanese officials should be allowed to enter the U.S. under "respectful conditions" and be able to meet U.S. officials; and (3) that the Taipei Economic and Cultural Representative Office (TECRO) and any other instrumentality established by Taiwan should be able to conduct business in the U.S.[1]

Welcomed by Taipei, the Taiwan Travel Act prompted accusations by Beijing that with this move Washington had contravened the "one China" policy, threatened the "status quo" and risked harming Sino-American ties. In reality, the bill acted more, as a reminder of what was already permissible under the "one China" policy than as a transformative agent of U.S. policy. Unofficial rules, as opposed to clear policy guidance, have resulted in the inability of senior U.S. and Taiwanese officials to visit their respective capitals. Those who expected that enactment of the Taiwan Travel Act would immediately result in reciprocal visits by senior officials from the two sides were in for a bit of disappointment, as they were when Washington failed to send anyone senior to the opening ceremony of the new AIT compound in Neihu in June 2018. While some had hoped that Trump's national security adviser, John Bolton, would attend the event, in the end the most senior U.S. official was Assistant Secretary of State for Educational and Cultural Affairs Marie Royce (more on this later).

In the end, it was clear that "permissions" and "reminders" notwithstanding, visits by senior officials would continue to depend on a cost-versus-benefit analysis by Taipei and Washington, with the knowledge that any sudden change in long-standing practices was bound to result in more punitive actions by Beijing against Taiwan. This, therefore, put a premium on a gradualist approach to closer engagement by senior officials; the symbolism of visits by top officials, gratifying though this might be, would have to wait. This explains in part why President Tsai, during her transit in the U.S., limited her visits to Houston and Los Angeles, and did not pressure Washington to be allowed to make additional stops in Washington and New York. Despite the Act, Washington remains jittery on the possibility of visits – or even the suggestion of such visits – to the capital by top Taiwanese officials, and will signal its displeasure to Taipei if such signals are made too publicly.

More significant to the reinforcement of U.S.-Taiwan ties is the NDAA for Fiscal Year 2018 and Fiscal Year 2019. Signed by President Trump on 12 December 2017, NDAA 2018 called for important steps – among them, strengthening the defense partnership between the U.S. States and Taiwan under the TRA and the "Six Assurances," and normalizing the transfer of defense articles and defense services to Taiwan. More specifically, it called on the U.S. to conduct regular transfers of defense articles and defense services necessary to enable Taiwan to maintain a sufficient self-defense capability, based solely on the needs of Taiwan; invite the military forces of Taiwan to participate in military exercises, such as the "Red Flag" exercises; carry out a program of exchanges of senior military officers and senior officials with Taiwan to improve military-to-military relations, as expressed in

108 The regional and global context

section 1284 of the NDAA 2017; support expanded exchanges focused on practical training for Taiwan personnel by and with U.S. military units, including exchanges among services; conduct bilateral naval exercises, to include pre-sail conferences, in the western Pacific Ocean with the Taiwan navy; and consider the advisability and feasibility of reestablishing port of call exchanges between the U.S. navy and the Taiwan navy.[2]

On the normalization of arms sales, NDAA 2018 stated that any requests from the Government of Taiwan for defense articles and defense services should receive a case-by-case review by the Secretary of Defense, in consultation with the Secretary of State, that is consistent with the standard processes and procedures in an effort to normalize the arms sales process with Taiwan. This was all parts of efforts to "de-bundle" or "de-package" arms sales to Taiwan so as to expedite the process of request and acquisition, and to reduce the political costs associated with Beijing's reaction to past multibillion-dollar arms packages (more on the subject of arms sales later).

As expected, Beijing bristled at the language in NDAA 2018. Already in August, China's ambassador to the U.S., Cui Tiankai (崔天凯), had expressed "grave concerns" over the Taiwan Travel Act and text in the Taiwan Security Act which eventually became part of NDAA 2018. Those measures, the letter said, represent "provocations against China's sovereignty, national unity and security interests," and "have crossed the 'red line' on the stability of the China–U.S. relationship" (Rogin 2017). One sentence in particular in NDAA 2018 – "consider the advisability and feasibility of reestablishing port of call exchanges between the U.S. navy and the Taiwan navy" – prompted strong reactions from the Chinese. Addressing hundreds of people assembled at a PRC embassy event in Washington in December, Li Kexin, the No. 2 at the embassy who, as we saw in Chapter 2 met the same month with members of the China Unification Promotion Party and New Party in New York City, warned that "the day that a U.S. Navy vessel arrives in Kaohsiung is the day that our People's Liberation Army unites Taiwan with military force" (Tsao 2017). Li's strong language was understandably part of Beijing's efforts to ensure that the U.S. would not commit to such visits by U.S. navy vessels. It should also be said that NDAA 2018 only recommended the U.S. government "consider the advisability and feasibility" of reciprocal port calls by U.S. and Taiwanese navy vessels; in no way did the Act encourage or call for such actions, which like the stipulations of the Taiwan Travel Act, will be acted upon based on careful consideration by Washington and Taipei. (The nature of a vessel involved in such visits would also play a role in the kind of response it is likely to prompt by Beijing: a visit by a U.S. navy vessel equipped with the Aegis combat system would cause more alarm in the Chinese capital than that by, say, a hospital ship.)

NDAA for Fiscal Year 2019, also known as the John S. McCain Act, was signed by President Trump on 13 August 2018. Described in the media as a "pro-Taiwan" act, NDAA picked up where its predecessor had left off by ramping up collaboration with Taiwan while adopting a stronger line on China. On U.S.-Taiwan ties, it recommended that the U.S. should seek to – and here it is wise to quote the language verbatim:

improve the efficiency, effectiveness, readiness, and resilience of Taiwan's self-defense capability in the following areas:

(1) Personnel management and force development, particularly reserve forces.
(2) Recruitment, training, and military programs.
(3) Command, control, communications and intelligence.
(4) Technology research and development.
(5) Defense article procurement and logistics.
(6) Strategic planning and resource management.

[...]

(1) Not later than 1 year after the date of the enactment of this Act, the Secretary of Defense, in consultation with the Secretary of State, shall submit to the appropriate congressional committees a report containing each of the following:

(A) A summary of the assessment conducted pursuant to subsection (a).
(B) A list of any recommendations resulting from such assessment.
(C) A plan for the United States, including by using appropriate security cooperation authorities, to –

(i) facilitate any relevant recommendations from such list;
(ii) expand senior military-to-military engagement and joint training by the United States Armed Forces with the military of Taiwan; and
(iii) support United States foreign military sales and other equipment transfers to Taiwan, particularly for developing asymmetric warfare capabilities.

[...]

(1) the Taiwan Relations Act (22 U.S.C. 3301 et seq.) and the "Six Assurances" are both cornerstones of United States relations with Taiwan;
(2) the United States should strengthen defense and security cooperation with Taiwan to support the development of capable, ready, and modern defense forces necessary for Taiwan to maintain a sufficient self-defense capability;

110 The regional and global context

(3) the United States should strongly support the acquisition by Taiwan of defensive weapons through foreign military sales, direct commercial sales, and industrial cooperation, with a particular emphasis on asymmetric warfare and undersea warfare capabilities, consistent with the Taiwan Relations Act;

(4) the United States should improve the predictability of arms sales to Taiwan by ensuring timely review of and response to requests of Taiwan for defense articles and defense services;

(5) the Secretary of Defense should promote Department of Defense policies concerning exchanges that enhance the security of Taiwan, including –

    (A) opportunities for practical training and military exercises with Taiwan; and

    (B) exchanges between senior defense officials and general officers of the United States and Taiwan consistent with the Taiwan Travel Act (Public Law 115–135);

(6) the United States and Taiwan should expand cooperation in humanitarian assistance and disaster relief; and

(7) the Secretary of Defense should consider supporting the visit of a United States hospital ship to Taiwan as part of the annual "Pacific Partnership" mission in order to improve disaster response planning and preparedness as well as to strengthen cooperation between the United States and Taiwan.[3]

Note, in the last point, the reference to a U.S. "hospital ship" rather than the vague "U.S. navy" contained in the previous year's NDAA. (In October 2018, the 3,250-ton scientific research ship *Thomas G. Thompson* T-AGOR-23 made a port call at Kaohsiung.)

On China, which it now classified as a "strategic competitor that seeks to shape the world toward their authoritarian model through destabilizing activities that threaten the security of the United States and its allies," NDAA 2019 made the following recommendations, which again are worth quoting in their original language. The NDAA:

- Prohibits any U.S. government agency from using risky technology produced by Huawei [華為技術有限公司] or ZTE [中興通訊], two companies linked to the Chinese Communist Party's intelligence apparatus. The NDAA also prohibits any entity doing business with the US Government from using Huawei or ZTE technology. The NDAA also prohibits the use in security related functions of equipment produced by several other Chinese companies with ties to the Chinese government (This Proposal enjoys wide bipartisan support and is in concert with recent unanimous regulatory actions by the Federal Communications Commission.)

U.S.–Taiwan rapprochement 111

- Directs a whole-of-government strategy on China to address the Chinese Communist Party's use of political influence, economic tools, cyber activities, global infrastructure and development projects, and military activities against the United States and allies and partners.
- Requires the Secretary of Defense to submit a 5-year plan for an "Indo-Pacific Stability Initiative" to bolsters DOD's efforts to plan for and provide the necessary forces and military infrastructure, and logistics capabilities in the Indo-Pacific region.
- Extends authority for the Maritime Security Initiative (MSI) for an additional 5 years, re-designates the Southeast Asia MSI as the Indo-Pacific MSI, includes Bangladesh and Sri Lanka as recipient countries of assistance and training, and adds India as a covered country with the aim to increase maritime security and maritime domain awareness in the South China Sea and Indian Ocean.
- Requires a strategy with specific benchmarks toward enhancing India's status as major defense partner and defense and security cooperation with India.
- Prohibits China's participation at the Rim of Pacific (RIMPAC) naval exercises unless the Secretary provides a national security waiver or certification requirements to do so.
- Requires a public report on the military and coercive activities of China in the South China Sea and encourages the Secretary of Defense to require the public release of information illustrating Chinese activities of concern.
- Modifies the annual report on Chinese military and security developments to include malign influence activities, including efforts to influence media, cultural institutions, business, and academic and policy communities in the United States, and the use of nonmilitary tools, including predatory lending practices, to its global security and military objectives.
- Limits DOD funds for Chinese language programs at universities that host a Confucius Institute.

The tone had clearly changed and reflected developing attitudes in Washington. It remains to be seen whether any or all of the recommendations made in NDAA 2019 will be acted upon. But the signaling of intentions was there. And it was loud and clear.

Then in September 2018, on the heels of Taiwan's loss of El Salvador to China, a new bipartisan bill, known as the Taiwan Allies International Protection and Enhancement Initiative Act (or Taipei Act) was introduced. Among other things, the bill, which was passed in a U.S. Senate vote in September 2019 in the wake of the loss of the Solomon Islands and Kiribati,[4] requires "a U.S. strategy to engage with governments around the world to support Taiwan's diplomatic recognition or strengthen unofficial ties with Taiwan." It also authorizes the U.S. State Department to downgrade U.S. relations "with any government that takes adverse action regarding Taiwan, including suspending or altering foreign assistance, such as military financing" (Chiang 2018). In a press release, Republican Senator Cory Gardner, Chairman of Senate Foreign Relations Subcommittee on Asia and the Pacific and

112 The regional and global context

one of the co-initiators of the bill, said that "this bipartisan legislation demands a whole-of-government approach to stand up to China's bullying tactics against Taiwan, and will send a strong message to those nations considering siding with China over Taiwan that there will be consequences for such actions."[5] As we saw earlier, soon after El Salvador switched diplomatic relations to Beijing, Washington recalled its top officials in the Dominican Republic, El Salvador, and Panama "for consultations related to recent decisions to no longer recognize Taiwan." The State Department said its diplomats would meet with U.S. government leaders "to discuss ways in which the United States can support strong, independent, democratic institutions and economies throughout Central America and the Caribbean" (Beech 2018). Based on the language and early responses, it was becoming clear that Washington saw continued official diplomatic relations between Taiwan and countries to its south as conducive to "strong, independent, democratic institutions and economies" in the region. In other words, Taiwan's interests were now aligned with those of the U.S. in Central America and the Caribbean, where in recent years China has been making substantial investments.

After years of delays, the new AIT compound in Neihu was officially dedicated during a ceremony on 12 June 2018. Surrounded as we saw earlier by speculation as to which senior official, if any, Washington would send to the event, and overshadowed by the summit in Singapore between President Trump and Kim Jong Un of North Korea, the event was a strong reaffirmation of longstanding ties between the two countries. Equal to a medium-size embassy with approximately 450 staff members, the quarter-of-a-billion-U.S.-dollar building was as clear a sign as any that the U.S. was here to stay, and that it was willing to make substantial investments to mark its presence in the country. (The former AIT building on Xinyi Road was in a state of disrepair and certainly did not reflect the importance of the U.S. diplomatic presence in Taiwan.)

During the ceremony, Assistant Secretary of State for Educational and Cultural Affairs Marie Royce told the audience that the new building "represents much more than steel and glass and concrete. The New Office Complex is a symbol of the strength and vibrancy of the U.S.-Taiwan partnership in the 21st century." Turning to the shared values of freedom and democracy, she continued:

> Over the past decades, Taiwan has formed its own deep convictions about the importance of democracy. With courage against long odds and great adversity, the people of Taiwan have constructed gleaming cities and developed an advanced economy. They have cultivated a robust civil society and built a vibrant multiparty democracy. We may be separated by a great ocean, but our shared convictions, values, and trust form a strong foundation for cooperation across a range of issues.
>
> *(AIT 2018)*

Speculation on whether U.S. marines would be deployed to the new AIT compound to ensure personnel security, as they are at U.S. embassies worldwide, came to end in September 2018 after reports stated that then-Secretary of Defense Jim Mattis had turned down the request from the Department of State. Instead, as with other de facto embassies and unofficial U.S. diplomatic outposts in the Middle East and Africa, private contractors were to provide security at the compound. Citing an unnamed defense official, CNN reported that the decision not to deploy Marines was made "due to resource constraint issues" and because the Department of State "had not told the Pentagon in advance that the completion of the new facility would require a Marine Security Guard detachment." The official denied the decision was made so as to avoid angering the communist government in Beijing (Browne 2018).

Whatever the actual reason for the decision, this turn of event dashed hopes among Taiwan's supporters that a marine contingent, which would have brought the AIT compound closer to an actual embassy, would materialize. At the symbolic level, this may have been disappointing for Taiwan; but in the end, what mattered was the evidence, in the form of the US$250 million building and its hardworking, dedicated personnel, that the U.S. was committed to continued and deepened engagement with Taiwan.

Another symbolic victory for Taiwan was President Tsai's transit in the U.S. during her state visits to Paraguay and Belize in August 2018. As we saw earlier, the Tsai administration did not insist on additional layovers in Washington, D.C., and New York, which could have added complexity to the visit by giving Beijing more reasons to retaliate against Taiwan. "Tsai's prudence and respect for the Trump administration," observed Liu Shih-chung (劉世忠) (2018), "have won a positive response from Washington for better transit treatment. . . . Tsai's team has worked closely with its American counterpart to ensure a surprise-free but more respectful and dignified transit for Taiwan's leader."

Building on those solid foundations, President Tsai made good use of her stops in Los Angeles and Houston, in what media described as the most high-profile stopover by a Taiwanese president in 15 years. There were a few precedents during the visit, including the U.S. "allowing" Tsai to give a public talk – which touched on politics – in Los Angeles, the release of her delegation's full schedule ahead of time, and permitting the Taiwanese journalists who accompanied her during the visit to publish articles while they were in the U.S. Tsai also held meetings with Senator Cory Gardner, as well as members of Congress Ed Royce, Brad Sherman, and Judy Chu (Lee 2018). Sherman, a Democrat, used the occasion to state that the U.S. should formally invite President Tsai to visit Washington.

The warm treatment reserved for the visiting Taiwanese president inevitably led to accusations by Beijing and questions in the media as to whether the U.S. had changed its "one China" policy, which U.S. officials denied it had. This, like many occasions before, was yet another example of Beijing – and inadvertently some media – using amnesia to add pressure on Taiwan and its allies in the international community. By raising a storm every single time Taiwanese engaged with another country, Beijing was giving the impression that states, as well as organizations and even individuals, were crossing red lines. Exchanges that, in the past, had taken

114 The regional and global context

place without Beijing making too much noise were now unacceptable; things that had been done a few years ago were now violations of "one China" which risked harming bilateral ties between China and the offending country. According to Beijing, the U.S. was breaking protocol by allowing a Taiwanese president to transit on its soil, something that has been done on a number of occasions over the years by Lee Teng-hui, Chen Shui-bian, and Ma Ying-jeou before Tsai (Beijing bit its lip when Ma did such transits, including one in New York City in 2013, ostensibly due to the warmer ties between Taipei and Beijing at the time. In 2006, Chen was asked to make a transit in Alaska rather than in a continental American city due to Chinese pressure. It was suggested at the time that the rebuke was Washington's response to the Chen administration's decision to abolish the National Reunification Council. Rather than limit his layover to a brief refueling stop, Chen cancelled the U.S. transit altogether (Hille and Dinmore 2006). In 2003, he too had been able to make a stopover in New York to receive a human rights award). Far too often, foreign media would parrot Beijing's strident accusations without checking the historical facts. By doing so, they helped amplify Beijing's pressure on Taiwan and other countries and created a sense of crisis that simply was not warranted (they would also do this with PLA live-fire exercises and U.S. navy transits in the Taiwan Strait).

Washington was in no way altering its "one China" policy by allowing President Tsai to transit in the U.S., meeting members of Congress, or even visiting the U.S. National Aeronautics and Space Administration's Johnson Space Center in Houston, which her public relations team certainly played up to great symbolic effect. Nor was the Taiwan Travel Act necessary for those to occur, although some presented the successful and high-profile visit as a "litmus test" for the Act. In fact, as a U.S. official told me after Tsai had returned to Taiwan, other than the aforementioned lifting of restrictions on the president's schedule and Taiwanese journalists' ability to file stories while in the U.S., no new precedent was made during the visit. The crisis, such as it was, resulted from Beijing's saber rattling – for example, the pressure which it brought to bear on the 85°C (85度C) coffee chain after Tsai made an impromptu stop at one of its chain stores in Los Angeles – and media looking for drama and sometimes failing to properly check the history.

Defense cooperation

No aspect of the U.S.-Taiwan bilateral relationship has captured more attention than U.S. arms sales to Taiwan, which under the Taiwan Relations Act (TRA) are part of a policy whereby Washington assists Taiwan in acquiring the military articles it needs to defend itself against aggression from China. Over the years, arms sales have become highly politicized, not only because of Beijing's reaction to them, but also because the size, composition, and frequency of the arms packages have been regarded as a barometer of U.S. political support for the democratic island-nation. Thus, long periods during which no arms sales occurred, as was the case during the

Bush Jr. and Obama administrations, were seen as indicators of sagging U.S. support for Taiwan. In his first year in office in 2009, Obama did not notify Congress of any major foreign military sale (FMS) to Taiwan; there also was a four-year gap between notifications in 2011 and 2015.

Anxieties over U.S. support for Taiwan surrounding Trump's transactional style and early flip-flopping on his relationship with China were compounded for several months after he came into office by the absence of a new arms sale notification. When one was finally made in late June 2017, Taipei sighed in relief, even though the US$1.363 billion release contained mostly leftover items that the Obama administration had failed to release (USTBC 2017).[6]

Part of the problem was the complex and time-consuming process by which Taiwan secured the release, through notification to Congress, of arms packages from the U.S. Although, from a purely symbolic perspective, the announcement of a, say, US$6.4 billion arms sale to Taiwan sent a clear — and headline-grabbing — signal of continued U.S. support for Taiwan, by their very nature arms packages were not time effective. In fact, the entire process created delays in the delivery of arms that were necessary for Taiwan's self-defense capabilities.

In recent years, efforts have been made to address this lacuna in the arms procurement process and to normalize arms sales. Above all, this has meant "de-bundling" or "de-packaging" arms sales — making them smaller, more frequent, and thereby ending what Shirley Kan, a longtime analyst of U.S. arms sales to Taiwan, has described as a "distorted practice" in approval and delivery caused by lumping everything into one large package. Under this, Taiwan would make requests based on current or future needs, and the request would be assessed — and notified to Congress — as a single program rather than a package of disparate programs. One of the most vocal proponents of a normalized arms sales process was Randall G. Schriver, who until December 2019, was U.S. assistant secretary of defense for Asian and Pacific affairs in the Trump administration.

One such arms release was announced in September 2018, with the approval of an estimated US$330 million Foreign Military Sales Order (FMSO) II for "stock replenishment supply of standard spare parts, and repair/replace of spare parts in support of the F-16, C-130, F-5, Indigenous Defense Fighter (IDF), all other aircraft systems and subsystems, and other related elements of logistics and program support" (DSCA 2018). This was followed by the announcement in July 2019 that the State Department had approved a US$2 billion sale of 108 M1A2T Abrams tanks to Taiwan (Judson 2019), and the following month, that of a US$8 billion sale of F-16 Viper combat aircraft (Gould and Yeo 2019).

Commenting on the announcement in September 2018, the U.S.-Taiwan Business Council (USTBC, 美台商業協會) wrote that it was "encouraged by this Congressional notification, which appears to move away from the previous 'bundling' method for Taiwan arms sales." It continued:

> Notifying each sale when it is ready is a positive development, and indicates more potential activity at the end of this year and into early 2019. It is the

116 The regional and global context

approach the Council has advocated for since the original bundling began in 2008.

(USTBC 2018)

Despite the promising sign of "de-bundling" which the September announcement suggested, observers still saw other issues with the arms sales process. Chief among them, as the USTBC pointed out, is the fact that since 2011, "U.S. arms sales have focused almost exclusively on sustainment and maintenance of Taiwan's existing military capabilities. There has seemingly been no willingness by the U.S. to assess new capabilities for Taiwan." According to the Council, requests for new systems have apparently been rejected or deterred prior to the initial stages of evaluation. In speeches and other statements, it continued, the State Department has referred to the need for "intelligent" arms sales to Taiwan,

> which leave unanswered questions both about the criteria for arms sales and the existing process. Is Taiwan free to make any request, or only those deemed 'intelligent?' Who makes the determination of what is 'intelligent,' and at what stage in the review process does this determination take place?

In the same press release, Rupert Hammond-Chambers, president of the USTBC, observed that it is the Trump administration's "stated policy" that Taiwan be able to submit a Letter of Request (LoR) for Pricing and Availability "for any platform or system Taiwan feels they need to mount a credible defense," and that Taiwan is "entitled to receive a full assessment and timely response to their request by the full interagency review process."

"This gets at the heart of normalizing the arms sales process," he said.

> Will Taiwan be able to ask for all that it feels it needs, to then have that LoR accepted – not deterred if deemed 'unintelligent' – and assessed on its merits? If the U.S. deems that a request is not doable at the moment, will they offer an alternative solution? It is not for any one department to determine what is 'intelligent,' but for the full interagency review process to be employed to ensure that Taiwan can mount a credible and full defense as required by U.S. law under the Taiwan Relations Act.

Given the widening capabilities gap in the Taiwan Strait (in part due to U.S. restrictions on what it sells to Taiwan and Beijing's ability to procure highly advanced systems from the Russian Federation), Taiwan's inability to procure new advanced platforms could be problematic. That being said, many defense analysts have argued that rather than spend large sums of money on new platforms from the U.S., Taiwan would get more "bang for the buck" focusing on indigenous programs and shifting from a large-platform-type defense posture to one that prioritizes dispersibility and survivability – in other words, small, rapid, radar-evasive, and relatively low-cost land-, air-, and sea-based "asymmetrical" platforms equipped with counter-landing capabilities, all with the aim of reinforcing Taiwan's "porcupine" strategy. Given, as we saw, the political weight attached of continued U.S. arms sales to Taiwan, the key for Taiwan is to find the right balance between foreign and domestic procurement and development. It should also be noted that Taiwan continues to rely on U.S. assistance for certain technologies that it cannot develop domestically, such as fire control systems for its Indigenous Defense Submarine or development/acquisition of a 4.5- or 5th generation combat aircraft (e.g., F-35) as its fleet faces aging problems. In April 2018 the Trump administration finally gave the green light for the issuing of a marketing license for U.S. defense firms seeking involvement in Taiwan's submarine program. The marketing license allows a determined U.S. firm to demonstrate the specifications of its submarine combat system to Taiwan, though an export license will be necessary for a sale to take place (MND 2018).

With the Tsai administration determined to bolster Taiwan's indigenous defense capabilities, new incentives have also been created for the Taiwanese defense sector to collaborate with foreign firms, including but not limited to U.S. companies, in developing and manufacturing weapons of tomorrow. Here again, Taiwan's ability to jointly develop and mass-produce defense articles with foreign firms will be contingent on the willingness of the U.S. government to work with Taiwan and to face pressure from Beijing, and in the government in Taipei persuading Taiwanese firms to carry out the necessary reforms to allow such collaboration.

Although this is a long way off, some defense analysts in Washington and Taipei have also called for the integration of Taiwan into regional intelligence-gathering architecture, such as the U.S.-South Korean-Japanese submarine tracking effort in the Asia Pacific. Here again, political will from all the players involved will be necessary. Moreover, for intelligence-sharing of this nature to be possible, Taipei will need to reassure its security partners that the highly classified information it receives will be secure and not be accessed by the Chinese. Integrity of systems, as well as longstanding laxness in classification and security clearances in Taiwan, will need to be taken much more seriously. Given Taiwan's geographical position and linguistic capabilities, it is ideally placed to provide regional allies with signals, electronic and human intelligence on the CCP and the PLA. It already hosts one of the most powerful early-warning long-range radar systems in the region at Leshan (樂山) in Hsinchu County. It only makes sense that Taiwan would share the information it collects using such systems with the U.S. and other regional allies, and in return, it should be able to obtain intelligence collected by those countries to improve its own situational awareness and early-warning responses. But to fully integrate into that regional architecture, Taiwan will need to earn the trust of the countries involved, chief among them the U.S. It has already taken some steps toward reassuring Washington; much more needs to be done, and it is hoped that the more high-level and more frequent contact between members of the armed forces from both sides, which is encouraged under the NDAA and Taiwan Travel Act, will further strengthen the bonds of trust between the two sides and facilitate solutions on how Taiwan can improve its ability to protect highly sensitive data.

118 The regional and global context

It is already very helpful that the U.S. Department of Defense understands the benefits of engagement with Taiwan and regards it as a strategic asset. It is high time that the Office of the U.S. Trade Representative (USTR, 美國貿易代表署) did so as well. Among other things, USTR should move beyond the Trade and Investment Framework Agreement (TIFA, 美台貿易暨投資架構協定) and begin thinking about a full free-trade agreement with Taiwan. Taipei could do a few things on its own to make it easier for advocates of a FTA with Taiwan in the U.S. by, among other things, addressing the problem, as USTR puts it, of "longstanding and unwarranted barriers to U.S. beef and pork, which is necessary for any deepening of our trade relationship," as well as strengthening IP protection, legislation, and enforcement. On the beef and pork dispute, the U.S. government could also do more to de-link those issues from the larger strategic context, in which closer U.S.-Taiwan engagement would be beneficial to both. The same holds for Taiwan, where unfortunately the beef and pork issue has been highjacked by domestic party politics, which is short-sighted and self-defeating given that the issue has been an impediment to greater engagement at the strategic level. The USTR recognizing, as the Pentagon has, that Taiwan is a strategic asset would be a considerable step in the right direction and could convince U.S. trade officials of the inadvisability of "linkage" on what is, at its core, a relatively minor issue in bilateral trade.[7]

In all, U.S.-Taiwan bilateral ties have made important progress in recent years, thanks to a careful approach to policy making by the Tsai administration and an increasingly institutionalized shift across the U.S. in reaction to threat perceptions of China. Rapprochement has been incremental rather than sudden, and much of it has consisted of quiet exchanges, which rarely make headlines. This is intelligent and by design, although perhaps unsatisfactory to Taiwanese and their supporters who would like to see more clear and overt top-level engagement between the two sides as a counter to Beijing. Given the high likelihood that reckless engagement with the U.S. would result in highly punitive countermeasures by Beijing against Taiwan, it remains essential that both Taipei and Washington weigh the actual benefits of new engagement against the costs imposed by China. This, as this chapter has argued, puts a premium on achieving concrete results rather than on highly symbolic, but ultimately low-impact, developments in the relationship, such as, for example, visits by top government officials.

In the next two chapters, we turn to the closer ties that have also developed between Taiwan and its neighbors amid efforts by Beijing to limit Taiwan's international space.

Notes

1 H.R.535 – Taiwan Travel Act, www.congress.gov/bill/115th-congress/house-bill/535/text

2 H.R.2810 – National Defense Authorization Act for Fiscal Year 2018, www.congress.gov/bill/115th-congress/house-bill/2810/text

3 John S. McCain National Defense Authorization Act for Fiscal Year 2019 Conference Report to Accompany H.R. 5515, https://docs.house.gov/billsthisweek/20180723/CRPT-115hrpt874.pdf

U.S.–Taiwan rapprochement **119**

4 Senate Foreign Relations Committee Passes the TAIPEI Act, September 25, 2019, www.gardner.senate.gov/newsroom/press-releases/senate-foreign-relations-committee-passes-the-taipei-act
5 Gardner, Markey, Rubio, Menendez Introduce Legislation to Defend Taiwan, September 5, 2018, www.gardner.senate.gov/newsroom/press-releases/gardner-markey-rubio-menendez-introduce-legislation-to-defend-taiwan
6 SM-2 Block IIIA All-Up Rounds, associated equipment and technical support; MK 54 Lightweight Torpedo Conversion Kits, spare parts and other support and assistance; MK 48 Mod 6AT Heavyweight Torpedoes, other support, spare parts, training, and assistance; Hardware, software, and other upgrades to the AN/SLQ-32(V)3 Electronic Warfare Systems supporting Taiwan's Keelung-class destroyers; AGM-154C JSOW Air-to-Ground Missiles, spare/repair parts and other support and assistance; AGM-88B HARMs and Training HARMs, spare/repair parts, testing, and other support and assistance; SRP (Surveillance Radar Program) Operations and Maintenance follow-on sustainment.
7 美豬牛輸出台灣議題 美貿易報告：嚴正關切: CNA, January 3, 2018, www.cna.com.tw/news/firstnews/201803010016.aspx

References

Akimoto, Satohiro (2018) "How Japan Can Save the Indo-Pacific Strategy," *Japan Times*, 24 July. www.japantimes.co.jp/opinion/2018/07/24/commentary/japan-commentary/japan-can-save-indo-pacific-strategy/#.W6yH3GVCJBw.
American Institute in Taiwan (AIT) (2015) "Remarks by AIT Director Christopher J. Marut at the 'Global Cooperation Training Framework' MOU Signing Ceremony," 1 June. www.ait.org.tw/remarks-ait-director-christopher-j-marut-global-cooperation-training-framework-mou-signing-ceremony/.
American Institute in Taiwan (AIT) (2018) "Remarks by Assistant Secretary Marie Royce at the Dedication Ceremony of AIT's New Office Complex," 12 June. www.ait.org.tw/remarks-by-assistant-secretary-of-state-for-educational-and-cultural-affairs-marie-royce-at-dedication-ceremony/.
Apple Daily (2018) "AIT主席透露美中關係改變原因　學者：美重新考慮一中政策," 25 September. https://tw.news.appledaily.com/sf/realtime/20180925/1435789.
Beech, Eric (2018) "U.S. Recalls Diplomats in El Salvador, Panama, Dominican Republic Over Taiwan," *Reuters*, 8 September. www.reuters.com/article/us-usa-china-taiwan/u-s-recalls-diplomats-in-el-salvador-panama-dominican-republic-over-taiwan-idUSKCN1LO00N.
Bohan, Caren and David Brunnstrom (2016) "Trump Says U.S. Not Necessarily Bound by 'One China' Policy," *Reuters*, 11 December. www.reuters.com/article/us-usa-trump-china-idUSKBN1400TY.
Browne, Ryan (2018) "Pentagon Turns Down Request to Send US Marines to Taiwan," *CNN*, 13 September. https://edition.cnn.com/2018/09/13/politics/taiwan-pentagon-marines-request/index.html.
Chan, Minnie (2017) "Mattis Outrages Beijing with Explicit Commitment to Defend Taiwan," *South China Morning Post*, 3 June. www.scmp.com/news/china/diplomacy-defence/article/2096762/james-mattis-outrages-chinas-military-delegation-taiwan.
Chiang, Jin-ye (2018) "美參議員提出台北法案 助台灣維繫邦交," *Central News Agency (Taiwan)*, 6 September. www.cna.com.tw/news/firstnews/201809060015.aspx.
Cole, J. Michael (2016a) "The Tsai-Trump Call: The Dynamics in Taiwan," *The Diplomat*, 9 December. https://thediplomat.com/2016/12/the-tsai-trump-call-the-dynamics-in-taiwan/.

Cole, J. Michael (2016b) "Taiwan, Not the US, Will Likely Pay the Price for the Trump-Tsai Call," *Lowy Interpreter*, 7 December. www.lowyinstitute.org/the-interpreter/taiwan-not-us-will-likely-pay-price-trump-tsai-call.

Defense Security Cooperation Agency (DSCA) (2018) Taipei Economic and Cultural Representative Office in the United States (TECRO) – Foreign Military Sales Order (FMSO) II Case, 18 September. www.dsca.mil/major-arms-sales/taipei-economic-and-cultural-representative-office-united-states-tecro-foreign.

Faries, Bill and Mira Rojanasakul (2018) "At Trump's State Department, Eight of Ten Top Jobs Are Empty," *Bloomberg*, 2 February. www.bloomberg.com/graphics/2018-state-department-vacancies/.

Feast, Lincoln (2017) "Timeline: Trump Questions then Honors 'One China' Policy," *Reuters*, 10 February. www.reuters.com/article/us-usa-trump-china-xi-timeline/timeline-trump-questions-then-honors-one-china-policy-idUSKBN15P0OQ.

Gould, Joe and Mike Yeo (2019) "Trump OKs F-16 Sale to Taiwan Amid China Tensions," *Defense News*, 16 August. www.defensenews.com/congress/2019/08/16/trump-oks-f-16-sale-to-taiwan-amid-china-tensions/.

Hille, Kathrin and Guy Dinmore (2006) "Taiwan's Chen Cancels US Stop After Perceived Snub," *Financial Times*, 4 May. www.ft.com/content/35d220dc-da49-11da-b7de-0000779e2340.

Judson, Jen (2019) "US State Dept. OKs Possible $2 Billion Abrams Tank Sale to Taiwan," *Defense News*, 8 July. www.defensenews.com/land/2019/07/08/state-okays-possible-2-billion-abrams-tank-sale-to-taiwan/.

Lee, Yihua (2018) "Warming US-Taiwan Ties on Display as President Tsai Visits LA," *Voice of America*, 14 August. www.voanews.com/a/warming-us-taiwan-ties-on-display-as-president-tsai-ing-wen-visits-la/4528549.html.

Liu, Shih-chung (2018) "Tsai's Overseas Visit and Transit a Counterbalance to Beijing's International Saber-Rattling," *Prospect Foundation Newsletter*, 12 September. www.pf.org.tw/article-pfch-2049-6349.

Ministry of National Defense (MND) (2018), 2 October. www.mnd.gov.tw/Publish.aspx?p=75211.

Nakamura, David (2017) "At Mar-a-Lago, Trump Welcomes China's Xi in First Summit," *Washington Post*, 7 April. www.washingtonpost.com/politics/at-mar-a-lago-trump-to-welcome-chinas-xi-for-high-stakes-inaugural-summit/2017/04/06/0235cdd0-1ac2-11e7-bcc2-7d1a0973e7b2_story.html?utm_term=.20032491a839.

Phillips, Tom (2018) "'Maybe We'll Give That a Shot': Donald Trump Praises Xi Jinping's Power Grab," *The Guardian*, 4 March 4. www.theguardian.com/us-news/2018/mar/04/donald-trump-praises-xi-jinping-power-grab-give-that-a-shot-china.

Rogin, Josh (2017) "China Threatens U.S. Congress for Crossing Its 'Red Line' on Taiwan," *Washington Post*, 12 October. www.washingtonpost.com/news/josh-rogin/wp/2017/10/12/china-threatens-u-s-congress-for-crossing-its-red-line-on-taiwan/?utm_term=.80b51bc206f4.

Tsao, Nadia (2017) "中國駐美公使嗆聲：美艦抵高雄之日 武統台灣之時," *Liberty Times*, 9 December. http://news.ltn.com.tw/news/politics/breakingnews/2278114.

U.S. Department of Defense (DOD 2018a) "Remarks by Secretary Mattis at Shangri-La Dialogue," 3 June. https://dod.defense.gov/News/Transcripts/Transcript-View/Article/1201780/remarks-by-secretary-mattis-at-shangri-la-dialogue/.

U.S. Department of Defense (DODb) (2018b) "Remarks by Secretary Mattis at Plenary Session of the 2018 Shangri-La Dialogue," 2 June. https://dod.defense.gov/News/Transcripts/Transcript-View/Article/1538599/remarks-by-secretary-mattis-at-plenary-session-of-the-2018-shangri-la-dialogue/.

U.S. Department of State (2018) "Briefing on the Indo-Pacific Strategy," 2 April. www.state. gov/r/pa/prs/ps/2018/04/280134.htm.

U.S. Taiwan Business Council (USTBC) (2017) "The Trump Administration Announces U.S. Arms Sales to Taiwan," 29 June. www.us-taiwan.org/pressrelease/2017june29cong ressionalnotificationsarmssalestotaiwan.pdf.

U.S. Taiwan Business Council (USTBC) (2018) "Comments on the September 24, 2018 U.S. Arms Sale to Taiwan," 25 September. www.us-taiwan.org/pressrelease/2018september25 congressionalnotificationsarmssalestotaiwan.pdf.

Yeh, Joseph (2019) "Taiwan Serves as Example for Religious Free Society: U.S. Official," *Focus Taiwan*, 11 March. http://focustaiwan.tw/news/aipl/201903110012.aspx.

6

THE FUTURE OF THE JAPAN-TAIWAN PARTNERSHIP

Besides the U.S., no country is as important for Taiwan's national security than Japan. This is due not only to the geographical proximity of the two countries, but also a result of history and the impact that half-a-century of Japanese rule over Taiwan (1895–1945) had on people from both sides. For Taiwanese of an older generation, such as my spouse's grandparents, Japanese was, or for those who are still alive today, is their mother tongue. The Japanese presence in Taiwan was formative in part because Japan, at the time it ruled over Taiwan, was in the process of modernizing itself based largely on Western models and, seeing itself as an imperial power in the making, wanted to turn Taiwan into a model colony. Unlike the Korean experience under the Japanese, which, like Manchuria, was largely repressive and for extractive purposes, controls over Taiwan, though they did exist, were certainly not as severe – with the exception of Japan's pacification of Aborigines.

The selective history, and in some cases amnesia, that characterizes remembrances of Japanese rule in Taiwan is also due to what came next. Soon after Japan's defeat in World War II, Nationalist (KMT) forces crossed the Taiwan Strait and imposed themselves on a population that was told it was to be "liberated" and reunified with a supposed Motherland. Rather than liberate the Taiwanese, a riffraff of shell-shocked Nationalist soldiers and officials imposed a much harsher rule on the Taiwanese people, starting with the 228 Massacre of 1947 and followed by decades of Martial Law rule known as the White Terror. Thus, the contrast between Japanese rule and what followed it contributed to a somewhat revisionist, if not beautified, view of the period that preceded the Nationalists' arrival in Taiwan, a perception that remains to this day.

That special bond is something that is not well understood by foreign academics who have spent long periods of time in China or Korea. Many of them have searched, in vain, for the kind of hostility and large protests that have been seen in those two countries over the issue of comfort women, visits to the Yasukuni

Shrine by Japanese leaders, or the territorial dispute over the Senkaku/Diaoyutai islets in the East China Sea. That special bond between the two peoples is also why, when natural catastrophes like major earthquakes, typhoons or tsunamis strike Japan or Taiwan, the two countries have always shown tremendous generosity and selflessness. Japanese visiting Taiwan never miss an occasion to thank the Taiwanese for their very generous donations after the 2011 Tōhoku earthquake and tsunami (2011年日本東北地方太平洋近海地震), which killed upwards of 16,000 people and caused an estimated US$360 billion in damage. Perhaps this is also animated by a sense of guilt, after the Japanese government failed to properly acknowledge Taiwan's contributions at the first commemorative ceremony of the disaster.

Of course the U.S. occupation of Japan, the imposition of a pacifist Constitution on the country and Japan's role since then as a non-belligerent major economy has also facilitated good relations with Taiwan, whose people no longer need fear an overbearing neighbor. People-to-people ties began under colonial rule when thousands of Taiwanese went to Japan to receive an advanced education, and as many more Japanese went to Taiwan to govern, have continued since, this time through business and tourism. Japan has left its mark on Taiwan's culture, fashion, food, language, music, literature, architecture, urban layout, railway system, medicine, and values, a legacy that, unlike Korea, has on the whole been embraced by the Taiwanese. Efforts by the Nationalist government during the Martial Law era to "re-Sinicize" the Taiwanese – and to ban the teaching of the Japanese language – only had modest results, though it can be argued that the ban did succeed in creating an entire generation of Taiwanese who did not speak Japanese well or at all, something which has repercussions today.

Despite the warm people-to-people relations that have existed since the end of the Second World War and survived Japan's recognition of the PRC in September 1972, for ordinary Japanese, Taiwan is not a key priority. They think of it with fondness, and some may take some pride in the fact that Japan played a role, for the most part positive, in its early development (and inadvertently to an early national consciousness as a form of resistance to rule by a foreign power). For the great majority of them, the Japanese public does not consciously link Taiwan's continued existence as a sovereign state with their own sense of security.

Like the U.S., Japanese attitudes toward China have shifted in recent years, though in a less overt fashion. This is largely due to the fact that, unlike the U.S., Japan is in China's immediate neighborhood and will be more directly affected by developments in the region. History also brings a complex baggage to the Sino-Japanese relationship, which the CCP has often used to its advantage and to fuel nationalist sentiment whenever public displays of anger are deemed necessary to make a point. On some occasions, as over the Senkaku/Diaoyutai dispute, protests initiated by the Chinese government got out of hand, resulting in injuries, damage and contributing to a reassessment by some Japanese firms as to the wisdom of continuing to have a presence in China.

At best, therefore, Japan and China are "frenemies" – overtly friendly toward each other in some cycles, but competitors and sometimes outright enemies whenever

124 The regional and global context

there is a downturn in the relationship. Bilateral ties have gone through several cycles over the years. At this writing, the Abe Shinzo government is using the trade war between China and the U.S., an inherent Chinese vulnerability, to encourage a "reset" with Beijing so as to reduce tensions. Reciprocal visits by Prime Minister Abe and Xi Jinping have been held, and Tokyo has even mulled possible cooperation with Beijing on the Belt and Road Initiative. However, we have seen such efforts in the past, and longstanding disputes over history and territory, the ardent nationalism that has been cultivated in China and the influence of conservative forces in Japanese politics, ensure that a final resolution to the dispute will likely remain elusive. As Smith (2015) writes in her study of the relationship between China's rise and Japan's domestic politics,

> Starting in 2006, Chinese and Japanese leaders sought to redefine their diplomatic relationship to reflect a new 'reciprocity' and 'mutual benefit.' But the idea that Japan and China could find a 'win-win' formula for building future cooperation seemed hollow in view of domestic grievances. Japan's leaders found it harder and harder to justify cooperation with Beijing as public opinion at home became more sensitive to Chinese behavior and more skeptical of Chinese motives.
>
> *(Smith)*

This is the natural outcome of natural rivalry between the two Asian powers, which by fate happen to be linked geographically. For Japan, the rise of China also threatens the status quo in Asia that has well served Japanese interests. More recently, skeptical and negative views of China among the Japanese have deepened as a result of China's greater assertiveness under President Xi. As with the U.S., Chinese bad behavior has broken the hold that Japan's elite and business community have traditionally had on Japanese foreign policy making and given more space for new, more skeptical interest groups to influence those policies. Repeated intrusions by PLA navy vessels and aircraft, as well as harassment in Japanese waters by Chinese coast guard vessels and fishing boats, which occasionally resulted in collisions, have also contributed to hardened views in Japan. Despite also being a claimant over the Senkaku islets in the East China Sea, Taiwan has not engaged in this type of dangerous brinkmanship with Japan; in fact, the two sides were able to set the dispute aside and sign a fisheries agreement on 10 April 2013, which was further amended in 2015 to expand the permitted zones for fishing (Blanchard 2013). Meanwhile, in a development that was sure to distress Japan, China announced in March 2018 that its coast guard was to fall under the control of the PLA Navy, signaling the militarization of a naval presence in the East China Sea (and elsewhere) that had hitherto been the remit of civilian organizations. One possible consequence of that decision is that Chinese coast guard vessels could become better armed while blurring the lines between civilian and military operations (Zhen 2018). Also complicating the relationship are suspicions in Japan over the patron–client relationship between China and North Korea, both of which regard Japan as one of their main

The future of the Japan-Taiwan partnership **125**

adversaries, as well as Beijing's permissive attitude toward Pyongyang's nuclear aspirations (Lee 2016).

To all this we must also add the Treaty of Mutual Cooperation and Security between the United States and Japan, which represents a major impediment to China's regional ambitions and goal of expelling the U.S. military from the Asia Pacific.

It is important to dive into Japan's security environment because this is directly related to Tokyo's ability and willingness to cooperate with Taiwan. In its 2017 White Paper, Japan's Ministry of Defense (2017) observed that

> while advocating "peaceful development," China, particularly over maritime issues where its interests conflict with others', continues to act in an assertive manner, including attempts at changing the status quo by coercion based on its own assertions incompatible with the existing international order. These actions include dangerous acts that could cause unintended consequences. China remains poised to fulfill its unilateral demands without compromise, which has included making steady efforts to turn these coercive changes to the status quo into a fait accompli. There is strong concern regarding the impact of these actions on the security environment of the region including Japan and of the international community.

Amid this shift in perceptions of a rising China, several supporters of Taiwan have advocated for a reassessment of Tokyo's generally careful relationship with Taipei and a deepening of bilateral ties, perhaps including the security field. The return to power of the DPP following its victory in the January 2016 elections was also seen as an auspicious coincidence, given the party's affinity toward Japan and Prime Minister Abe's positive views of the green camp – not to mention the greater influence of conservative "hawks" in Japan, who naturally would be more favorable to greater engagement of Taiwan.

That things did not turn out this way entirely can be explained by several factors. Chief among them are Tokyo's ongoing efforts to improve the relationship with Beijing. As long as this is the chief policy for the Japanese government, Tokyo will feel compelled to limit the scope and visibility of its relations with Taiwan. As a number of Japanese officials have told me – and this is bound to disappoint those who hoped for a quick deepening of Taiwan-Japan bilateral ties – Tokyo feels more comfortable doing more with Taiwan when its relationship with Beijing is stable. What this means is that notwithstanding changing attitudes in Japan toward China, more frictions between Tokyo and Beijing will not necessarily translate into immediate closer ties with Taiwan. The influential "China School" at Japan's Ministry of Foreign Affairs (MFA), for one, would not allow this to happen.

On the military side, Tokyo has, like the U.S., maintained a position of strategic ambiguity as to whether, and if so in which fashion, it would intervene in a Taiwan contingency. According to some, revised Guidelines to the Treaty of Mutual Cooperation and Security, adopted in September 1997, include provisions that would make it possible for Japan to take action in reaction to a military attack on Taiwan by China. Conservative Japanese media have on occasion encouraged this view in their articles. This ambiguity is by design, and I would argue that the text of the Treaty contains language that is vague enough ("situations that may emerge in the areas surrounding Japan and which will have an important influence on the peace of security of Japan [and] the Asia–Pacific region") that, under some circumstances in which Japan's national security is compromised, Tokyo could initiate responses to a military contingency in the Taiwan Strait. One possibility would be for the Japan Self-Defense Forces (JSDF, 自衛隊) to play a support role for the U.S. military (McGregor 2017).

As McGregor argues, the new clause may have been "laboriously worded," but "its intent was clear: the Taiwan [missile] crisis [of 1995–96] had crystallized a sea change in Japanese policy toward China, converting Tokyo's mainstream policy makers into 'reluctant realists' about the growing threat from Beijing." And that was in the late 1990s!

What most defense experts and military planners agree on is that in the opening phase of a major war in the Taiwan Strait, the PLA would feel it necessary to disable bases used by the U.S. military in Okinawa – "the only place in the region within reasonable tactical combat range of Taiwan" (Bush and O'Hanlon 2007) – so as to prevent their intervention over Taiwan. Any missile attack on Japanese territory would trigger Article 5 of the Treaty of Mutual Cooperation and Security, which stipulates that "Each Party recognizes that an armed attack against either Party in the territories under the administration of Japan would be dangerous to its own peace and safety and declares that it would act to meet the common danger in accordance with its constitutional provisions and processes" (MFA 1960). Okinawa houses about 50 percent of the 54,000 U.S. troops that are stationed in Japan and accounts for 64 percent of the land space used by the U.S. bases in the country. In all, Okinawa is home to 30 military bases. Among them, Kadena Air Base, as well as Marine Corps Air Station Futenma (slated for relocation to Henoko Bay), would be a prime target for a PLA ballistic missile barrage in preparation for an invasion of Taiwan, both to knock out current U.S. Air Force and Marine capabilities there, and to prevent reinforcements.

The host unit at Kadena Air Base is the U.S. 18th Wing, which, according to the air base's official web site (2018), "can deliver unmatched combat airpower and a forward-staging base to provide sovereign options that promote peace and stability in the Asia-Pacific region, ensure the common defense of our allies, and enhance the United States' unparalleled global engagement capability."[1] Key capabilities based at Kadena include the 44th Fighter Squadron and 67th Fighter Squadron of F-15C/D Eagle; 909th Air Refueling Squadron of KC-135 Stratotanker; and 961st Airborne Air Control Squadron of E-3 AWACS. Additionally, as part of a "long-planned deployment . . . designed to demonstrate the continuing U.S. commitment to stability and security in the region," the U.S. military has begun deploying F-35As at Kadena (Insinna 2018). F-22 Raptors have also been routinely deployed

The future of the Japan-Taiwan partnership **127**

at Kadena AB over the past decade, and returned to the island for the first time in 2018 after a four-year hiatus (Kadena).

Futenma Air Station houses approximately 4,000 U.S. Marines and features a 2.7 km-long runway. The 1st Marine Aircraft Wing, the aviation combat element of the III Marine Expeditionary Force, also operates in the complex. Its mission is to carry out air operations in support of Fleet Marine Forces, offensive air support, air defense, assault support, aerial reconnaissance (including active and passive electronic countermeasures, ECM), as well as control of aircraft and missiles. Futenma operates a variety of fixed wing, rotary wing, and tilt rotor aircraft, such as the MV-22 Osprey, in support of the III Marine Expeditionary Force.

As one Japanese academic told me, a PLA attack on Okinawa would immediately trigger a Japan entry into a war against China. That is why Beijing is believed to have attempted to exert political influence on Okinawa, with the aim of fueling calls by residents of Okinawa for the relocation, or outright removal, of the controversial – and at times socially harmful – U.S. military presence on the island. The neutralization of Okinawa as a possible staging ground for U.S. forces intervening in a Taiwan Strait scenario would remove a major obstacle to Beijing's aspirations over Taiwan. If there no longer were U.S. forces based on Okinawa, the U.S.' ability to enact a timely response to a Taiwan Strait crisis would be severely compromised; and just as important, China would no longer need to knock out U.S. forces based there by bombarding airfields and other military facilities. By removing that, China would no longer need to launch attacks against Japanese territory, which would reduce the likelihood of a Japanese entry into a Taiwan Strait military contingency.

To achieve this objective, China has exploited longstanding discontent with the U.S. military presence on the island. The environmental impact of those bases, as well as controversies over the rape of young Japanese girls by U.S. military personnel and accidents resulting in deaths of Japanese citizens, has sparked controversy in Japan's domestic politics – a rift between the governments of Okinawa and central authorities in Tokyo – and been the subject of many rounds of negotiations between Tokyo and Washington on force relocations, either in Japan or elsewhere, including Guam. Those efforts have encountered various difficulties, and to this day the military presence remains. Meanwhile, protests have emerged over Prime Minister Abe's plans to construct a new airfield on reclaimed land at Henoko Bay, forcing him to put the project on hold. Opinion polls have shown that a majority of the residents oppose the new construction project and want the base to be moved out of the prefecture – or out of Japan altogether (Reynolds 2018).

For Abe's Liberal Democratic Party (LDP), the base relocation project is a crucial part of Tokyo's efforts to demonstrate to the U.S. and to President Trump that Japan remains a committed and reliable partner to the U.S. Tokyo faced a new challenge in October 2018 when the LDP's favorite in elections in Okinawa was defeated by Denny Tamaki, an outspoken opponent of the plan to relocate Futenma to Henoko and a former Lower House member of the Liberal Party. During his campaign, Tamaki told voters he would ask the U.S. and Japanese governments to

128 The regional and global context

close Futenma, return the land to Okinawa, and move the air station off the island (Kageyama 2018).

Although it is difficult assess the impact of Beijing's strategy, what is known is that pro-CCP organizations, such as the Chinese Ryukyu Study Society and the Ryukyu Independence Study Association, are known to have collaborated with pro-Taiwan unification groups such as Chang An-le's China Unification Promotion Party (CUPP) and New Party. These groups have promoted an end to the U.S. military presence on the island, opposed Abe's "Japanese militarism," and called for Okinawa's independence. All these positions dovetail with the CCP's efforts to expel the U.S. from the Asia–Pacific (Cole 2015). China also lays territorial claims to the Ryukyus (McCurry 2013). A 2013 editorial in the *Global Times* (2013), warned that "if Japan seeks to be a pioneer in sabotaging China's rise, China can carry out practical input, fostering forces in Okinawa that seek the restoration of the independence of the Ryukyu Chain." It continued: "If Japan, binding itself with the US, tries to threaten China's future, China should impose threats on the country's integrity." During anti-base protests in 2013, a number of Okinawan protesters were seen wearing Chinese military uniforms, and their vehicles were plastered with anti-U.S. military placards as well as portraits of Mao Zedong, Kim Il Sung, and Kim Jong Un. Loudspeakers railed against the U.S. and blasted pro-China slogans (Tritten and Sumida 2013).

Such incidents have fueled speculation that pro-CCP elements may be engaging in political warfare to hijack and redirect natural opposition to Futenma and calls for the base's relocation toward a more outright anti-U.S. campaign. The mock pro-China protests – "dirty tricks," as one Japanese has described those – also risked being picked up by traditional media and create tensions between Okinawa and Tokyo, as well as between Tokyo and Washington. The infiltration and warping of democratic institutions, including elections, is one means by which China has compromised the electoral choices of its opponents, something it has done in Taiwan. It is therefore likely that it would seek to achieve similar goals in crucial places like Okinawa. Japanese officials have also told this author privately that Chinese nationals pretending to be Japanese have also attempted to obtain employment at U.S. military bases in Okinawa; some of them have reportedly succeeded.

The role of organized crime in the promotion of CCP policies also should not be underestimated, both as a mechanism for intimidation and to move money around to influence politicians. As we have already seen, the CUPP and New Party have in the past had interactions with pro-Beijing organizations in Okinawa that advocate for independence and the ouster of the U.S. military. In January 2018, Chang An-le's son, Chang Wei (張瑋), along with dozens of members of the Bamboo Union triad (竹联帮), visited Naha, the capital of Okinawa, where they held meetings with the violent 沖繩旭琉會 criminal organization (*Okinawa Times* 2018). It is also known that members of the two organizations had made reciprocal visits in 2015 and 2017 and that a working relationship has been established. The young Chang has already fallen afoul of the law in Taiwan for physically assaulting Taiwanese protesters at National Taiwan University and Hong Kong democracy

The future of the Japan-Taiwan partnership **129**

activists at Taiwan Taoyuan International Airport. Although it is highly possible that his visit to Okinawa and interactions with Japanese criminal organizations are part of purely criminal business operations, experiences with the Bamboo Union in Taiwan also suggest that such activities may also overlap with, or be reinforcing, activities that are political in nature. What is certain is that political warfare operations targeting Okinawa, if they are indeed occurring, would be directly related to China's claims over Taiwan.

Pro-Beijing groups in Taiwan, such as Chang's CUPP and the Concentric Patriot Association of the ROC (CPAROC, 中華愛國同心會), have also taken aim at the DPP's close relationship with Japan, often accusing the ruling party of acting on behalf of the Japanese. At one point, dozens of CUPP members dressed up as Japanese Imperial Army soldiers gathered outside the DPP headquarters and tried, in vain, to break through police barricades. Although no harm was done and people at the site were rather amused by the elderly protesters' attempt to sing Japanese songs, the reference to Japan's dark past caused anger among Japanese diplomats posted in Taiwan.

Those organizations have also repeatedly harassed Japanese officials at the Japan-Taiwan Exchange Association (公益財團法人日本台灣交流協會) office in Taipei, which ironically is located less than a five-minute walk from the CUPP main office. In early September 2018, pro-unification groups splashed paint all over the building's entrance, foyer, and glass panels during a protest organized by the KMT over the issue of comfort women (Chen 2018). The same groups have also held protests over the Senkaku/Diaoyutai territorial dispute (ostensibly for violating the rights of Taiwanese fishermen in the area), while in August 2018 members of the New Party deposited a "comfort woman" statue outside the de facto embassy in Taipei (*China Times* 2018). Over the years, the CCP has exploited war guilt – the claim that Tokyo never formally apologized for World War II atrocities – and the comfort women issue to leverage against Japan and tarnish its reputation internationally. On several occasions in the past two years, members of the CPAROC or the CUPP have protested outside the building and used loud speakers to bombard its occupants with insults. On a few occasions, Japanese officials felt compelled to call the police.

Pro-unification groups have also attacked symbols of Japan's past presence in Taiwan. In June 2017, four CUPP members were indicted for destroying century-old guardian "lion-dog" statues at an elementary school in Beitou District the previous month (Huang 2017).

Although protests targeting Japan in Taiwan did occur prior to 2016, they tended to be limited to key dates, such as "comfort women day," or over the Senkaku/Diaoyutai dispute. Since then, the protests have become much more frequent and disruptive, no doubt a reflection of Beijing's growing assertiveness and as part of efforts to cause a split between Taiwan and Japan. So far Japanese officials appear to have distinguished between pro-CCP troublemakers from the CUPP and CPAROC and the rest of Taiwanese society. But the constant harassment certainly had created a sense of siege among Japanese diplomats posted in Taiwan; should

130 The regional and global context

the situation escalate, the Japanese side could understandably call upon Taiwanese authorities to ramp up police protection at the de facto embassy and for officials and their families.

Ironically, the ramped up protests outside the Japanese mission were also ostensibly in response to its renaming, from Interchange Association (Japan) (公益財團法人交流協會) to Japan-Taiwan Exchange Association, in January 2017. In May that same year, Taiwan's own diplomatic presence in Japan, the Association of East Asian Relations, Taiwan (臺灣日本關係協會), saw a name change to Taiwan-Japan Relations Association (台灣日本關係協會). Both symbolized a closer relationship and, by placing the names of the countries in the official names of their diplomatic missions, signified a more normalized relationship, even though Tokyo continued to abide by its own version of the "one China" policy. An official at the Japanese mission in Taipei said the name change was to "boost recognition."

As expected, the Chinese foreign ministry said it was "extremely dissatisfied" with the name changes and referred to Tokyo's decision as a "negative move by Japan on the Taiwan issue" (Blanchard 2016).

Alongside the name changes, collaboration between Taiwan and Japan has become closer in recent years, although it has mainly occurred behind closed doors given the sensitivity of the relationship and possible reactions by Beijing. As with Americans and others, Track II delegations and academic exchanges between Taiwan and Japan have become more frequent, and Japan has expressed interest in joining U.S.-Taiwan GCTF initiatives. From 2019, Japan has committed to co-hosting GCTF summits and did so at the "Defending Democracy Through Promoting Media Literacy II" round in September 2019.

On the security side, members of the armed forces have met frequently, but do so without wearing uniforms. Japan has a de facto military attaché in Taiwan, who historically has been a retired officer from the JSDF.

In March 2017, Senior Vice Minister of Internal Affairs and Communications Jiro Akama made history by visiting Taiwan on official business. Akama was the most senior Japanese official to visit Taiwan in the past 45 years, since Japan established official diplomatic relations with the People's Republic of China (Ihara 2017). As expected, Beijing issued a protest, saying the visit "has caused serious disturbance to the improvement of Sino-Japanese ties" (Blanchard 2017). Of course, Beijing's anger and threats were entirely survivable, and the sky didn't fall on either Taiwan or Japan. That same week, Prime Minister Abe called Taiwan "an important partner that shares Japan's values and interests" (*Nikkei Asian Review* 2017).

Tokyo has also signaled its interest in institutionalizing the relationship by establishing more formal channels of communication. Chief among them is a plan to direct communication between the two countries' National Security Councils (NSC). Such plans were actually first floated during the Ma Ying-jeou administration, but the Japanese side did not want to do so as long as the KMT was still in office. Despite claiming to have cordial ties with Japan, President Ma often failed to hide his apparent contempt for the Japanese, which undermined trust between the two sides. In one incident, a Japanese delegation to Taiwan was treated by MOFA to a visit at an

The future of the Japan-Taiwan partnership **131**

exhibit on comfort women at Chiang Kai-shek Memorial Hall in Taipei. Needless to say, the diplomatic *faux pas* made the visiting Japanese rather uncomfortable.

With the DPP now in office, the feasibility of establishing a NSC–to–NSC channel between Taipei and Tokyo should be greater; however, according to a retired Japanese official, the Abe administration has made such a move contingent on Taipei lifting a ban on certain food products from Fukushima Prefecture, which suffered a nuclear plant catastrophe in the wake of the 2011 earthquake. Such "linkage," similar to the U.S.' insistence on the lifting of bans on certain pork and beef products, has combined with the politicization of food issues in Taiwan – the KMT will describe any move by Taiwan to reopen its doors to products from Fukushima as the DPP administration caving in to Japanese pressure and, worse, not caring about the health of Taiwanese – to make progress very difficult.

On the Japanese side, the issue of food safety was compounded by the fact that Tokyo only recently began to make available publicly – and in a manner that is comprehensible to ordinary consumers – scientific data demonstrating that food products from the affected region are now safe for human consumption. Among other things, Japanese authorities have brought Taiwanese media, academics, and others on all-expenses-paid trips to Fukushima Prefecture, where they were able to taste various foods as well as witness progress in reconstruction and rehabilitation years after the natural catastrophe.

According to the same former Japanese official, a perceived lack of initiative on the part of Taiwan's envoy to Tokyo has frustrated Japanese efforts to engage Taiwan on certain subjects and forced them to bypass the representative office and instead contact Taipei directly.

More controversially but something that has been discussed in some circles is the possibility of involving Taiwan, in some capacity, in the Free and Open Indo–Pacific (FOIP) strategy. As Japan, the U.S., Australia, and other states begin to pay more attention to China's designs upon Pacific islands (discussed in Chapter 4), they are also realizing that continued official diplomatic relations between those small states and Taiwan are in their strategic interests. Although Tokyo has insisted that FOIP should not be construed as an attempt to "contain" or "encircle" China, there nevertheless is no doubt that the initiative intends to regroup countries that share certain values and at least have in common a desire to prevent the further spread of China's authoritarian model. Above all, what all these countries want is the preservation of a rules-based system, with the realization that the very structure of government within a given region has geopolitical implications. Greater engagement with those weak and vulnerable states, therefore, both in the form of security provisions and the offer of an alternative model of economic assistance, will be necessary if China's nefarious influence in the region is to be mitigated, or countered altogether. For one thing, developed countries such as the U.S., Japan, Australia, Singapore, India, South Korea, and Taiwan could endeavor to bring more high-spending tourists to countries, like Palau, that have become victims of China's "weaponization" of tourism to punish them for insisting on retaining their official diplomatic relations with Taiwan.

132 The regional and global context

A possible role for Taiwan would include being part of a more synchronized effort with Japan, the U.S. and others to bring development assistance to small island-states in the Pacific, to help build up their law-enforcement capabilities, and to deepen its promotion of and support for democratic institutions in those countries. All of this need not be conducted with fanfare. As with many other things, quiet but effective diplomacy and engagement is, more often than not, more beneficial to Taiwan than highly symbolic and publicized efforts.

Such efforts would also signify a greater role for Taiwan's International Cooperation Development Fund (ICDF, 財團法人國際合作發展基金會) and better coordination between such agencies and its counterparts in participating countries in FOIP. In this, Taiwan could also deepen its collaboration with Japan in other areas of the Asia Pacific. Although much attention has been paid in recent years to China's Belt and Road Initiative (BRI), many have forgotten that Japan remains the largest investor and donor in the region. In 2016, Prime Minster Abe announced a US$200 billion plan, over five years, to build roads, ports, and power plants in Asia and Africa (reorganization at Japan's MOFA has also meant that an increasing number of Mandarin-speaking diplomats in the China Division are being dispatched to Africa, which Tokyo has identified as a new area of competition with China).

Japan's economic outreach in the region has in fact been going on for decades. Using financing vehicles like the Asian Development Bank (ADB) and the Japan International Cooperation Agency (JICA), Japan has provided "massive amounts of money and direction" for the development of roads, rail lines, metro systems, and ports across Asia. In December 2016, Japan also launched a joint venture, funded by Mitsubishi UFJ Lease & Finance, Hitachi Capital and Bank of Tokyo-Mitsubishi UFJ, known as the Japan Infrastructure Initiative (JII). The Initiative intends to invest as much as US$878 million into various Japanese-directed infrastructure projects, including railways and power plants, across Asia, Europe, as well as in the U.S. (Shepard 2016).

Recognizing this potential, in July 2018 then-premier William Lai opined that Taiwan and Japan should deepen economic ties by jointly exploring business opportunities in emerging markets across South and Southeast Asia, adding that Japan's current policy dovetailed with the Tsai administration's New Southbound Policy (*United Daily News* 2018). Taipei should also continue to encourage Tokyo to support Taiwan's joining the Comprehensive and Progressive Agreement for Trans-Pacific Partnership (CPTPP).

While Tokyo has indicated its intention to collaborate with China on BRI – doing so also serves Japan's strategic interests – it remains to be seen how long and how far such joint efforts between the two competitors will last. Should bilateral relations sour, as they likely will again at some point, Tokyo will have an even greater incentive to deepen its investment and assistance program for the region as a counterbalance to growing Chinese influence. Even if relations remain stable, there are still several areas where Japan is likely to go it alone and not bandwagon on BRI.

It is in those areas that Taiwan's ICDF, NGOs and other entities can play a role, working alongside Japan in sectors that play to its strengths. Collaborating with

JICA, or even joining the JII in some capacity, could help position Taiwan as a key participant in major infrastructure initiatives that provide an alternative to China's BRI – an alternative that emphasizes good governance, human rights, and that will avoid the "debt trap," which now has a number of recipients of Chinese largesse worried about the cost to their sovereignty.

By early 2019, Japan had also co-sponsored two GCTF events with Taiwan and the U.S., one on combating corruption in the Indo Pacific (Yeh 2019), and the other on combating drug-resistant tuberculosis (*Taiwan Today* 2019). This demonstrated a willingness on Tokyo's part to play a role in the successful bilateral arrangement between Taipei and Washington, D.C., and to explore mechanisms by which Taiwan can be more proactively integrated into multilateral efforts tackling issues of shared interests.

Other areas of possible collaboration between Japan and Taiwan include freedom of navigation patrols – Japanese naval forces including, for the first time since World War II, a submarine (Kato 2018), as well as a helicopter carrier, are now involved in exercises and joint patrols alongside the U.S. in the South China Sea, an economic lifeline for Japan – maritime security, search-and-rescue operations in waters near and between Taiwan and Japan and elsewhere in Southeast Asia, as well as humanitarian assistance and disaster relief (HADR). While mil-to-mil exchanges remain highly sensitive and are bound to prompt a vitriolic response from Beijing, cooperation at the civilian level – including coast guards, law enforcement, and so on – is far less controversial, and much more could be achieved in that domain, provided that both sides show the willingness to do so. In July 2018, Taiwan's Industrial Technology Research Institute (ITRI) and the Maritime Disaster Prevention Center (MDPC) – Japan's only authorized maritime disaster prevention institute – signed a MOU to cooperate on responses to toxic chemical disasters. The pact will facilitate and encourage exchanges of ground- and sea-rescue expertise, bolster toxic chemical disaster response capabilities, and make both sides better at handling environmental pollution accidents (Shu and Hsu 2018).

On the military side, as we saw, exchanges do occur but generally do so in an unofficial capacity and setting. Proper channels could facilitate intelligence sharing, provided that Taiwan can give enough reassurances to its partners in the Japanese intelligence community and the JSDF that the information will be safely stored and not leaked to the Chinese.

With PLA aerial and naval passages in international waters around both Taiwan and Japan, through their Exclusive Economic Zones, Air Defense Identification Zones (ADIZ), contiguous zones, and even territorial waters and airspace, becoming more frequent in recent years, Tokyo and Taipei should increase communication and better coordinate their response so as to better manage this growing concern. Some defense experts, including retired admiral Dennis Blair (2018), have argued that Taiwan's and Japan's military should stop their longstanding practice of scrambling aircraft on every occasion to intercept and "escort" Chinese intruders. "Although this intercept and escort policy seems a sensible way of protecting a country's sovereignty, demonstrating that a country's armed forces are on their

134 The regional and global context

guard and can defend their territory," Blair observes, "it comes at a cost in military effectiveness." He continues:

> "Scrambles" of alert aircraft to intercept Chinese aircraft, and rapid sorties of alert surface ships to intercept Chinese ships, are simple tactical evolutions that provide little training value in wartime skills. The pattern of reactions provides intelligence insights to the People's Liberation Army about Japanese and Taiwanese surveillance and reaction capabilities, insights that can be used to the PLA's advantage in combat operations.
>
> The budget effects of these "intercept and escort everything" policies are more important. They use up flying and steaming hour budgets, leaving less money available for complex exercises to hone more difficult skills that will be needed in wartime. Within limited defense budgets, purchasing replacement or additional aircraft and ships for intercept and escort competes with the purchase of larger inventories of long-range surface-to-air missiles, submarines or other systems that are of greater utility in defeating Chinese attempts to take and hold islands.

With these "intercept everything" policies, Blair writes, Japan and Taiwan are "degrading their readiness to defend their territory in conflict [and] lowering deterrence of Chinese military aggression." Blair argues that the Taiwanese and Japanese military should decide how much they want to allocate to intercepts and could counter with intrusions of their own, which would spark complaints by Beijing and, in the process, expose the contradiction in its own argument. He adds that Taiwan and Japan should also time military exercises to coincide with passages by the PLA so as to send a stronger signal both to Beijing and their respective publics.

Blair rightly recognizes that the governments in Tokyo and Taipei are under "strong political pressure to intercept and escort every Chinese sortie near their territory." Indeed. And it is not difficult to imagine how pan-blue media and the opposition KMT would politicize such a decision by portraying President Tsai as weak on defense and unable to uphold the nation's sovereignty. All of this, of course, would be for domestic consumption. It would help alleviate such politicking if Tokyo and Taipei *jointly* developed and announced a strategy to deal with and manage the PLA passages in waters and airspace near their respective territories.

The defense industry sector is another area that shows promise, with the two sides, possibly in collaboration with U.S. defense firms, jointly developing and mass-producing various defense articles. Technical assistance by "retired" Japanese engineers for ongoing programs in Taiwan, such as the Indigenous Defense Submarine, is also within the realm of possibility, although such initiative will need to be carried out quietly. Direct arms sales by Japan to Taiwan remain unlikely for the foreseeable future, both due to the China factor and to export controls in Japan that, despite recent revisions, continue to make arms transfers difficult.

Expectations that Prime Minister Abe would consider a Japanese version of the U.S.' Taiwan Relations Act (TRA) or some sort of defense treaty are unlikely to be fulfilled any time soon. Japan's engagement with Taiwan, though improving, will remain careful. Unlike the U.S., Japan is not a superpower and therefore must do more balancing to protect its national interest; carelessly sabotaging its relationship with China does not serve Japan's interest. While close ties with Taipei are arguably also in Tokyo's interest, its engagement with Taiwan must be pragmatic, strategic, and perforce will continue to occur mostly at the unofficial level.

As I mentioned in the opening section of this chapter, the majority of ordinary Japanese have highly favorable views of Taiwan, but such perceptions have not translated into recognition that Taiwan is also an important element in Japan's national security. Knowing this, and in light of the fact that Japanese assistance is essential to Taiwan's survival, it is incumbent upon Taipei to launch a major public diplomacy initiative to educate the Japanese about this aspect of the relationship. In other words, it is for Taiwan to explain to the Japanese why a free and sovereign Taiwan is in *their* interest, and why Japan should therefore do more to help Taiwan retain its freedom. This means much greater outreach, and identifying individuals who have the right skill sets – including Japanese-language abilities – to go to Japan and address university students, communities, and others. Exchanges with government agencies and think tanks, which occur regularly and are undoubtedly useful, are not sufficient to persuade the Japanese public. And if Taiwan remains passive in such efforts, we cannot expect the Japanese to ask that their government do more in that respect. Taiwan cannot afford to wait for other countries to see the light about Taiwan's essentiality for a free and open Indo-Pacific, or to expect that the world will come to its assistance simply because it is a democracy.

Note

1 Kadena Air Base, 18th Wing Fact Sheet, www.kadena.af.mil/About-Us/Fact-Sheets/Display/Article/417045/18th-wing/

References

Blair, Dennis (2018) "Commentary: Japan, Taiwan Must Re-Evaluate How They're Intercepting Chinese Threats," *Military Times*, 26 August. www.militarytimes.com/opinion/commentary/2018/08/26/commentary-military-confrontations-in-peace-and-war/.

Blanchard, Ben (2013) "China Angered as Japan, Taiwan Sign Fishing Agreement," *Reuters*, 10 April. www.reuters.com/article/us-china-japan-taiwan/china-angered-as-japan-taiwan-sign-fishing-agreement-idUSBRE93909520130410.

Blanchard, Ben (2016) "China Upset at Name Change of de Facto Japan Embassy in Taiwan," *Reuters*, 28 December. www.reuters.com/article/us-china-japan-taiwan/china-upset-at-name-change-of-de-facto-japan-embassy-in-taiwan-idUSKBN14H0GQ.

Blanchard, Ben (2017) "China Upset as Japanese Minister Visits Self-Ruled Taiwan," *Reuters*, 27 March. www.reuters.com/article/us-china-japan-taiwan/china-upset-as-japanese-minister-visits-self-ruled-taiwan-idUSKBN16Y0R7.

Bush, Richard C. and Michael E. O'Hanlon (2007) *A War Like No Other: The Truth About China's Challenge to America*, Hoboken: John Wiley & Sons, p. 116.

Chen, Chih-hsien (2018) "統促黨日台交流協會潑漆 李承龍3人各5萬元交保," *China Times*, 11 September. www.chinatimes.com/realtimenews/20180911001789-260402.

China Times (2018) "新黨「很震撼」連線將慰安婦阿嬤像請下車," 28 August. www.chinatimes.com/realtimenews/20180828004698-260407.

Ching Min, Lee (2016) *Fault Lines in a Rising Asia*, Washington: Carnegie Endowment for International Peace, p. 320.

Cole, J. Michael (2015) "Chang Wei-shan's Troubling Connections," *Thinking Taiwan*, 14 September. http://thinking-taiwan.com/thinking-taiwan.com/political-warfare-watch-chang-wei-shans-troubling-connections/comment-page-1/index.html.

Global Times (2013) "Ryukyu Issue Offers Leverage to China," 10 May. www.globaltimes.cn/content/780732.shtml#.UbCOBUA-bK1.

Huang, Jie (2017) "破壞兩尊「石狛犬」 李承龍等4人被起訴," *Liberty Times*, 6 June. http://news.ltn.com.tw/news/society/breakingnews/2090837.

Ihara, Kensaku (2017) "Japan Vice Minister Officially Visits Taiwan," *Nikkei Asian Review*, 26 March. https://asia.nikkei.com/Politics/Japan-vice-minister-officially-visits-Taiwan2.

Insinna, Valerie (2018) "Air Force F-35 Put Through Its Paces in First Asia-Pacific Deployment," *Defense News*, 5 February. www.defensenews.com/digital-show-dailies/singapore-airshow/2018/02/05/f-35-put-through-its-paces-in-first-asia-pacific-deployment/.

Kadena Air Base (2018) "F-22 Raptors Return to Kadena Air Base," 30 May, 2018. www.kadena.af.mil/News/Article-Display/Article/1535851/f-22-raptors-return-to-kadena-air-base/.

Kageyama, Yuri (2018) "Okinawa's New Governor Has a Big Problem: What to Do About the U.S. Military and Its Bases," *Associated Press*, 2 October. www.militarytimes.com/news/your-military/2018/10/01/okinawas-new-governor-has-a-big-problem-what-to-do-about-the-us-military-and-its-bases/.

Kato, Masaya (2018) "Japanese Submarine Conducts Drill in South China Sea," *Nikkei Asian Review*, 17 September. https://asia.nikkei.com/Politics/International-Relations/Japanese-submarine-conducts-drill-in-South-China-Sea2.

McCurry, Justin (2013) "China Lays Claim to Okinawa as Territory Dispute with Japan Escalates," *The Guardian*, 15 May. www.theguardian.com/world/2013/may/15/china-okinawa-dispute-japan-ryukyu.

McGregor, Richard (2017) *Asia's Reckoning: China, Japan, and the Fate of U.S. Power in the Pacific Century*, New York: Viking, p. 158.

Ministry of Defense (2017) "White Paper." www.mod.go.jp/e/publ/w_paper/pdf/2017/DOJ2017_1-2-3_web.pdf.

Ministry of Foreign Affairs (MFA) (1960) "Japan-U.S. Security Treaty." www.mofa.go.jp/region/n-america/us/q&a/ref/1.html.

Nikkei Asian Review (2017) "Japan's Abe Calls Taiwan 'Important Partner'," 30 March. https://asia.nikkei.com/Politics/Japan-s-Abe-calls-Taiwan-important-partner2.

Okinawa Times (2018) "台湾マフィア、幹部ら十数人が来日　沖縄の暴力団と接触," 2 January. www.okinawatimes.co.jp/articles/-/202723.

Reynolds, Isabel (2018) "U.S. Serviceman's Son Is Latest Threat to Abe's Trump Strategy," *Bloomberg*, 28 September. www.bloomberg.com/news/articles/2018-09-27/u-s-serviceman-s-son-is-latest-threat-to-abe-s-trump-strategy.

Shepard, Wade (2016) "Japan Ups Its Game Against China's Belt and Road," *Forbes*, 1 December. www.forbes.com/sites/wadeshepard/2016/12/01/japan-ups-its-infrastructure-game-against-chinas-belt-and-road/#4c579d283223.

Shu, Wei and Elizabeth Hsu (2018) "Taiwan, Japan Sign MOU on Toxic Chemical Disaster Response," *Focus Taiwan*, 16 July. http://focustaiwan.tw/news/ast/201807160017.aspx.

Smith, Sheila A. (2015) *Intimate Rivals: Japanese Domestic Politics and a Rising China*, New York: Columbia University Press, p. 238.

Taiwan Today (2019) "Taiwan, US, Japan Stage GCTF Workshop on Drug-Resistant TB," 1 May. https://taiwantoday.tw/news.php?unit=2,6,10,15,18&post=154093.

Tritten, Travis J. and Chiyomi Sumida (2013) "Protests on Okinawa Aren't Always What They Appear to Be," *Stars and Stripes*, 23 May. www.stripes.com/news/protests-on-okinawa-aren-t-always-what-they-appear-to-be-1.222240.

United Daily News (2018) "出席台日交流高峰會 賴揆期待日本助台加入CPTPP," 7 July. https://udn.com/news/story/6656/3240079.

Yeh, Joseph (2019) "Japan Co-Hosts a Taiwan-U.S. Training Workshop for the First Time," *Focus Taiwan*, 26 March. http://focustaiwan.tw/news/aipl/201903260007.aspx.

Zhen, Liu (2018) "China's Military Police Given Control of Coastguard as Beijing Boosts Maritime Security," *South China Morning Post*, 21 March. www.scmp.com/news/china/diplomacy-defence/article/2138257/chinas-military-police-given-control-coastguard-beijing.

7

TAIWAN AND THE WORLD

Isolation vs. creative engagement

Besides the U.S. and Japan, unofficial diplomatic allies have begun to figure more prominently in Taiwan's outreach efforts. Although it would like to keep the official diplomatic allies it has left – 15 at this writing – Taipei appears to have realized that it cannot hope to win a fight that has very much been waged on Beijing's terms. The sheer size of China's economy, for one thing, means that this will never be a battle between equals, especially when the countries dragged into this diplomatic tug-of-war need substantial development assistance. If it's about money alone, Beijing will, in most cases, win.

Aware of this, and cognizant of the limited influence (perhaps with the exception of the Vatican, discussed later in this chapter) that all of Taiwan's official allies have in international politics, the Taiwanese government has reached out to the large and democratic economies, as well as countries within the region, in an effort to strengthen and diversify its engagement, even if much of this occurs at the unofficial level. As we saw earlier, a changing global context, in which China's assertiveness and growing fears that it may have embarked on a colonial project of its own through its Belt and Road Initiative and "debt trap" diplomacy, has also opened doors for Taiwan that, a few years ago, had been closed. China's ambitions to rewrite the rules-based global order, and rising apprehensions over the impact of its influence operations on major democracies worldwide, have also increased the appeal of Taiwan as a stable, responsible, democratic partner.

Taiwan's physical proximity to China, its decades of experience striking a balance between risk and opportunities in its relationship with its neighbor, and of course the cultural and linguistic elements it also shares with it, have contributed to making Taiwan an alluring source of information for countries that are just now beginning to ask themselves how to deal with a global power that, on many issues, does not share our ideology. Taiwan has experienced it all: the military threat, espionage, cyber warfare, political warfare, disinformation, crime syndicates, intellectual property theft; and, on the more positive side: business, investment, joint partnerships, tourism, cultural exchanges, religion, people-to-people interactions, and so on.

Taiwan is still learning how to appropriately respond to many of these challenges, and therefore it cannot be expected to be in a position to provide solutions for all of them. But over the years it undoubtedly has developed an awareness of the situation, and an ability to identify actors and practices, that is unequalled elsewhere.

Taiwan's relationship with the rest of the world, therefore, has been becoming more mutually beneficial, and this is an opportunity that Taipei cannot miss. This particular moment in time has opened a window for Taiwan to develop new relationships and deepen existing ones in a way that ties Taiwan more tightly into the international system and within the community of democratic nations. We do not know how long that window will remain open, though here I would argue that as long as Xi Jinping remains in charge, the logic of reassessing the value of Taiwan to the international community will remain.

This situation has given rise to an irony: as Beijing intensifies its campaign to isolate Taiwan by luring its official diplomatic allies and preventing it from joining or participating in multilateral institutions – both areas where it has scored a number of successes since 2016 – the world is gradually becoming more interested in doing things with Taiwan. Taipei has seized this occasion by agreeing to the reality that a large component of those interactions has to occur both quietly and at the unofficial level. Taiwan's odd situation within the international system has compelled it to become more pragmatic, even though, on the symbolic side, this has proven frustrating to diplomats who covet assignments as ambassadors to real embassies, as well as to ordinary Taiwanese who resent the very idea of unofficial relations, which in their minds belittles Taiwan and its existence as a sovereign state.

None of this is ideal, nor is it fair. But that is the hand that the Taiwanese have been dealt, and they must make the most of it by being pragmatic and strategic.

Several countries besides the U.S. and Japan, both discussed in the previous chapters, have expressed renewed interest in working with Taiwan. Within the region, this includes Australia, New Zealand, Singapore, India – whose importance to Taiwan is finally being recognized – and seven or eight of the 18 countries targeted by the administration's New Southbound Policy (NSP): Singapore, Vietnam, Indonesia, the Philippines, Malaysia, Thailand, Cambodia, Brunei, Myanmar, and Laos from ASEAN, and India, Sri Lanka, Bangladesh, Bhutan, Nepal, and Pakistan, along with New Zealand and Australia from South Asia. With Australia, Taiwan has also made its advanced medical services available to more than 10 seriously ill asylum-seekers, who were being held on Nauru, under an MOU with Canberra (Ku and Kao 2018). The agreement was not without controversy, with some critics accusing the Taiwanese government of complicity in an asylum program in Australia that is seen as unjust and possibly in violation of human rights. Nevertheless, the case can be made that, by providing emergency medical services, Taiwan's efforts saved lives.

With regards to India, in May 2018, Taiwan opened a new Taiwan External Trade Development Council (TAITRA, 中華民國對外貿易發展協會) office in New Delhi, India. The new office, TAITRA's fourth in India and its 61st around the world (including 10 in China), was charged with providing more assistance to Taiwanese businesses seeking to expand their markets in South Asia (Kang and Kao 2018). Taiwan has also developed incentive programs to attract more graduate students from India in the tech sector and to foster future cooperation. Taiwan and India have signed a total of 12 agreements so far, although none were signed through government institutions.

Elsewhere, engagement has also deepened with countries like Germany (green energy), France (education), the U.K. (culture and education, aerospace technology, financial technology, offshore wind power), as well as the European Union (technology, wind energy, intellectual property). In May 2018, TAITRA and the Israel Export & International Cooperation Institute agreed to increase cooperation between the two countries in trade and economic development in the private and public sectors. That same month, a high-level TAITRA delegation, which included heads of venture capital funds and executives of high-tech firms, was in Israel to explore strategic opportunities with the "startup nation" and "hub for global high-tech industries" (Kempinski 2018; Shoshanna 2018).

Taiwan has also made important inroads with other countries like the Czech Republic, and this despite the heavy influence that China has had on that part of the world and "elite capture" by firms like the embattled China Energy Fund Committee (CEFC). Taiwanese diplomats in those countries have learned to navigate the fears and desires of governments, pushing for events – trade, cyber, culture, and so on – as well as contact at the official and semiofficial level. They have learned to proactively seek partnerships but also to be patient when governments believe the timing is not appropriate, such as when a head of state is about to embark on an official visit to China, or when a Chinese official is expected to visit the country. Taiwan representative offices in those countries (again the Czech Republic comes to mind) have also learned to work around the aggressiveness of Chinese embassies, which have no compunction in repeatedly browbeating host governments to force them to sever all ties with Taiwan (it also helps that in many countries, the promised investments from China simply do not materialize, and in many cases, Taiwan is a source of larger investments that contribute to local job creation). Successes – and they are many – have occurred quietly and with pragmatism in several countries. The fact that we rarely hear about them is largely by necessity; one thread at a time, Taiwan is tightening its relationships with several unofficial allies all over Europe and elsewhere. The hard work that Taiwanese diplomats do to ensure such successes does not receive the recognition it deserves. This author has had the chance through his travels of meeting many of them all around the world; several have shared their hopes, apprehensions, and frustrations over the years. (Many feel that the work they do is misunderstood by the Taiwan public. I take this occasion to salute their hard work – several of them I now count as friends.)

Although there undoubtedly were some successes, Canada has proven to be a bit of a challenge since the election of Justin Trudeau's Liberals on 19 October 2015. This is largely due to the party's historical ties with China, the grip that pro-Beijing elements have had on Trudeau's small circle of advisers and within the intellectual community, as well as the Trudeau government's desire to sign a free-trade agreement (FTA) with China, a goal that became more pressing as President Trump began threatening the very existence of the North American Free Trade Agreement (NAFTA). It remains to be seen whether an eleventh-hour agreement, reached on 30 September 2018, that saved the North American FTA and renamed it the United States–Mexico–Canada Agreement (USMCA), will force a recalculation in Ottawa, especially a provision buried in the USMCA which stipulates that member states could be barred from signing FTAs with non-market economies – a clause that many saw as directly aimed at China (Lawder 2018).

The Trudeau government's silence on the Air Canada controversy, where the carrier gave in to Chinese pressure and began referring to Taiwan as "Taipei, CN," was also indicative of Ottawa's reluctance to push back against China on the Taiwan "issue." According to sources, Taiwanese diplomats posted in Canada have also seen their ability to interact directly with Canadian officials somewhat reduced since the Liberals came back to power in 2015. Despite this, a number of MOUs between Taiwan and Canada were signed in 2015 and 2016, and on 15 January 2016, the Canadian Trade Office in Taipei and the Taipei Economic and Cultural Office in Canada signed an *arrangement* – not an agreement – on the avoidance of double taxation and the prevention of fiscal evasion (Canadian Department of Finance 2016). The deal was the result of many years of hard work by officials from both sides, and represented a good step toward increasing bilateral trade and investment.

The Trudeau government's reluctance to deal with Taiwan in a manner that reflects the shared values of our two countries is highly frustrating (Lehre 2018). These examples serve as an important lesson – and reminder – about which priorities truly influence and drive a country's foreign policy. These suggest that democracy alone is insufficient to convince a country, however liberal and democratic it may be, that it is in its interest to do more with and for Taiwan. If liberal, democratic and progressive Canada cannot get it, this means that those who care about Taiwan's future must think of new strategies, new language, and a new framework to educate the rest of the world on *why*, as Shelley Rigger (2011) has put it in a book of this title, Taiwan matters.

It goes without saying that Ottawa is not the only capital that has engaged in risk-avoidance when it comes to engaging Taiwan over fears of earning Beijing's wrath, as may have been the case following China's kidnapping of two Canadian nationals, Michael Kovrig and Michael Spavor, in apparent retaliation over the arrest by Canadian officials, and possible extradition to the U.S., of Huawei Technologies CFO Meng Wanzhou (孟晚舟) on 1 December 2018, on allegations of violating U.S. sanctions on Iran and committing bank fraud (Monga and Mackrael 2019). In many cases, officials have simply refused to consider new initiatives or contact with Taiwan on the *assumption* that China would react negatively. Beijing and vocal Chinese envoys, therefore, do not even have to do or say a thing: fear – and in some cases the feeling that a faux pas concerning Taiwan could cost one's ability to get a coveted promotion – does that for them. Much of this has also ridden on confusion, encouraged by Chinese officials and propagandists, between a country's "one China" *policy* and Beijing's "one China" *principle*.

142 The regional and global context

A number of countries have allowed official delegations from Taiwan, but insisted on certain protocols to limit the damage should Beijing find out. Here again, Taiwanese officials have swallowed their pride and focused on achieving their objectives rather than seek visibility and recognition for their efforts. A few countries have also been pondering renaming their representative offices in Taiwan, as Japan has done, so as to better reflect the near-embassy functions performed by those offices (in 2015 the U.K. representative office in Taiwan changed its name from British Trade and Cultural Office to the British Office, though officials were quick to emphasize that this was simply "rebranding") (*Taipei Times* 2015). Reluctance on the part of the governments back home, due to fears of "angering" Beijing if such efforts were discovered, or resulting from a wrong understanding of their government's "one China" policy, has resulted in delays and caused frustration among a number of officials and representatives posted in Taiwan, many of whom have endeavored to deepen their countries' ties with Taiwan.[1]

From bilateral security talks at the Track II level to the Quad and the Free and Open Indo-Pacific strategy, to exploring new investment opportunities and collaborating on combating emerging risks to the region, Taiwan and its counterparts have made good progress since 2016, in some cases building upon initial efforts that had been made by President Tsai's predecessors. For example, an ongoing, decade-plus-long program in which the Ministry of Justice Investigation Bureau (MJIB, 法務部調查局) provides training to hundreds of law-enforcement officers across Asia has been quite successful. The U.S.-Taiwan Global Cooperation and Training Framework (GCTF) (see Chapter 5), has also appealed to other regional partners who have expressed the desire to become involved in future rounds of meetings. Some have also begun assessing whether they should have their own version of GCTF with Taiwan. As we saw, Japan joined the initiative in 2019, as did Sweden for the summit on media literacy in September 2019. Much of this engagement has occurred at the academic or semiofficial level, although in a number of instances active government officials, in some cases at the minister level, have also participated. There is a lot going on at this level, including activities that even experts may not be aware of. Due to the sensitive nature of many of those, I have chosen not to discuss them in this book.

While GCTF-type forums, regular bilateral meetings or *ad hoc* measures are not ideal, they nevertheless represent important first steps in helping Taiwan work around the barriers that China has erected in its way, especially in Taipei's efforts to be invited to participate at multilateral organizations that require statehood or UN membership, such as Interpol, ICAO, the WHA, and others. Despite backroom efforts by democratic allies of Taiwan, including Japan and the U.S., to encourage those institutions to allow Taiwan to participate in a "meaningful" way (or simply as an observer), so far Beijing has prevailed upon those institutions, which is a key reminder of the level of influence it has built up, often with the complicity of many small undemocratic UN member states at the UN General Assembly (many of those organizations have also been headed by Chinese nationals in recent years). Unless this changes, Taiwan and its allies will need to find ways to institutionalize and widen the membership of platforms like GCTF in a way that gives Taiwan the ability to both contribute to the international community and draw from it the data, experience, and resources it may need in time of crisis (e.g., a new SARS outbreak, a major terror attack, or an airline disaster). Through a campaign organized by MOFA, Taiwan has signaled its intention of playing a full, constructive role within the international community, and pointed out the dangers of allowing politics to hijack Taiwan's integration, which has created a "blind spot" in the global network that one day could come back to haunt us. As some observers have put it, diseases, transnational crime, terrorists, smugglers, and air traffic do not recognize or care about artificial borders or Beijing's sovereignty claims over Taiwan. A global response to emerging threats to health and human security should also operate under this philosophy.

In several areas, government-organized nongovernmental organizations, known as GONGOs, have taken the lead in projects with their foreign counterparts and officials where direct contact with Taiwanese government agencies would have been more "controversial" to the host countries. Active and suitably empowered GONGOs have therefore been able to establish channels that would otherwise have been unavailable to the Taiwanese.

Official outreach by Taiwan with countries worldwide has also tended to depend on the personality of the heads of mission sent by Taipei. In countries where the representative is motivated, as in the U.K. Czech Republic and Germany, to use three European examples, relationships have developed in a promising direction. In others, as is the case at Taiwan's missions in much of the Middle East, lack of initiative has cost Taiwan.

Besides government-to-government and Track II exchanges, Taiwan has made good use of its role – or that of some of its political parties – in organizations like the Council of Asian Liberals and Democrats (CALD), Liberal International (LI) and the Community of Democracies (CD), although the latter has been reluctant to give Taiwan the visibility and full membership it deserves as a major donor country. Through these networks and others, Taiwan has developed ties with the civil societies in countries across the region, and helped promote and consolidate sound democratic practices, human rights, and transparency, all values that have gained currency as part of fledging efforts, by countries like Japan and the U.S., to provide a liberal-democratic alternative to the BRI authoritarian model proposed by China. Moreover, in some cases, members of civic organizations across Asia were eventually elected into government, as was the case with Malaysia's Bersih 2.0. There is a strong possibility that governments thus constituted will be more amenable to doing more engagement with Taiwan. In other words, cultivating ties at the level of civil society is an investment – not only does it encourage good governance across the region, but it can also create future partners who, one day, will be the rulers of the countries involved.

Much of this has also dovetailed with the NSP, a major initiative of the Tsai administration, which focuses not only on diversifying Taiwan's business and investment destinations to reduce its reliance on China (a phenomenon that had already

144 The regional and global context

begun in the last three years or so of the Ma Ying-jeou administration), but also on people-to-people ties, culture, science and technology. On business alone, exports to NSP countries grew 12 percent in 2017, the first full year of the policy's implementation. And as we saw earlier, tourism arrivals from select NSP countries have seen tremendous growth since 2016, more than making up for the drop in tourists from China.

Furthermore, while previous iterations of Taiwan's go-south policy focused primarily on Taiwanese businesses establishing a presence in Southeast Asia, under the NSP, ASEAN and South Asian businesses have also been invited to come and invest in Taiwan, "allowing for a mutual-cooperation system based on a two-way benefit channel." Conversely, while earlier policies sought to attract students from ASEAN and South Asia to come to Taiwan to study, the NSP also encourages Taiwanese to go study or have internships in the region, a policy that aims to establish closer ties culturally and linguistically between Taiwanese and future partners across the region. As of 2017, more students from ASEAN and South East countries were studying in Taiwan than there were from China. In March 2017, the Ministry of Education unveiled a New Southbound Talent Development Program (新南向人才培育計畫), which includes a NT$1 billion (US$3.3 million) investment to fund projects promoting education cooperation with NSP target states.

The more wholistic approach to the NSP, which emphasizes people-to-people relations, streamlined visa treatment for Southeast Asian visitors, city-to-city initiatives, and "soft power" – even ensuring that halal meals and restaurants are easily accessible to Muslim visitors – is therefore "an expansion of Taiwan's foreign policy."

As mentioned in the previous chapter, Japan's growing engagement with the region, alongside other key democratic players, could result in various opportunities for Taiwan to collaborate under the NSP, either as part of infrastructure projects or on many of the "softer" areas, which will nevertheless have an impact on democracy (where it exists) and good governance. Taipei has already expressed its desire to ride that wave; its ability to do so will be contingent on the willingness of the players involved to let it play a role. Itself a victim of devastating earthquakes and typhoons, Taiwan also has a wealth of experience in disaster relief and rescue operations that could be better utilized as part of its foreign policy and as a component of the NSP.

Despite the progress, the NSP remains vulnerable to political interference by China and the fact that Taiwan does not have official diplomatic relations with a single of the 18 countries targeted by this initiative. Consequently, should Beijing decide that the NSP is becoming too successful for its comfort, it could threaten retaliation against Taiwan's partners and pressure them under the "one China" policy. As Chen and Chattaraj (2018) have pointed out, two universities in the Philippines have already turned down a proposal by Kaohsiung's National Sun Yat-sen University (國立中山大學) to open a Southeast Asian research center there, largely due to the fact that Chinese universities have much greater resources to start similar initiatives. As a large number of agreements and MOUs are not signed at the government level, this can also pose a challenge in terms of future funding and long-term sustainability.

Thus far, the Chinese have mostly derided the NSP and downplayed its significance, in part to signal that the Tsai's administration's efforts to diversify Taiwan's economic partners are futile, and also because the NSP does not threaten China's much more ambitious BRI. There are two schools of thought on whether a larger role for the NSP, as part of, say, the FOIP strategy or Japan's new infrastructure investment initiative for the region, would make Beijing pay more attention to Taiwan's efforts: either it would compel Chinese authorities to crack down, or, conversely, the subsumption of Taiwan into a larger, multinational effort would confer greater protections. As this has yet to be tried, we can only speculate as to how Beijing would respond.

Finally, a few words on the Vatican, Taiwan's last official diplomatic ally in Europe. It is no secret that Beijing has long sought to encourage the Vatican to de-recognize Taiwan and embrace the PRC, home to an estimated 12 million Catholics, who are split between the state-approved Catholic Patriotic Association (中國天主教愛國會) and those who have sworn loyalty to the Vatican. Over the years, a dispute over the appointment of bishops, and the crackdown by Chinese authorities on non-state-sanctioned "underground" churches across China, have gotten in the way of the establishment of official ties between the two sides.

However, Beijing and the Vatican signed a landmark provisional agreement on 22 September 2018, giving the Holy See a say in the appointment of bishops in China and the Pope's decision to recognize seven Chinese bishops who had been appointed by the Chinese government without papal mandate (for the Vatican, those were regarded as "illicitly ordained"). Soon afterward, the Holy See also announced that Chinese bishops would for the first time be able to attend the synod – high level meetings – at the Vatican (Pullella 2018).

In a message to the Church in China on 26 September, Pope Francis admitted that the agreement had its limits, but saw hope in the fact that for the first time, "the stable elements of cooperation" had been set up so that Chinese authorities and the Vatican can "provide good shepherds for the Catholic community." The agreement is just an instrument, not a solution to all the existing problems, he said, adding "it will prove ineffective and unproductive, unless it is accompanied by a deep commitment to renewing personal attitudes and ecclesial forms of conduct" (Brockhaus 2018).

While the Vatican insists that the agreement is not political, many analysts regard this development as a precursor to just that. With this "deal with the devil," as some have put it, Beijing may have dangled the hook that will drag the Vatican inescapably toward official recognition. Through a gradual approach – by addressing existing problems one by one – Beijing could condition the Holy See and eventually make the entire deal conditional on the de-recognition of Taiwan. At this point, it will be very difficult for the Vatican to step back, even if it realizes that the CCP will continue to regard all religions with deep suspicion and therefore will not cease to impose various restrictions on assembly and practices. The long-elusive

146 The regional and global context

agreement Beijing has reached with the Vatican is not about religious freedom in China, despite what some optimists have alleged. Anyone who has seen what the CCP is doing to the practice of Islam in Xinjiang, to Buddhism in Tibet, or to Falun Gong practitioners knows that the party regards organized religion as a threat rather than an element of civil society that should be allowed to exist freely. The provisional agreement reached in September 2018 is primarily about control, and despite what the Holy See says, it is ineluctably political.

In concrete terms, the loss of the Vatican as an official diplomatic ally would have little impact on Taiwan. However, the psychological impact of such a development – and the loss of Taiwan's sole remaining official ally in Europe – would be felt, especially among Taiwan's own 300,000 or so Catholics. The loss of the Vatican would cause some administrative problems, such as finding new mechanisms by which the Catholic Church would administer Fu-Jen (輔仁大學) and Wenzao Ursuline (文藻外語大學) universities, but it would be entirely survivable, as was the loss of other small allies since 2016.

As this chapter has demonstrated, Taiwan continues to face a difficult international environment and must elaborate creative policies to engage partners in what often has to be unofficial capacity. While "quiet" and unofficial engagement can be injurious to Taiwan's dignity, this approach remains necessary for the time being, something that the Tsai administration appears to understand well. With the exception of the U.S. and Japan, the willingness of other countries to engage Taiwan cannot be taken for granted and is largely contingent on factors that are beyond Taipei's ability to control, chief among them global perceptions of China. So far the Tsai administration has benefited from a shift among many democratic countries, which has resulted in a harder stance on China. As we saw in Chapter 5, much of this can be attributed to Xi Jinping's megalomania. Taiwan should use this window of opportunity to build as many networks internationally as it can.

Revising domestic (oftentimes protectionist) regulations, which have long had a detrimental impact on the appeal of the Taiwanese market to foreign investors, is also largely overdue but should now be regarded as a matter of national security. Taiwan must urgently level the playing field for foreign firms, investors, and talent, under the assumption that the greater the presence of foreign interests in Taiwan, the least likely it is that China will use force to annex Taiwan as doing so would compromise the safety of a larger number of non-Taiwanese. In other words, foreign investment in Taiwan would help bolster Taiwan's deterrent capability – as does anything that tightens its connection with the international community. The Tsai government has taken important steps in achieving this objective. Much more needs to be done, and this is an effort that will need to be sustained for years to come, regardless of the party in power.

Note

1 To protect their identity (and governments), I do not name the many foreign officials who have discussed such matters with me over the years.

References

Brockhaus, Hannah (2018) "Pope Francis Urges Reconciliation in Message to Church in China," *Catholic News Agency*, 26 September. www.catholicnewsagency.com/news/pope-francis-urges-reconciliation-in-message-to-church-in-china-51391.

Canadian Department of Finance (2016) "Tax Arrangement Signed Between the Trade and Economic Offices of Canada and Taiwan," 18 January. www.fin.gc.ca/treaties-conventions/notices/taiwan-eng.asp.

Chen, Mumin and Saheli Chattaraj (2018) "New Southbound Policy in India and South Asia," *Prospect Journal*, Volume 18, p. 42. www.pf.org.tw/files/5976/80FADDFA-2240-4DE5-929E-76CED6C4D169.

Kang, Charles and Evelyn Kao (2018) "Taiwan Unveils Opening of New Trade Office in New Delhi," *Focus Taiwan*, 18 April. http://focustaiwan.tw/news/aeco/201804180019.aspx.

Kempinski, Yoni (2018) "Israel and Taiwan Growing Closer and Closer," *Arutz Cheva*, 2 May. www.israelnationalnews.com/News/News.aspx/245299.

Ku, Chuan and Evelyn Kao (2018) "Australia Sent Refugees to Taiwan for Urgent Medical Care: MOFA," *Focus Taiwan*, 24 June. http://focustaiwan.tw/news/aipl/201806240010.aspx.

Lawder, David (2018) "Trade Pact Clause Seen Deterring China Trade Deal with Canada, Mexico," *Reuters*, 3 October. www.reuters.com/article/us-trade-nafta-china/trade-pact-clause-seen-deterring-china-trade-deal-with-canada-mexico-idUSKCN1MC305.

Lehre, Eric (2018) "Rethinking the Taiwan Question: How Canada Can Update Its Rigid 'One China' Policy for the 21st Century," MacDonald-Laurier Institute, September. https://macdonaldlaurier.ca/files/pdf/20180828_MLI_Taiwan_PAPER_FINAL_Webready.pdf.

Monga, Vipal and Kim Mackrael (2019) "Court Filings Shed New Light on Arrest of Huawei Executive," *Wall Street Journal*, 23 August. www.wsj.com/articles/court-filings-shed-new-light-on-arrest-of-huawei-executive-11566581148.

Pullella, Philip (2018) "After Vatican-China Deal Taiwan Says Beijing Wants to Make It Irrelevant," *Reuters*, 3 October. www.reuters.com/article/us-pope-china-taiwan/after-vatican-china-deal-taiwan-says-beijing-wants-to-make-it-irrelevant-idUSKCN1M-C2BH.

Rigger, Shelley (2011) *Why Taiwan Matters: Small Island, Global Powerhouse*, Plymouth: Rowman & Littlefield.

Shoshanna Solomon (2018) "Israeli chutzpah, Taiwan's Confucian Culture Can Be a 'Great Match' in Business," *Times of Israel*, 6 May. www.timesofisrael.com/israeli-chutzpah-taiwans-confucian-culture-can-be-a-great-match-in-business/.

Taipei Times (2015) "Representative Says British Office Name Only 'a Rebranding'," 28 May. www.taipeitimes.com/News/taiwan/archives/2015/05/28/2003619366.

PART 3
The road ahead

8
DEMOCRACY UNDER THE DPP
A scorecard

As this book and its predecessor have argued, Taiwan's strongest prophylactic against Beijing's annexationist designs is its robust democracy. While authoritarians revel in their ability to dictate means and outcomes in their countries, and benefit from similar mechanisms in countries with which they conduct business, democracy imposes a series of accountability rules, checks and balances, and inherent correctives that often will frustrate the aspirations of autocrats. As I argued in *Convenient*, the CCP resents Taiwan's democracy not because, as is often argued, it challenges the prevailing system of governance in China, but primarily because it erects a firewall around Taiwan that makes achieving Beijing's objectives – on Beijing's terms – a nearly impossible task.

The CCP's multifaceted assault on Taiwan's democratic institutions, described in this volume and its predecessor, is therefore an attempt to erode, undermine, discredit, and bypass the institutions and codes of conduct agreed upon by Taiwanese society so as to facilitate the achievement of its political objectives. For all its "cumbersome inefficiency," as Grayling (2017) describes it, democracy offers in return "civil liberties and the involvement of the enfranchised part of the population in legitimizing government." By ensuring civil liberties and empowering the public, democracy makes it likelier that people will have a say in the formulation and implementation of policies, especially on matters that pertain to the very existence of the state. It provides insurance against abrupt changes in policy by government officials, and in Taiwan's case, it makes it highly unlikely that a president or government will be able to sell Taiwan out to the Chinese, as some alleged former president Ma intended to do. A good indication of the robustness of Taiwan's democracy – and of the authorities' need to bend to its will – was the Sunflower Movement of 2014, which nixed a controversial cross-Strait services trade agreement and prevented the Ma administration from getting closer to Beijing for the remainder of its term. Without checks and balances, the promise of electoral

152 The road ahead

retribution and an empowered civil society that can step in when democratic institutions are seen to be failing, the Ma administration would have enacted the controversial agreement, and Beijing most assuredly would have followed with a series of additional measures meant to further draw Taiwan into its sphere of influence. Thanks to Taiwan's democracy and the willingness of political parties to respect its rules, the Taiwanese public decided how far they wanted the Ma administration to go in its rapprochement with China. And with the 2016 elections, they chose to elect a leader who promised a more cautious approach to cross-Strait relations – a choice that the outgoing KMT had to respect.

Democracy, however, is a pendulum, not an end state. Thus, it is in constant need of maintenance and must be improved upon to ensure its ability to adapt to a changing environment. It is not sufficient to say that a country has a democracy and to expect that this means of governance will ensure the state's well-being in perpetuity. It is therefore important to constantly assess how well a government is doing in terms of its respect for democratic norms and efforts to ameliorate the country's democratic institutions. If a government behaves in such a manner as undermines the good functioning of democratic instruments, the firewall will inevitably be weakened.

This chapter briefly discusses some of the key democracy-related issues that have emerged under the Tsai administration and assesses their impact on the status of Taiwan's democracy. *Convenient* was rather critical of the KMT administration's track record on democracy, and somewhat more favorable of the DPP, if only because the latter was part of the opposition during the period covered in that book. Now that the DPP is in power, the health of Taiwan's democracy is primarily its responsibility. And one thing is certain: governing is far more difficult than being the opposition, and the ideals that one espouses outside government will often be compromised – or become the objects of compromise – once an individual or organization has joined the system.

Two items that were at the top of the Tsai administration's agenda after it entered office have sparked controversy and raised alarms among the government's critics. Those are pension reform and transitional justice. In the first case, reform of an overly generous pension system for public servants, teachers, and members of the armed forces, was seen as necessary, both for the preservation of state coffers and from the perspective of generational rights. For far too long, retired public servants had received pensions that were regarded as overly generous, unfair to new entrants in the workforce, and a real threat to the nation's finances. Both the Chen Shui-bian and Ma Ying-jeou governments had signaled their intention to tackle the issue, only to back down after facing opposition from pensioners themselves and the system that upheld that unjust tradition – a legacy, as many saw it, of the patronage system implemented by the KMT during the authoritarian era to keep public servants on side.

President Tsai came into office determined to reform the cash-strapped pension system, come what may. This was an instance where the usually careful president put her foot down, deflecting heavy criticism from some circles, mass protests, and even threats to her personal safety when it was discovered that her security detail had likely been penetrated by protest groups (e.g., the "800 Heroes") with close ties to the security/military establishment (among other things, protesters had an uncanny way of knowing the president's schedule wherever she went).

Pension reform

At the heart of the controversy was the preferential savings rate that retired public servants were entitled to. That rate has undergone several adjustments since its introduction, from 21.6 percent initially to 14.25 percent in 1970, then 16.7 percent in 1979 and 18 percent in 1983. Following the implementation of a new pension system in 1995, the preferential interest rate was scrapped, while civil servants' pension benefits were increased by permitting part of an employee's monthly income to be deposited in the pension fund. In other words, from 1995, the government no longer was the sole contributor to a public servant's pension.

However, public servants who were hired before 1995 were still entitled to the saving rate of 18 percent after retirement (how much of a retiree's pension payment was eligible for the interest rate was contingent on pre-retirement income and the number of years of service prior to 1995). According to the Presidential Office's Pension Reform Committee, as of June 2016, as much as NT$462 billion (US$15 billion) in pension payments for an estimated 457,000 public-sector retirees were stored in bank accounts eligible for the 18 percent interest rating. This meant an unsustainable NT$82 billion draw on government coffers each year. According to some estimates, the pension system could have gone bankrupt as early as 2020 for military veterans, 2030 for public school teachers, and 2031 for civil servants.

The new pension reform is affecting about 130,000 public servants, 140,000 public school teachers, and 63,000 military veterans. According to the bill, the preferential 18 percent interest rate on savings for those who receive NT$32,160 per month or more in retirement income was reduced to 9 percent from 1 July 2018 to 31 December 2020, and cut to zero starting on 1 January 2021. The income replacement rate for pensioners who are receiving NT$32,160 per month or more is also to be gradually lowered. The income replacement rate for public servants with 35 years of service will be reduced from 75 percent to 60 percent over a decade, and those with 15 years of service will see a decrease from 45 percent to 30 percent over the same period. The minimum age of retirement with full pension for civil servants will be 60 starting in 2021, and will be raised by one year until 2026, when it will be set at 65. Retirement for hardship jobs will remain lower (Lee and Low 2017).

Cuts to military pensions, meanwhile, were relatively milder and, no doubt, were meant to avoid straining relations with the armed forces. Under the reformed pension program, military veterans will see a 20 percent cut or so to their monthly stipend over a decade. For example, the monthly stipend for a retired lieutenant colonel will initially be cut from approximately NT$71,000 to a little more than

NT\$69,000, and eventually to approximately NT\$56,400 after a decade (Agence France-Presse 2018).

Reforms to the pension system have undoubtedly created losers, at least as seen from the perspective of one's monthly allowance. Some disgruntled targets turned to fabrication and "fake news" to depict themselves as hapless victims who could no longer afford to have a decent meal. In reality, many retired public servants had ample savings, fully paid houses, and spent their retirement money on themselves and other family members vacationing abroad. The relatively low cost of living in Taiwan, furthermore, meant that reduced pensions were still more than sufficient to meet a retiree's basic needs. That retired public servants and military veterans should be looked after for the services they rendered to the nation is obvious. But the preferential rate had become unsustainable and was utterly unfair to young Taiwanese, whose salaries are in many cases lower than the pension received by retirees, and who cannot afford to purchase a house in big cities. As President Tsai made clear, this endeavor was about generational justice and a reallocation of money for future generations. While this income redistribution did create losers, it was a necessary affair, and despite the loud protests by the groups affected, the public was supportive of the government's efforts.

Transitional justice

Meanwhile, in May 2018 a Transitional Justice Commission (促進轉型正義委員會) was launched, which was charged with uncovering political repression during the White Terror era. Among other things, the Commission, which operates under the guidance of the Act on Promoting Transitional Justice (促進轉型正義條例) passed in December 2017, was to launch systematic truth-seeking investigations to establish responsibility and to set up a legal mechanism for the rehabilitation of victims. Additionally, political archives, which have long been inaccessible to the public, will be made more readily available, and a report on the history of the period is to be produced. The first outcome of the Commission's efforts occurred in early October 2018, when a total of 1,270 victims of the White Terror, who suffered political persecution during the martial law period, were pardoned by President Tsai following an investigation by the Commission. Their records of "illegal activity" during the martial law era were cleansed.

Although Commission chairman Huang Huang-hsiung (黃煌雄), who resigned in October 2018, emphasized that the main task of the Commission was to seek and disclose the facts of the authoritarian era rather than settle old scores, critics of transitional justice – including many in the KMT – depicted the effort as an attempt by the DPP to create new enmities and bring the party to its knees. Many of the perpetrators of political repression during the White Terror are still active today, and some were even candidates in the November 2018 local elections. Many say they were simply following orders and that, moreover, the KMT has transformed itself since democratization and should therefore not be targeted for the sins of the past.

The Tsai administration has had to strike a balance between uncovering past wrongs, attributing blame, and ensuring justice for the many victims of political repression. In a highly politicized environment like Taiwan, efforts to redress past wrongs and to bring perpetrators to some sort of account were sure to cause controversy and spark accusations that the Tsai government had unleashed a "green terror" against its opponents. Any society that has undergone transitional justice, such as South Africa, Rwanda, and the former Czechoslovakia, has struggled with the contradictions inherent to truth and reconciliation (T&R). For many of the victims, no healing is possible without the perpetrators being brought to justice; in some cases, it will be sufficient for only the top officials involved in the formulation and implementation of repressive policies, while in others, punishment should be imposed on the whole of the perpetrators. In some countries, contrition is sufficient for reconciliation; in others, imprisonment is seen as a necessary form of redress. There is no easy formula, and each country that has had to deal with a dark past has to come up with its own formula, even if informed by the precedents set in other countries. As the South African experience has shown us, full transitional justice cannot solely be limited to identifying perpetrators and victims, and some process of reconciliation. The systemic imbalances created by authoritarianism, in which one group of people lorded it over another group, must also be addressed otherwise that imbalance will perpetuate itself well after T&R has completed its efforts. Consequently, in Taiwan, alongside the opening of archives, the attribution of blame and reconciliation, it will be necessary for the Commission to return to their initial owners property that was illegally seized by the KMT after 1949 and from which the party profited immensely over decades, giving it an unfair financial advantage over its opponents. South Africa, with its emphasis on reconciliation, neglected to address the systemic imbalance created by apartheid, and as a result South Africans of color today remain at a disadvantage against their white cohorts (Msimang 2018).

As with pension reform, transitional justice creates winners and losers and can widen divisions within society. If T&R efforts emphasize the punitive aspects too much and are seen to be largely retributive, the backlash can be severe and the process of reconciliation can be undermined. Conversely, if efforts are too focused on reconciliation, victims and their descendants will accuse the government of failing to punish perpetrators accordingly and the wounds of the past will continue to bleed. And as just mentioned, the very infrastructure of domination that characterizes authoritarian and totalitarian rule must also be dismantled if transitional justice is to have any long-lasting impact on society. It will be years before Taiwan can settle this matter, and whatever the outcome, it is certain to spark discontent on either side of the divide. Given Taiwan's precarious position and Beijing's tendency to exploit every division in Taiwanese politics, the government will have to tread carefully on this subject, and must not act in a way that threatens major hostilities between the two sides. It must also avoid exploiting its current advantage as the party in power to exact vengeance on its political opponents, which would risk sparking a new cycle of attacks and counterattacks that can only result in a

156 The road ahead

weakening of the nation's political fabric. Taiwan is probably alone in all the countries that have undergone truth and reconciliation in that it began the process while facing an external existential threat.

Indigenous rights

Alongside transitional justice efforts targeting Taiwan's authoritarian past, the Tsai administration has also appealed to Taiwan's indigenous communities, who have long been the victims of colonization and unfair treatment by successive governments. A special committee for transitional justice for Indigenous peoples was also set up by the Tsai government. The first step began with an official apology by President Tsai in early August 2016 for "centuries of pain and mistreatment" (Ramzy 2016). Tsai said:

> In the future, we will push for policies to ensure that succeeding generations of indigenous tribes and all ethnic peoples in Taiwan never lose their languages and memories, that they are never separated from their cultural traditions, and that never again are they lost in a land of their own.

The landmark apology, which received international coverage, also reflected a conscious effort by the Tsai government to celebrate the indigenous aspects of Taiwan's culture. However, despite the apology and embracing of indigenous culture on the national stage, the corporate predations of aboriginal land has continued under the DPP, as has the divide between local tribes and officials at the Council of Indigenous Peoples (CAP, 中華民國原住民族委員會) who have been appointed to look after their interests. Among other things, indigenous activists from the Indigenous Youth Front and other groups have expressed discontent over the government's Regulations for Delimiting Indigenous and Tribal Range Land, which only apply "natural territory" to public land and exclude privately owned land. According to activists, many plots of private land owned by corporations today were forcibly seized from indigenous populations in the colonial era, then transferred to state-owned enterprises under the KMT and eventually privatized. Indigenous activists argue that the new regulations implemented by the Tsai administration amount to "justifying a theft of the 1 million hectares of indigenous land (out of 1.8 hectares of indigenous lands on the East Coast) that have been designated as private property" (Simon 2017).

Privately owned land on territory that once belonged to Indigenous peoples has also been used for various development projects over which local tribes have had no say. Indigenous groups have held sit-ins in front of the Presidential Office and called on the Tsai government to return sovereignty of such lands to Indigenous peoples. A 20-year extension of mining rights for Asia Cement Corp (亞洲水泥) to continue its activities on Truku traditional territory in Hualien County's Hsiulin Township (秀林) also sparked protests in June 2017, this time bringing together indigenous activists as well as environmental groups.

Despite dialogue between the government and indigenous representatives, vertical tensions remain and indigenous communities remain wary of the central government's intentions, and practices of co-optation are still very much active at various levels. Thus, despite progress and promising signaling by the Tsai administration, longstanding tensions between indigenous rights and corporate/political needs remain an unresolved issue, even under the DPP. Lack of progress on the controversies has led some indigenous activists to question the legitimacy of President Tsai's apology to Indigenous peoples and to transitional justice for the first occupants of this land.

Besides issues surrounding traditional indigenous land, land issues in general continue to be a source of discontent around Taiwan, highlighting tensions between individual rights on the one hand, and urban renewal as well as development on the other. Although there have not been as many cases as during the Ma presidency – some incidents, such as the forced evictions in Taipei's Huaguang Community (華光社區) and Miaoli County's Dapu Borough (大埔), sparked massive protests in 2013 and the brief occupation of the Ministry of the Interior in August that year – land remains a precious and highly lucrative commodity in Taiwan, and weaker members of society are regularly the losers in the resulting battles.

Death penalty

The Tsai administration has also come under criticism for the execution of a death row inmate in August 2018, the first since the DPP assumed office (the last execution occurred on 10 May 2016, ten days before Tsai's inauguration). Despite the high support among the population for the death penalty, state executions attract condemnation from the international community and human rights activists, and put Taiwan alongside a number of countries with poor human rights records. Only four advanced industrialized states still carry out the death penalty – the U.S., Japan, Singapore, and Taiwan. A total of 53 countries worldwide still carry out executions (Smith 2018). Furthermore, the timing of executions has often led to speculation that such measures are meant to bolster support for the ruling party ahead of elections or to rescue an embattled administration. With the execution, Tsai broke with a "freeze" that had been imposed by former president Chen Shui-bian in 2006, and which, after their resumption under president Ma, had been expected to continue now that the DPP was once again in power. Before the freeze, a total of 32 inmates on death row had been executed during the Chen presidency. A total of 33 inmates were executed during the Ma administration between 2008 and 2016. There was little secret that Tsai's first minister of justice, Chiu Tai-san (邱太三), was not keen on the death penalty, and that as long as he held office, no execution was likely to take place, this despite his public remarks that abolishing the death penalty was not on the government's agenda. Ironically, Tsai Ching-hsiang (蔡清祥), who replaced Chiu as minister of justice in July 2018 and ordered the execution, later said that the government's policy to gradually move toward abolition of the death penalty remained unchanged. It was clear, therefore, that there was disagreement

158 The road ahead

within the administration. But public pressure, especially in the wake of a series of gruesome murders in Taiwan, compelled the authorities to resume executions. Whether this was part of political calculations ahead of the November elections was anyone's guess. For Taiwan's signaling to its allies in the international community, the resumption of executions was a blemish on its track record. Unlike what some critics have argued, the death penalty is not prohibited under the International Covenant on Civil and Political Rights (ICCPR), which Taiwan ratified in 2009.

From a human rights perspective, it once again raised the possibility of wrongful executions – such as that of 21-year-old Air Force private Chiang Kuo-ching (江國慶) in 1997 – while reinvigorating the debate on whether the death penalty acts as a deterrent against acts of murder. In this author's view, it does not, simply because any individual who is ready to kill another human being (other than in a war situation) is already in a state of mind where rational cost-versus-benefit analysis of one's actions no longer applies. A better way of ensuring that murderers cannot be repeat offenders would be for Taiwan to adopt life sentences without parole; otherwise, the public – and the families of victims – will understandably be opposed to any possible release of an individual who murdered a loved one.

As with land and indigenous issues, the resumption of executions cost the DPP administration support among the more progressive, and often younger, members of Taiwanese society, as well as within the NGO community.

Same-sex marriage, conservative forces, direct democracy

The issue that may have hurt the Tsai government the most – at least for the first three years – is that of marriage equality, which had been one of the major components of the DPP's election campaign in 2016. In the lead-up to the elections, the DPP had released several campaign videos in which same-sex couples were featured, and many items in the party paraphernalia bore LGBTQI colors and symbols, including the lanyards that many government employees who came in with Tsai still wear in the office today.

Of all the issues that attracted international attention in the run-up to 2016 – from cross-Strait relations to the likelihood that Taiwan would get its first female head of state – marriage equality was one that captivated the imagination abroad, especially as it meant that Taiwan could become the first country in Asia to legalize same-sex unions. For young Taiwanese, 80 percent of whom support legalization, according to various opinion polls, LGBTQI rights was also an issue of self-identification: it helped position Taiwan as a progressive nation, in sharp contrast with the situation in China and elsewhere in the region.

With the DPP gaining control of the executive and legislative branches of government, it appeared that the stars were aligned and that Taiwan, which already was host to the largest gay pride parade in Asia, would soon make history. Rather than deliver, the Tsai administration stalled. It soon became evident that, notwithstanding the campaign rhetoric, legalization of same-sex marriage was not a top priority for the new government, which instead moved on matters such as pension reform, transitional justice, and labor laws. All those were no doubt pressing issues, but for the LGBTQI community and observers abroad, the lack of interest in marriage equality was a letdown, if not inexplicable. Worse, it soon led to accusations that the DPP had raised the issue to attract votes in the 2016 elections. Whether that was true or not (and there were many ardent supporters of the cause in the DPP), the optics were bad, and those who awaited legalization – either for their own personal needs or to celebrate the progress made by Taiwanese society – were sorely disappointed. Even worse, the administration's foot-dragging on the issue provided the time and space opponents of legalization needed to organize and ramp up their activities. Soon, groups purporting to defend the rights of the family and of children unleashed a series of protests and campaigns pressuring the Tsai administration and seeking to convince society of the terrible fate that awaited them should same-sex marriages be permitted by law.

The anti-legalization movement was largely led by conservative Christian churches, which replicated the memes spread by similar religious organizations in the West, such as the International House of Prayer (IHOP). One U.S.-based group, MassResistance, even became involved in the campaign in Taiwan and provided literature that was distributed at rallies (Cole 2017). Despite being a minority, those groups were well organized, resourceful, and they sensed weakness. The more noise they made, the more concessions the Tsai administration made, such as stating that more dialogue and understanding, more hearings, were needed. Rather than deliver, the Tsai government created a false moral equivalence between those who advocated for the extension of human rights, and those who, using an unscientific and intolerant religious worldview as their basis, sought to curtail the rights of certain individuals based on their sexual identity.

What made matters worse was the fact that the Presbyterian Church of Taiwan also came out in opposition to the legalization of same-sex marriage. Due to its historical ties with the DPP as part of the *dangwai* (黨外) movement, the Presbyterian Church had long advocated for human rights. But on the issue of same-sex marriage, the institution chose to side with conservative forces within Taiwanese society. That variable made the DPP more reluctant to act on its campaign promise, as members of the Church threatened to boycott the DPP in future elections if it moved toward legalization. Some DPP legislators, among them Tainan's Wang Ding-yu (王定宇), were even threatened with recall action should they continue to express their support.

Then for a while it looked like the Tsai administration would no longer have to make a decision when the Council of Grand Justices, in a landmark ruling on 24 May 2017 announced that it was unconstitutional to deny individuals of the same sex to get married. The ruling gave the government two years to formulate appropriate legislation; failing that, the law would automatically come into force. While the unprecedented move by the Grand Justices gave wings to the LGBTQI movement, opponents also saw it as illegitimate. After all, it wasn't the government that had made the decision, but simply a small group of judges (14 out of 15 after one recused himself) appointed by Tsai and Ma over the years. Rather than see this

160 The road ahead

as a defeat, conservatives redoubled their efforts to pressure the government and convince society.

As the issue ground to a halt, conservative groups like the Greater Taipei Stability Power Alliance (安定力量), which was associated with the Faith and Hope League (信心希望聯盟), a political party that ran on an anti-same-sex marriage platform in 2016, began targeting politicians with recall action. Ironically, reforms to the Civil Servants Election and Recall Act (公職人員選舉罷免法) initiated by progressive legislators who tended to favor same-sex marriage legalization now made it easier to initiate, and to pass, attempted recalls against elected politicians. One such effort was made against Huang Kuo-chang (黃國昌) of the New Power Party (NPP). Votes in favor of recalling Huang totaled 48,693, against 21,748 who opposed. Under new recall rules, one-fourth of the 255,551 constituents in the electoral district needed to take part in the vote, and of them 63,888 needed to vote in favor of a recall for Huang to be unseated (*Commonwealth Magazine* 2017). Turnout was 27.75 percent. Although the highly publicized recall attempt failed, it nevertheless demonstrated the problems associated with referenda and recall mechanisms. The same groups then threatened similar action against Wang Ding-yu and Hsiao Bi-khim (蕭美琴), both of the DPP (recall action was among the strategies proposed by MassResistance for its campaign in the U.S.).

The most troubling aspect of the recall attempt against Huang was the dangerous precedent it would have set had it been successful. At issue was the negative impact such recalls can have on Taiwan's democracy, regardless of who the targeted official is. With it, a marginal group demonstrated that it is now possible to unseat just about any elected official who won by a close margin in an election, regardless of that official's actual performance (Citizen Congress Watch 公民監督國會聯盟 gave Huang top grades). All that is needed is an argument – in the present case religious-based opposition to marriage equality – and the mobilization of enough voters who supported the runner-up in the previous election (e.g., the KMT candidate), and one of the key elements of a healthy democracy – regular elections – could be thrown out the window.

Concretely, what this means is that democratically elected legislators – and those who elected them – no longer have the assurance that they will be able to complete their full four-year term in office. Delinquency, the reason why a recall should be launched (and which, like him or not, certainly does not apply to Huang), is no longer the sole justification for a recall to be initiated. This is a serious flaw in the current recall laws in Taiwan and a recipe for instability in electoral processes, especially in the age of disinformation (i.e., "fake news"), where a small group like the Greater Taipei Stability Power Alliance can now succeed, using fabrication, social media, and money, in creating enough momentum to initiate a recall attempt, and maybe one day in unseating an elected official. Recalls should only be initiated in exceptional circumstances; they should never turn into an instrument for narrow-interest groups (in this case ultraconservative religious churches) or crass politicians who seek to undo electoral results by expediting the ouster of one's opponent and thereby derail the regular course of democratic politics. Since lower thresholds are now law, there ought to be some evaluation committee in charge of determining whether a recall attempt is made on reasonable grounds.

Huang was duly elected, and his views on same-sex marriage were well known before and during the election campaign. As a participant in Taiwan's democratic experiment, the Alliance should therefore respect the wishes of the majority, and must not be allowed to turn democracy against itself in the pursuance of its bigoted policies. Conservatives are welcome to field their own candidates in 2018 and 2020, and see whether they can attract enough votes. Before then, they must respect the outcome of the previous elections.

Undeterred by the failed recall attempt, conservative groups then initiated a referendum to prevent implementation of same-sex legislation, in a signature drive that was marred by claims of irregularities. As with the recall attempt, opponents of same-sex marriage relied on fear and disinformation – spread on Facebook, Line, and other social media – to gather signatures, even when canvassing neighborhoods. The referendum, held concurrently with local elections on 24 November 2018, played in the conservative's favor and marked a setback for those who hoped Taiwan would become the first country in Asia to legalize same-sex marriage (Hsu 2018). The Tsai administration's ostensible lack of leadership on the issue had allowed religious-conservative groups to hijack the policy process (the same groups have now signaled their intent to initiate a referendum that would make it illegal to seek an abortion beyond eight weeks into a pregnancy).

A disorganized oversight of the elections and 10 concurrent referendum questions also reflected poorly on Tsai's appointment to head the Central Election Commission (CEC, 中央選舉委員會), who stepped down after the election.

Then, in another turn in a long and eventful journey, the Taiwanese legislature in May 2019 finally passed a bill legalizing same-sex unions, although it did not amend the constitution which states that marriage could only occur between a man and a woman. The bill came into effect on 24 May 2019 (Hollingsworth 2018). Undeterred, conservative organizations and at least one candidate in the 2020 presidential elections – the KMT's Han Kuo-yu – have vowed to seek ways to overturn the bill.

Lowering thresholds for referenda was probably a mistake in Taiwan at this point, due to the high political polarization, and exposed policy making to the vagaries of populism and disinformation. It is a dangerous instrument, which, ironically, the current government and its allies in the NPP have unleashed.

Fishing industry, migrant workers, human trafficking

Another area where conditions have not improved markedly since President Tsai took office include the fishing industry, where labor and human rights violations involving migrant workers on fishing vessels operated by Taiwanese – especially distant-water fishing (DWF) – remain frequent. In a report titled "Misery at Sea," Greenpeace (2018) writes that "Plagued by environmental and human rights abuses, Taiwan's DWF fleet has become a major embarrassment for a global fishing power that relies on its credibility and reputation for market share." Despite legislative

162 The road ahead

attempts in recent years to tackle the problems with the industry, "systemic IUU [illegal, unreported and unregulated] fishing, egregious human rights abuses, and an ineffective Taiwanese Fisheries Agency (FA) [have been] repeatedly failing to uncover, prosecute, or resolve widespread offending," the report continues, adding that "Taiwan's governmental and Fisheries Association's actions in response to earlier exposed cases have been largely ineffective." Forced labor, exploitation and "poor working conditions of foreign fishing crews on Taiwan-flagged long-haul vessels" remain an issue. The Taiwan International Workers' Association and other civic organizations have called on Taiwanese authorities and ship owners to better protect foreign fishermen. In 2017, amendments were made to the Labor Standards Act (勞動基準法) to fill the gaps in the Human Trafficking Prevention Act (人口販運防制法) of 2009, which excluded distant-sea fishing from Taiwan's jurisdiction. However, insufficient resources and education, and a lack of willingness on behalf of legislators, have undermined efforts to end the rampant violations.

Abuses of migrant workers by brokerage firms, including what critics have called "exorbitant fees" for basic services, also continue, and a grading system by the Ministry of Labor does not appear to have had a significant impact on the practice. The Taiwan International Workers Association (TIWA, 臺灣國際勞工協會) and other advocacy groups have called for the abolition of exploitative brokerage firms. In its 2017 human rights report on Taiwan, the U.S. Department of State Bureau of Democracy, Human Rights and Labor (2017) stated that the high fees that are commonly charged by brokers leave workers "vulnerable to debt bondage." In April 2017, amendments were made to the Standards for Fee-Charging Items and Amounts of the Private Employment Services Institution (私立就業服務機構收費項目及金額標準), which reduced the maximum fee a broker can charge a migrant worker to no more than NT$1,500 per month more than NT$1,500 from a worker's third year. Revisions have also removed a provision requiring that migrant workers who have worked for three years – the maximum period allowed by contract – to leave Taiwan for at least one day before they could be rehired. Under the new law, migrant workers no longer have to leave the country before signing a new contract. While conditions for migrant workers remain imperfect and subject to exploitation, these measures have improved the system. As part of the New Southbound Policy, the Tsai administration's outreach to South and Southeast Asians, where the majority of foreign workers come from, has also fostered a friendlier environment for individuals from this part of the world, which hopefully will be conducive to further improvements in regulations. Doing so is essential for Taiwan's image and a reputation in a part of the world that is increasingly important for Taiwan's future.

Countering foreign forces and subversion

One area, which has already been touched on in this volume, is the participation in Taiwan's democratic processes of groups and parties whose objectives may very well run counter to the democratic ideal and therefore to Taiwan's security. Although

Taiwanese can take great pride in having a democracy that is mature enough it can countenance participation by individuals and political parties that espouse a great variety of views and ideologies – which certainly contrasts with the closed political environment across the Taiwan Strait – there nevertheless should be limits to what parties can do as part of their political activities. Parties, such as the China Unification Promotion Party (CUPP) and the Taiwan Red Party (TRP), that ostensibly seek to subvert Taiwan and which, if proved by an investigation, are receiving illegal funding from the a foreign government, should not be allowed to participate in the nation's democratic processes.

Plurality of opinion is an important component of democracy, but parties and their representatives should be accountable to the system that permits their activities and demonstrate their willingness to play by certain established rules. Permissiveness and toleration of different views are strengths of democracy, but if elements within it have a demonstrated commitment to undermining the system, then allowing their continued existence turns into a dangerous exercise in naivety and carelessness. Given their stated aims and suspected practices – illegal funding, ties to organized crime, intimidation tactics, pro-unification views, and relationship with an exogenous anti-democratic regime – parties like the CUPP and the TRP (discussed in Chapter 2) inarguably constitute a threat to Taiwan's democratic institutions and should be dealt with accordingly. Negligence will come at a cost. For most of the period under Ma, the CUPP and its affiliates were able to operate with impunity. Since Tsai took office, the CUPP and its affiliate, the Bamboo Union crime syndicate, have been targeted by raids and their funding investigated by prosecutors. Arguably much more needs to be done to ensure that such parties, as well as other suspected proxies of the CCP, are compliant and do not pose a subversion risk.

To this end, in 2019 the Tsai administration made several revisions to bills governing national security, with changes to the Criminal Code (刑法), the Act Governing Relations between the People of the Taiwan Area and the Mainland Area (兩岸人民關係條例), the Classified National Security Information Protection Act (國家機密保護法), and the National Security Act (國家安全法). Among other things, the revised bills impose more serious sentences for individuals who pass classified information to CCP agents. As of the end of 2019, the ruling DPP was also trying to introduce a "foreign agents bill" modeled on the U.S.' Foreign Agents Registration Act and Australia's national security and foreign interference laws enacted in 2018. Opposition KMT lawmakers have attempted to block the bill, alleging that it would put Taiwanese working in China – *Taishang* and the heads of Taiwan Business Associations representing their interests in China, who must collaborate with representatives of the TAO at the local level (Schubert 2016) – in a difficult position; the DPP rejects the claim that this measure is aimed at this category of Taiwanese.

While such laws were long overdue and necessary to defend Taiwan's democratic institutions against hostile activities both domestic and external, every effort should nevertheless be made to ensure that parties which comply with the law, regardless of their views and ideology, are allowed to participate in Taiwan's democratic processes and to field candidates in elections. When addressing existential threats, there is always a risk that the government will overshoot or engage the nation on a slippery slope that can eventually undermine the health of a democracy. Despite accusations by some KMT lawmakers and Chinese officials who have sought to create a "moral equivalence," there is no reason to conclude at this point that the Tsai administration has violated the cardinal rules or that it is using the threat of external influence to gain an unfair advantage over its political opponents in Taiwan.

Related to this is oversight of the nation's law-enforcement and intelligence agencies, primarily the Ministry of Justice Investigation Bureau and the National Security Bureau (NSB, 中華民國國家安全局). Currently, oversight of those agencies is mostly carried out in the legislature, whereby the director generals are called in for regular grilling by members of parliament. There are several problems with this practice. For one, legislators often "grandstand" for political effect, with little attention being paid to the actual issues. A number of them are not qualified to discuss the complexities of law enforcement and intelligence collection. Moreover, legislators will occasionally bring human rights activists along, resulting in review sessions that achieve little more than to humiliate the head of agency. The echoes of Taiwan's authoritarian era still reverberate through the ages and continue to taint public perceptions of security and intelligence bodies, who are still often regarded as untrustworthy or the enemy, even. Yet another problem is the fact that legislators (let alone civil society) do not have the appropriate security clearance to discuss such matters, and the venue itself, the Legislative Yuan, is not secure. This situation compels agency director generals to speak in vague terms or to hide information, which in turns sparks accusations that they are acting unaccountably.

To address this deficiency, Taiwan should adopt the system already in place in other advanced democracies and establish proper oversight agencies and review committees that are staffed with individuals who have the right background and a security clearance. Such oversight mechanisms are not perfect, and their ability to access all classified information is often curtailed by the very agencies being scrutinized, but such mechanisms are nevertheless in a much better position to ensure both that security agencies remain accountable and that sensitive information is not released accidentally, which can in turn compromise an ongoing investigation.

Despite the lacunae described in this chapter, Taiwan remains the freest country in Asia in terms of freedom of the press, something that has continued under the DPP. It also remains a champion of human rights and democracy, and through organizations such as the Taiwan Foundation for Democracy (TFD, 臺灣民主基金會) it has empowered various individuals, groups, and parties around the world who also espouse the values of democracy. Though imperfect and rambunctious, Taiwan's democracy remains an essential firewall, and an instrument of its foreign policy. The democratic ideal is now indivisible from how Taiwanese identify themselves, even if they are critical of the very institutions that are charged with its protection. Despite its flaws, it is not, as a poster promoting a speech by former premier under Ma Ying-jeou, Jiang Yi-huah (江宜樺), stated

> tainted by a serious divide of national identity, relentless partisan politics, disfunction of government, disrespect of the law, and notorious manipulation of mass media. The shortcomings of Taiwanese democracy is [sic] so appalling that more and more people become suspicious of the desirability of democracy in general, and the feasibility of democracy for the Chinese people in particular.[1]

Nor is it, as Ma himself has said, an "illiberal democracy," a term which he used to discredit President Tsai following her National Day speech in 2018.

According to experts on democracy, an illiberal democracy (also known as "partial" or "empty" democracy) limits the democratic process to regular elections while curtailing civil liberties. Under such a regime, citizens are cut off from the government and the press is muzzled. In his classic *Developing Democracy: Toward Consolidation*, Diamond (1999) describes an illiberal democracy as a system where "political institutions that constrain executive authority are weak, the rule of law is tenuous and human rights may seriously be abused." For all its problems, Taiwan's democracy today certainly cannot be described in such terms, and Ma was simply politicking – crass politics by a former leader who should know better than to disparage a country he once ruled.

Note

1 The Successes and Failures of Taiwanese Democracy and Its Meaning 臺灣民主政治的成敗及其意義, www.cb.cityu.edu.hk/cityseminar/past/20170216.html

References

Agence France-Presse (2018) "Taiwan Passes Controversial Bill Cutting Veterans' Pensions," 21 June 21. www.straitstimes.com/asia/east-asia/taiwan-passes-controversial-bill-cutting-veterans-pensions.

Cole, J. Michael (2017) "U.S. Hate Group MassResistance Behind Anti-LGBT Activities in Taiwan," *Taiwan Sentinel*, 2 January. https://sentinel.tw/us-hate-group-anti-lgbt/.

Commonwealth Magazine (2017) "【黃國昌罷免案】安定力量如何拿到近5萬的「罷昌」票？" 16 December. www.cw.com.tw/article/article.action?id=5086907.

Diamond, Larry (1999) *Developing Democracy: Toward Consolidation*, Baltimore: Johns Hopkins University Press, p. 42.

Grayling, A.C. (2017) *Democracy and Its Crisis*, London: Oneworld, p. 200.

Greenpeace (2018) "Misery at Sea: Human Suffering in Taiwan's Distant Water Fishing Fleet," 24 May. https://storage.googleapis.com/p4-newzealand-production-content/new-zealand/wp-content/uploads/2018/05/9fdf62aa-greenpeace_misery_at_sea-report-lowres.pdf.

Hollingsworth, Julia (2018) "Taiwan Legalizes Same-Sex Marriage in Historic First for Asia," *CNN*, 17 May. https://edition.cnn.com/2019/05/17/asia/taiwan-same-sex-marriage-intl/index.html.

166 The road ahead

Hsu, Elizabeth (2018) "Taiwanese Vote Against Gay Marriage, Back 6 Other Referendum Questions," *Focus Taiwan*, 25 November. http://focustaiwan.tw/news/aipl/201811250002.aspx.

Lee, Ming-tzung and Y. F. Low (2017) "Bill Passed to Cut Civil Servants' Retirement Benefits," *Focus Taiwan*, 23 June. http://focustaiwan.tw/news/aipl/201706270017.aspx.

Msimang, Sisonke (2018) "All Is Not Forgiven: South Africa and the Scars of Apartheid," *Foreign Affairs*, January–February, pp. 28–34.

Ramzy, Austin (2016) "Taiwan's President Apologizes to Aborigines for Centuries of Injustice," *New York Times*, 1 August. www.nytimes.com/2016/08/02/world/asia/taiwan-aborigines-tsai-apology.html.

Schubert, Gunter (2016) *Routledge Handbook on Contemporary Taiwan*, London: Routledge.

Simon, Scott (2017) "The Roots of Taiwan's Indigenous Peoples Protests," *Taiwan Insight*, 9 October. https://taiwaninsight.org/2017/10/09/the-roots-of-taiwans-indigenous-peoples-protests/.

Smith, Oliver (2018) "Mapped: The 53 Places That Still Have the Death Penalty – Including Japan," *Telegraph*, 6 July. www.telegraph.co.uk/travel/maps-and-graphics/countries-that-still-have-the-death-penalty/.

U.S. Department of State Bureau of Democracy, Human Rights and Labor (2017) "Country Reports on Human Rights Practices for 2017: Taiwan," www.state.gov/j/drl/rls/hrrpt/humanrightsreport/index.htm?year=2017&dlid=277119#wrapper.

9

REINVENTING TAIWAN FOR THE 21ST CENTURY

Taiwan has been in a process of transformation as the world around it changes. So far, despite the great challenges it has faced – chief among them China's extraordinary rise – Taiwan has been able to weather the ride and to continue the consolidation of its democracy. The journey has been an arduous one, with many setbacks and periods when everything seemed lost, when China seemed unstoppable. Unable to transform the international system, which on many fronts has excluded it, Taiwan has instead bought time, hedging against China, while seeking to strengthen its ties with the international community. President Tsai's New Southbound Policy, along with ramped up efforts by Taipei to connect with likeminded counterparts around the world, even if at the unofficial level, are part of this process of adaptation, which in the past two years has been given a push by the international community's long overdue awakening to the reality of China in the 21st century. Global reactions to a China that, after decades of engagement did not turn out to be like us, are creating unprecedented opportunities for Taiwan, and those have been seized carefully by the Tsai government. However, Beijing's own reaction to an external environment that suddenly no longer seems as amenable as before to engaging it, will in turn have a transformative, and possibly disruptive, effect in the Asia Pacific. At the heart of all this lies Taiwan, a coveted object which, depending on how it reacts, the CCP could put aside for the time being or, conversely, turn into an even immediate target of its expansionist aspirations.

Although Beijing has intensified its punitive activities since 2016, it can be argued that other matters – from the South China Sea to the North Korean nuclear issue, the trade war with the U.S. to mounting instability within China – have been higher priorities for Xi Jinping. The problem with closed authoritarian regimes is that they are unpredictable. That is especially so under Xi, whose megalomania and high level of paranoia, along with his unprecedented consolidation of power, make him a leader like no other since Mao Zedong. Therefore, amid changing regional

168 The road ahead

and global circumstances, we cannot know with certainty what China will do tomorrow, let alone next year or five years from now.

While predictions are futile, Taiwan can nevertheless prepare for a variety of scenarios. And decision makers in Taipei need to ensure that the country has the ability to survive in even the worst cases. To assume that the future will be somewhat similar to the past – the famous $T=T-1$ formula of political science – would be to take an irresponsibly careless view of tomorrow. Xi has demonstrated that the China with which Taiwan must conjugate today is no longer the China of Deng Xiaoping, Jiang Zemin, or Hu Jintao. Xi has unleashed a new era in Chinese behavior, one that has far more in common with the Chinese imperial rule of old than that of a normal country in the Westphalian sense of the word.

To meet the challenges ahead, Taiwan will therefore have to continue on the road to reform. In this chapter I discuss some areas where change is urgently needed and which can be brought about irrespective of developments in its external environment. In other words, the needed changes I discuss here are well within Taiwan's own ability to implement, provided there is a national will to do so.

Chief among them is the longstanding divide, which I already touched upon in my previous book. The green-blue division, or that pitting Taiwanese against *Waishengren*, remains highly problematic. I cannot emphasize enough how such dynamics continue to undermine Taiwan's ability to meet the challenges ahead. Although the Sunflower Generation promised a shift away from that binary view of Taiwanese society, the division remains very much a problem at the institutional level – in government, and between political parties. Parties in particular remain locked in the old zero-sum mentality, which undermines cooperation, weakens Taiwan's resilience, and creates opportunities for the CCP to exploit. This is an artificial divide that not only refuses to acknowledge the many overlapping interests that exist among Taiwan's disparate groups, but that also puts the survival of the nation at risk at a time when the nation's main external threat is very much of one mind on what its objectives are and how to accomplish those. The Taiwanese public has every reason to have little faith in its politicians when the scorched-earth politics they engage in weaken the nation as a whole. As Snyder (2018) writes in *The Road to Unfreedom*, "This level of partisanship, where the enemy is the opposing party and the outside world is neglected, creates a vulnerability that can be exploited by hostile actors in the outside world."

What is particularly irksome is the fact that much of the party bickering is conducted not due to ideology, but rather for short-term political gain. The aim is to disrupt and discredit, not as a means to bring about a policy change, but to cause logjam. Disruption is not the means, but the end. Opposition parties often engage in this type of behavior to demonstrate the supposed inefficiency of their opponents in government, and with a view to securing an advantage in the next elections. Allegations are made against government officials and employees in government-sponsored nongovernmental organizations not because of irregularities or corrupt practices (although they do occur), but simply to cause trouble and to bolster one's image within the opposition party. Time and time again, good, honest, hardworking officials and their employees have spent days, weeks even, responding to groundless allegations, both in the media and at the legislature. Complicit media, always eager for controversy, have unfortunately provided the platform for the airing of such allegations, often by reprinting the musings of politicians on their Facebook page. Depending on one's political beliefs, news reports on alleged irregularities, collusion, corruption, or nepotism further inflame the belief that the other side cannot be trusted. This practice, which rarely if ever gets punished, perpetuates a vicious cycle of actions that weaken mutual trust and undermine institutions. It has been normalized, largely thanks to social media, and is now part of a vile form of evening entertainment on TV talk shows.

The system grinds on. It works, but the endless bickering causes unnecessary friction and undermines the government's ability to deliver. It is difficult to see how such behavior benefits the nation. At its worst, this phenomenon also encourages the view, helped by the media, that the main political parties are all the same, and equally to blame for dysfunction. This gives ammunition to those who seek to discredit democracy, even though politicians, not democracy itself, are the source of the problem. This practice can also lead the public to turn to populist independent candidates who are not beholden to the intra-party checks and balances that ensure a certain level of policy continuity. There is danger in that, especially if such independents collaborate with, or are supported by, external regimes like the CCP. As Levitsky and Ziblatt (2018) observe in their book *How Democracies Die*,

> stable artisan rivalries eventually give way to perceptions of mutual threat. As mutual toleration disappears, politicians grow tempted to abandon forbearance and try to win at all costs. This may encourage the rise of antisystem groups that reject democracy's rules altogether. When that happens, democracy is in trouble.

Voters should therefore demand an end to this kind of behavior. As some countries have done, Taiwan should establish a "committee of achievers" at the legislature, which would bring together legislators from all parties who are willing to work together on various issues. Although the situations are markedly different, Taiwan could still learn a few things from Israel, which also faces an existential threat from outside forces. Although Israeli society has its own deep divisions stemming from religious views to ethnicity, there nevertheless is agreement, among all parties, that on issues that pertain to national survival, differences should be set aside until a particular problem has been resolved. This ability to transcend the divide has given Israel the strength and cohesiveness it needs to survive in a difficult environment. Before it's too late, Taiwan should find a way to foster a similar coming-together of its society and politicians. The seeds are there, as most already agree on the fundamentals. But these need to be spelled out and to become part of a whole-of-nation strategy. Otherwise, the continuation of that self-inflicted wound could cost Taiwan dearly in the future.

170 The road ahead

As mentioned earlier, the "ethnic" and "color" divide also continues to haunt appointments to various positions in government. Appointees with the "wrong" pedigree or party affiliation are often regarded with suspicion and targeted by the other camp in ways that make their lives miserable. Those suspicions run deep, and often result in the creation of cliques, which work against each other, even within the same institution. Decades after the lifting of martial law and well into the nation's democratization, individuals should be judged on merit and not based on who their parents were, who they worked for, or where they came from. The baseline should be a commitment to Taiwan's democracy and liberal institutions, not one's "genes," party affiliation, or which university he or she attended. Both sides in that divide are to blame, and I have seen it in action far, far too often. As an "outsider" in all this, I cannot help but shake my head in despair when I witness this, and keep wondering why the two sides cannot set aside artificial differences and collaborate on the essentials, which far more often than not happen to coincide. The young generation, what with its civic nationalism based on shared values, has demonstrated repeatedly that, when their interests overlap, they have no problem transcending the old divide. In fact, for many of them the divide is ancient history. The problem is that political parties, government institutions, and the media continue to be largely run by members of the older generation, whose behavior only serves to perpetuate practices that should have been abandoned a long time ago.

The "color" divide has also undermined the government's ability to reform institutions, especially government agencies like MOFA, which are historically conservative, jealous of their institutions, and still dominated by the old "blue" guard. Resistance to change has been particularly strong in such institutions, and would-be reformers – often appointees who come from outside the system and therefore did not climb the ranks – encounter obstacles every step of the way. This, among other things, is one of the principal reasons why the public should be patient in its expectations of rapid change after a new government comes to power. At best, change will be incremental. Moreover, the government needs to work with the people it has; it cannot, in one fell swoop, fire thousands of its employees.

The old generation's refusal to trust, or to make room for younger people within institutions, is partly to blame for this as well. Far too many people who should have retired several years ago still occupy positions in government and government-affiliated institutions, shutting off job opportunities for young people and preventing the generation of new ideas. A sense of entitlement, and a tendency to blackmail government (often using the aforementioned color cliques), have ensured that people who refuse to retire continue to hold positions and to receive an income – salaries that often are substantially higher than those of younger employees, not to mention the many instances when such elders "double-dip." Purely from the perspective of Taiwan's interactions with foreign officials and academics, the far too-large presence of octogenarians at various institutions in Taiwan is bad optics, something that several foreign officials have pointed out to me.

In the same vein, entitlement has also served as a mechanism by which "elders" secure funding, grants, and other forms of largesse from the government for their pet projects. This practice was long associated with the KMT. Sadly, the green camp has had a tendency to do so as well, although perhaps not in as rampant a fashion. Former vice presidents and ministers do it. Not only is this unfair to younger generations, it also takes precious money from finite government budgets that, on many occasions, could have been put to much more effective use. Stopping the flow of money to party elders will require government to ignore threats and blackmail, and to realize that it does not have a responsibility to reward former officials in perpetuity. That would not be a problem if Taiwan had infinite resources to work with, but that is not the case. And while this happens, several talented, driven young Taiwanese with ideas that can bring real change struggle to make ends meet and simply do not have sufficient funds to make their projects a reality.

Besides stopping the flow of money to satisfy the enlarged egos and self-entitlement of elders, the government should thoroughly revise regulations on how it dispenses money to contractors, where the skills needed for special projects often are found. Existing rules were likely written decades ago, and the amounts involved no longer reflect current costs of living. The low wages and funding offered are stunningly uncompetitive and largely insufficient to attract – and to retain – the outside talent Taiwan needs to reinvent itself for the 21st century.

In light of the immensity of the resources that China has at its disposal to wage its propaganda and united front campaign against Taiwan, the self-defeating political/ethnic divisions and wastage of precious resources must stop. Given the possibility that, in the next few years, Beijing could make Taiwan even more of a priority than it has thus far, Taiwan will need to find ways to maximize the return on its investments in human capital. Far too much money is wasted at present on projects that contribute little to the maintenance and future-creation of Taiwan.

Finally, the political divisions at home have sometimes been exported abroad as well, where they have caused confusion. For example, in Washington, Taiwan is represented by the Taipei Economic and Cultural Representative Office (TECRO), and both the KMT and DPP have offices there as well. For U.S. officials, the mixed, and at times contradictory, messages they receive from these three representations, not to mention lobby groups such as the Formosan Association for Public Affairs (FAPA, 台灣人公共事務會) and think tanks like the Global Taiwan Institute (GTI), can undermine the effectiveness of Taiwan's engagement with its longstanding partner. Moreover, the government in Taipei has on some occasion mistrusted officials at TECRO and will instead deal directly with party offices, a bypassing of official government that does harm to Taiwan's cohesion and represents a failure of separation of powers. "These conflicting inputs," Calder (2014) writes in *Asia in Washington*, his study of Asian lobbying in the U.S. capital, "make it difficult for Taiwan as a whole to communicate a unified message. As Taiwan's political-economic challenges in asserting a distinct identity in Northeast Asia continue to deepen, its problems of coherent representation in Washington do so as well."

Another problem associated with the funding of projects that are beneficial to Taiwan needs elaboration. It is the dried-up non-state funding for projects that are part of Taiwan's "soft power," largely as a result of Beijing's punitive policies

172 The road ahead

targeting individuals and enterprises that are deemed to support independence. Increasingly, the private sector with a lot of money to dispense has become apprehensive about getting caught sponsoring projects – publications, TV series, films, and other initiatives – that are pro-Taiwan and supportive of democracy. The fear that has installed itself has led to the abortion or untimely demise of various initiatives, which could have made great contributions to Taiwan's image abroad.

Related to this is the problem of short-termism, which far too often has resulted in the untimely demise of projects that were beneficial to Taiwan's visibility abroad. Both state and non-state actors are responsible for this lack of long-term thinking. Given the billions that China spends on its own global media and propaganda presence, Taiwan cannot afford not to find ways to fund projects that contribute to its image. In the grand scheme of things, many of those projects cost peanuts. But for an individual, the sums are large enough to be a challenge, not to mention that one needs to draw a salary to pay the bills and feed the family. There is a dire need, therefore, for Taiwanese with both vision and money to step in to ensure the long-term viability of such projects. Taiwan's culture industry is seriously underfunded yet represents an area where Taiwan could do much, much more to strengthen its visibility overseas and counter China's propaganda.

The country remains far too conservative in its regulations concerning the employment of foreign nationals. Rules are such that foreign nationals often cannot be hired by agencies in the sectors of national security or diplomacy. Such regulations often are the result of protectionist tendencies in Taiwan – keeping jobs for Taiwanese – and an inability to see the advantages of foreign input. If Taiwan is to attract and retain the foreign talent it needs to combat China's efforts to isolate it on the international stage, it will have to change its mentality. The Taiwan-nationals-only policy for government positions is perfectly understandable as it pertains to one's allegiances, and most countries have those in place. But such restrictions are unnecessary for think tanks and government-sponsored non-governmental organizations. Taiwan needs to develop a brain trust, and foreign input is needed – not because foreigners inherently know better, far from it, but simply because their background allows them to look at issues from a different perspective.

Taiwan is in the process of becoming a multicultural nation, and should continue to open its doors to foreign immigrants. For demographic reasons, opening up to immigration is a matter of survival, if only because Taiwan's birth rate is at sub-replacement fertility levels (anything below 2.1 children per woman). In 2016, Taiwan's birth rate was 1.2, statistics from the National Development Council (中華民國國家發展委員會) (2018) show. According to Ministry of the Interior statistics, in 2017 Taiwan saw its third lowest number of births – 8.3 births/1,000 population – in the past four decades except 2009 and 2010. The same year, the rate of natural increase – the difference between the crude birth and death rates – was at 0.96 per 1,000 people, the second lowest in the nation's history (Liu and Liu 2018). The following year, Taiwan experienced its lowest birth rate in either years, with 181,601 births, or 7.56 per 1,000 people (Chen 2019).

Foreign workers and their children will be the necessary tax payers of tomorrow and ensure the sustainability of many of Taiwan's social programs, chief among them health and pension amid a rapidly aging society. Additionally, the influx of immigrants is having a transformative effect on the nation's very fabric, what with the cultures, languages, food, and religions it brings to the country, adding to its richness and diversity. New immigrants now account for about 3 percent of Taiwan's total population, at approximately 600,000 people. According to statistics from the Ministry of Education, 10.07 percent of the student population in the nation's elementary and junior high schools are new immigrants (Chiang and Yang 2018). With all this comes connectivity with Southeast Asia, which can strengthen Taiwan's foreign policy. And lastly, the presence of a large non-Han cohort of Taiwanese citizens will help undermine Beijing's claims of ownership of the island-nation, a curveball with which the CCP is ill-equipped to deal.

Another area where Taiwan should think differently is in its longstanding efforts, frustrated since 2016, to join the UN and UN-affiliated institutions. Under its current composition, the UN is unlikely to become a friendly body to Taiwan. Security will not even allow Taiwan-passport-holding students to enter UN a building in Geneva (Tong 2017), and will even prevent a woman wearing a Taiwan T-shirt having her photo taken *outside* the UN headquarters in New York City! China's veto power at the UN Security Council and growing influence at the bloc-voting General Assembly, not to mention its influence at the United Nations Educational, Scientific and Cultural Organization (UNESCO) and the Human Rights Council (Tisdall 2018), and control of various UN bodies like ICAO, the WHO, and Interpol – until Meng Hongwei's disappearance in China in October 2018 after he was accused, as we saw in Chapter 2, of bribery – ensures that the UN will remain unattainable to Taipei. Although the case can be made that Taiwan should continue its campaign to join the UN, or to secure observership at specialized UN agencies, if only to generate publicity for Taiwan's situation, Taiwanese authorities and civil society should recognize that, under current circumstances, most of its outreach efforts should focus on strengthening bilateral ties with unofficial diplomatic allies and establishing new alternative forums, such as Global Cooperation and Training Framework, which can help connect Taiwan with the international community outside of traditional UN channels.

Amid a greater desire by foreign governments and think tanks to collaborate with Taiwan on various security-relates issues – Chinese espionage, disinformation, cyber attacks, and "sharp power," among other subjects – Taiwan should strive for better coordination of ongoing efforts and create go-to portals for interactions with foreign counterparts. In the those sectors, various ongoing initiatives by the National Security Council (NSC), the Executive Yuan, the National Security Bureau (NSB), the Ministry of National Defense (MND), the MJIB, and other agencies, public and private, seem to be operating independently of each other, without much coordination. Orchestration of those efforts should be centralized at the NSC. As things stand, foreign entities that seek to collaborate with Taiwan on those issues do not know who to turn to. Centralization would ensure better

174 The road ahead

connectivity with the outside world and help reduce redundancy. Improving the language skills of employees at the NSC and at other government institutions would also go a long way in helping Taiwan interact with foreign partners.

On the military side, Taiwan should give serious thought to establishing a properly trained reserve force, which would play a crucial role in an invasion scenario. Building on the U.S.' NDAA 2019, which mentions U.S. assistance to Taiwan's reserve forces, Taiwan should seek to establish a force that would augment Taiwan's deterrent capability by demonstrating that it has sufficient civilians who can be mobilized to mount a resistance campaign against an occupation force. Regular training, as well as ready access to arms, would ensure that Taiwan could quickly mobilize such a force to counter the PLA. While a return to conscription is impractical, Taiwan should nevertheless adopt measures that ensure that ordinary Taiwanese have sufficient proficiency to bear arms and defend the nation when called upon to do so. A public relations campaign that explains the requirement for readiness, and which emphasizes the probability of a war scenario in the Taiwan Strait, would go a long way in encouraging Taiwanese to join such a program. Rebuilding the image of, and trust in, military institutions is an ongoing effort, and more should be done to position the military as a viable career choice for talented young Taiwanese men and women. Follow-up programs, which ensure placement and careers in other fields after service in the military, or that fund future education, should also be given greater consideration.

Taiwan should also address lax practices for classified material by implementing a uniform government-wide security clearance system for all government employees, with levels of classification similar to those used by Western countries. Security awareness training should be offered to all employees, and proper safe storage made available to all agencies. Such measures would help address foreign apprehensions about the handling of sensitive material by their Taiwanese counterparts.

Another question that is often asked is whether Taiwan should continue to abide by the "status quo," as the Tsai administration has chosen to do, or shift to a more proactive strategy to break out of what many regards as a straitjacket. Those who argue that Taipei should abandon the "status quo" do so on the basis that Beijing has itself abandoned the "status quo" and has been gradually altering the environment to its advantage. That is indeed the case. However, the case could be made that Taiwan has also been changing the "status quo" through its engagement with various actors within the international community. Or, for that matter, that the "status quo" has itself been changing by a rapidly transforming global environment that has turned far more skeptical of China than it was a few years ago. This, no doubt, has benefited Taiwan, and has helped it maintain a certain balance in the Taiwan Strait, notwithstanding Beijing's efforts to shift it in its favor. At this point, and given the variables at play, I would argue that Taipei should remain committed to the "status quo" for two key reasons – to reassure its partners in the international community that it is not about to embark on a dangerous new path, and to avoid giving hawkish elements within the CCP and the PLA the justification they need to use force against Taiwan. Taiwan cannot win this fight on its own and must therefore continue

Reinventing Taiwan for the 21st century **175**

to buy time with the hope that the external environment (not to mention that inside China) will continue to shift in its favor. A sudden policy shift, for example a declaration of *de jure* independence, would risk compromising all the goodwill that Taiwan has accumulated in recent years, with absolutely no guarantee that the more skeptical stance that has been developing worldwide toward China would translate into willingness to come to Taiwan's assistance should Beijing react belligerently.

Finally, and related to the previous point, Taiwan must redouble its efforts to demonstrate that its survival as a free and independent nation is indispensable to, and inseparable from, efforts to ensure that authoritarian China does not rewrite the global order. It, like other democracies, must operate under the assumption that an unwavering commitment to the liberal-democratic order is the best defense against revisionism that seeks to upend the values that have underpinned the system since the end of World War II. Taiwan and like-minded allies should echo the view of the British ambassador to Berlin, who wrote in 1935 that "the rapidly-growing monster of German militarism will not be placated by mere cooings, but will only be restrained from recourse to its *ultima ratio* by the knowledge that the Powers who desire peace are also strong enough to enforce it" (Brendon 2000).

President Tsai Ing-wen encapsulated that spirit during her National Day address in 2018, observing that

> The best way to defend Taiwan is to make it indispensable and irreplaceable to the world . . . We will continue to make Taiwan stronger, and irreplaceable in the global community. This is Taiwan's niche for sustainable survival . . . The first element in fortifying our national security is to strengthen value-based diplomatic links, and establish Taiwan's irreplaceable strategic importance. Taiwan occupies an important geostrategic position
>
> *(Focus Taiwan 2018)*

References

Brendon, Piers (2000) *The Dark Valley: A Panorama of the 1930s*, New York: Alfred A. Knopf, p. 414.

Calder, Kent E. (2014) *Asia in Washington: Exploring the Penumbra of Transnational Power*, Washington: Brookings Institution Press, p. 168.

Chen, Yu-fu (2019) "Birthrate Hits an Eight-Year Low," *Taipei Times*, 7 January. www.taipeitimes. com/News/taiwan/archives/2019/01/07/2003707502.

Chiang, Jeremy and Alan Hao Yang (2018) "A Nation Reborn? Taiwan's Belated Recognition of Its Southeast Asian Heritage," *The Diplomat*, 28 September. https://thediplomat. com/2018/09/a-nation-reborn-taiwans-belated-recognition-of-its-southeast-asian-heritage/.

Focus Taiwan (2018) "Full Text of President Tsai Ing-wen's National Day Address," 10 October. http://focustaiwan.tw/news/aipl/201810100006.aspx.

Levitsky, Steven and Daniel Ziblatt (2018) *How Democracies Die: What History Reveals About our Future*, London: Viking, p. 116.

Liu, Lee-jung and Kuan-lin Liu (2018) "Taiwan Recorded Lowest Population Growth in 2017," *Focus Taiwan*, 27 January. http://focustaiwan.tw/news/asoc/201801270006.aspx.

National Development Council (2018) "林至美、樓玉梅: 國發會「人口推估報告(2018 至2065年)」新聞稿," 30 August. www.ndc.gov.tw/News_Content.aspx?n=114AAE17 8CD95D4C&sms=DF717169EA26F1A3&s=E1EC042108072B67.

Snyder, Timothy (2018) *The Road to Unfreedom: Russia, Europe, America*, New York: Tim Duggan, p. 255.

Tisdall, Simon (2018) "Why Are World's Worst Violators Joining UN Human Rights Council?" *The Guardian*, 11 October. www.theguardian.com/politics/2018/oct/11/ eritrea-joining-human-rights-council-membership-undermine-work-hrc.

Tong, Elson (2017) "Not Just Officials: Taiwan Students Blocked from Visiting UN Public Gallery in Geneva," *Hong Kong Free Press*, 15 June. www.hongkongfp.com/2017/06/15/ not-just-officials-taiwan-students-blocked-visiting-un-public-gallery-geneva/.

10

WHAT'S NEXT? 2019 AND BEYOND

We have nearly come to the end of our journey. By this point, some readers will surely feel that some important elements have been left out, or that others have received too much emphasis. The fact of the matter is, the Taiwan Strait, and the larger issue of Taiwan's unique, troubled, and often frustrating relationship with the world, is of such complexity that no work could possibly discuss all its aspects. One must therefore prioritize and focus on the aspects of this situation that are, in the author's mind, of greatest importance. Some effort was also made to avoid repeating what was already discussed in *Convenient*, though by necessity there is still some overlap.

This concluding chapter attempts to do what one should normally seek to avoid – that is, try to predict the future. Given the high complexity of the issue and the many variables involved, many of which cannot be fully controlled by the main protagonists and antagonists in this story, the game of prediction is an exercise in futility. Because of the lack of transparency, the best we can do when it comes to understanding where China is going is to estimate based on sets of (often flawed) assumptions and the limited information we have at our disposal.

(One prediction: the CCP will *not* collapse anytime soon, as some analysts continue to argue is about to happen. That is due largely to its ability to adapt and its studious approach to learning from the past mistakes of other authoritarian regimes, chief among them the Communist Party of the Soviet Union, CPSU, 蘇聯共產黨.)

Add to this mix the immense challenges – economic, environmental, political, and demographic – the Chinese government will have to resolve in the coming decades, and it becomes clear that any attempt to predict what China will be like five years hence, let alone what its behavior will be like on the external front, is highly presumptuous. We cannot really know. And since China is the single most

178 The road ahead

important variable in the Taiwan Strait equation, those unknowns also entail that the future of the Taiwan Strait will itself be unknown to us.

Related to this is the uncertainty over the future relationship between the U.S. and China, which will also influence how Beijing behaves toward Taiwan. The unpredictability is also compounded by the fact that any future change of government in Washington – say, in the 2020 elections – could also bring about a policy chance vis-à-vis Beijing, although one could argue that even if the Democrats returned to power, it is unlikely we would see a return to the permissive, if not naive, policies that were adopted in the past. On China, and thanks largely to Xi Jinping, who will likely be around for a while yet, the genie is out of the bottle. We now know who we're dealing with, and it is now clear that past hopes that engagement would help turn China into an entity that is somewhat like us in its values and behavior were self-deception.

The best that can be attempted, therefore, is to elaborate a number of possible scenarios. And if we're 'lucky', one of several of those will come to pass. Scenario planning is a useful tool for governments and society to prepare for and defend against future situations that may arise that would imperil the nation's existence. Of course, due to limited resources, governments cannot prepare against every single possible scenario and must therefore prioritize, often doing so in descending order of likelihood.

Scenario #1: Continuity, accompanied by an intensifying assault on Taiwan's democratic institutions. In this scenario, Beijing refrains from using direct military force against Taiwan but continues to apply tremendous pressure on the island-nation in order to break its morale and force it to the negotiation table. Such negotiations would, by default, advantage Beijing and result in some loss of sovereignty for Taiwan. Despite China's growing military strength, decision makers in Beijing and within the PLA recognize the high levels of uncertainty and unpredictability that would be involved in an invasion of Taiwan, and the risks that things could go wrong in the "fog of war." This scenario assumes continued rational decision-making on the part of the Chinese leadership and therefore a domestic political situation in China where the CCP does not feel compelled to use external distractions to ensure its survival (see scenario #3). As part of this mid- to long-term strategy, the Chinese continue their campaign to erode and undermine belief in Taiwan's democratic institutions through disinformation, co-optation, social penetration, and espionage (discussed in Chapter 2). China seeks to bypass traditional political parties – both the DPP and the KMT, the latter having lost much of its appeal as a potential partner in unification – and reaches out to independent candidates as well as local leaders, business people, and so on. The success of this strategy would be contingent on how Taiwan responds to this challenge to its democracy. Unless Taipei shows a willingness to crack down on the pro-CCP anti-democratic forces that are now seeking to subvert Taiwan, Beijing is expected to make increasing use of this "magic weapon," which has the advantage of plausible deniability (the CCP can claim it has nothing to do with it), a relatively low cost, and is almost entirely risk-free for China (other than reputational costs and the possible arrest of

Chinese agents, few if any Chinese lives would be at risk). Such a scenario is likely regardless of the outcome of the 2020 elections – President Tsai's re-election or a return, unlikely as of this writing but not entirely unimaginable, of the KMT. Only the election of a populist independent candidate to the presidency, and of one who, moreover, demonstrated a willingness to shift Taiwan's cross-Strait policy to one that is more on Beijing's terms, would reduce, at least initially, the incentives for Beijing to bypass and corrode Taiwan's central institutions. In October 2018, as the nationwide November municipal elections approached, the MJIB said it was investigating as many as 33 cases involving suspected Chinese funding for specific candidates in the elections (Tu, Lin and Hetherington 2019). According to reports, the PLA's Strategic Support Force (中國人民解放軍戰略支援部隊), along with other organs involved in cyber, electronic, and psychological warfare, were using the November elections as a "testing ground" for various tactics ahead of the January 2020 general elections, in which their efforts would focus on securing the election of a pro-Beijing candidate. If successful, this endeavor would confirm Beijing's intention to ensure that Tsai Ing-wen was a one-term president. Interference in democratic mechanisms was also intended to undermine belief in and support for democracy among Taiwanese, and to create an atmosphere of mistrust, which would break the bonds that unite the Taiwanese as citizens of a democracy. The best way for Taiwanese authorities to prepare for this scenario is to adapt national security laws (e.g., classify Chinese perpetrators as foreign hostile agents), modernize the court/legal system, strengthen the capabilities and mandate of intelligence and law-enforcement agencies, and demonstrate the political will to take actions that may be uncomfortable. There comes a time when the defense of democracy compels the political leadership to make difficult choices.

Scenario #2: Xi meant what he said and unleashes the furies of Chinese ultra-nationalism. There is an ongoing debate as to whether Xi Jinping's harder line on Taiwan is simple nationalistic rhetoric to bolster his credentials within the CCP or that it constitutes something new and more dangerous for Taiwan. Given his break with precedent, Taiwan cannot afford to get it wrong and must therefore prepare against the possibility that Xi means what he says, and sometime in the third decade of the 21st century decides that the PLA has sufficient capabilities to launch an all-out assault against Taiwan to resolve the Taiwan "issue" once and for all. Under this scenario, international conditions would appear to be favorable to such a risky endeavor. Beijing has concluded that Washington does not have the will to come to Taiwan's assistance or is distracted by or overstretched as a result of another contingency somewhere else on the planet – e.g., war with Iran or North Korea. Beijing also calculates that other regional powers, chief among them Japan, also will not intervene in the Taiwan Strait. In sum, the international situation is such that the CCP convinces itself that Taiwan has been sufficiently isolated and that a quick, clean, high-intensity war in the Taiwan Strait can be won by China. Such a scenario could also come about if developments in Taiwan, such as a declaration of *de jure* independence, "forced" Beijing to activate the Anti-Secession Law and launch a "defensive" war against the island. The best way to ensure against this scenario is

180 The road ahead

for Taiwan, working with its allies, to bolster its deterrent capability and to avoid, as President Tsai has done so far despite pressure from the deep greens, giving Beijing any reason to lash out. Stronger signaling by Washington that an unprovoked attack on Taiwan would trigger a U.S. military response – in other words, moving away from the longstanding policy of "strategic ambiguity" – would also reduce the risks of miscalculation on Beijing's part. The community of democracies (U.S., E.U., and others) must also rebuild its credibility on "red lines" against state aggressors, which was severely undermined after its inaction over Georgia, Crimea/Ukraine, Syria, and the South China Sea.

Scenario #3: An embattled CCP uses the external card. Serious instability inside China, resulting either from a sharp economic downturn, a scandal involving the highest echelons of the CCP, or from a trade war turned hot war with the U.S., could compel the Chinese regime to use an external distraction to rally the Chinese people around the CCP flag. In this scenario, fear of losing control of Chinese society would encourage the embattled CCP regime to portray instability as being caused by outside agents. The regime would play up the sentiment of victimhood that has been cultivated by the CCP for decades. Beijing would accuse external forces of colluding to "keep China low" through encirclement and other devious strategies. The CCP would thus have no choice but to launch a "defensive" war against the external aggressors, preferably one which it can win quickly so that it can rebuild its reputation with the Chinese public. Given the promises Xi Jinping has made to the public since he assumed office, and the personalization of Chinese policy under his guidance, anything that threatens the "China dream" will be seen by Xi and his close circle as a direct threat to their survival and legacy. In the highly charged and cut-throat environment that is China today, any loss of face can become deadly business, and therefore the leadership has every incentive to do whatever it takes to remain in power. This, in turn, makes irrational behavior – a warped cost-versus-benefit analysis of one's actions – much likelier. Taiwan is one of several potential targets that the CCP, facing domestic crisis, could turn to in order to manufacture a crisis and thereby attempt to rebuild its legitimacy. Other areas – parts of the South China Sea, the Senkaku/Diaoyutai islets in the East China Sea, the border with India, islets claimed by Beijing and Seoul, the border with Russia, Central Asia, and elsewhere – also offer potential for an external distraction. With regards to Taiwan, an attack also need not include Taiwan proper, but could be limited to its outlying islands or possessions in the Spratlys (南沙). External distraction is a gamble, a desperate attempt to rebuild one's fortunes by sparking crisis elsewhere and redirecting public and institutional anger at an outside opponent. Given the need for success (debacle would only accelerate the demise of the troubled leadership), and assuming that some degree of rationality still informs decision-making, in such a situation the CCP would likely concentrate on the weakest targets within the region – in other words, not Taiwan, which remains a difficult opponent and which could spark a U.S. intervention, but rather countries like the Philippines and Vietnam – or areas where military clashes are unlikely to prompt a response by the U.S. Therefore, as with scenario #2, bolstering Taiwan's deterrence capabilities, and clarifying the signaling on the U.S.' and Japan's "red lines" in the Taiwan Strait would further reduce the likelihood that Taiwan would become an inviting target for a CCP external distraction.

Scenario #4: CCP collapse. For almost two decades, some analysts have predicted the eventual collapse of the CCP. Those predictions relied primarily on using the Communist Party of the Soviet Union (CPSU) as a template for the CCP. It is clear, by now, that the CCP has closely studied, and learned from, the many factors that contributed to the CPSU's demise and the collapse of the Soviet Union, with a view to avoiding making the same mistakes. Thus, while an end of CCP rule in China is not altogether impossible, it is unlikely the factors that brought about the spectacular collapse in the CPSU will be those that see the end of the CCP. The CCP has become a master of adaptability and benefits from historical hindsight; moreover, where the Soviet Union's economy was closed and inefficient, China's has contrariwise embraced capitalism ("with Chinese characteristics") and become inextricably enmeshed into the global economy. The experience of CCP rule in China is therefore idiosyncratic, and past models are of little utility in projecting its trajectory. The international community should nevertheless prepare for a collapse scenario, if only because such a development, given the CCP's near-total control of Chinese society, would have tremendous repercussions for China and the region as a whole. For Taiwan, the highly destabilizing effects of collapsed CCP rule in China would have economic repercussions due to the close supply-chain relationship that exists between the two sides and heavy investment by Taiwanese firms in coastal and other areas of China. On the security side, there is absolutely no guarantee that the end of CCP rule would bring about a change of heart in China with regards to claims over Taiwan. In fact, whoever and whatever comes after Xi and the CCP could be even more nationalistic and expansionist; conversely, rogue elements within the PLA, or a regional "warlord," could seize the opportunity caused by a chaotic situation in China and the collapse of centralized rule to launch what would conceivably be a limited attack on Taiwan. While such a scenario remains unlikely for the time being, it is an eventuality against which Taiwanese authorities must prepare. In general, what needs to be done differs little from the necessary preparations that must be taken against the contingencies discussed in scenarios #2 and #3.

Scenario #5: Taiwan capitulates. This scenario projects a successful intimidation campaign by China against Taiwan and an international environment in which Taiwan finds itself completely isolated. Perhaps as a result of a blockade, a successful military campaign, or the coming to power in Taiwan of a politician who is no longer bound by the constraints imposed by democratic institutions, capitulation would bring Taiwanese and Chinese to the table and an agreement of sorts would be reached under which Taiwan would become part of the People's Republic of China. Whether under "one country, two systems" or another formulation, Taiwan would lose its ability to carry out foreign relations, and if the Hong Kong example is any indication, the agreement would result in the curtailment of certain political rights. While Beijing could perhaps succeed in convincing enough Taiwanese that

182 The road ahead

a bright future as part of China is possible, or cow them into submission through scare tactics, due to the high level of opposition to Chinese rule in Taiwan, this transition would inevitably lead to resistance and instability, and thus compel law enforcement and military units now under the control of Beijing to take action. Several thousands would be arrested, and possibly as many killed in the process. The PLA, Ministry of State Security (MSS, 中華人民共和國國家安全部), People's Armed Police (PAP, 中國人民武裝警察部隊), and paramilitary units could also send detachments to Taiwan to pacify the island if instability there threatened Chinese rule. Chinese control, or the threat thereof, would also spark a mass exodus of Taiwanese abroad, a hollowing out that would turn the island-nation into a "ghost island," a mere plot of land – what the CCP wants is territory, not the Taiwanese people – from which China could project power. Given Beijing's larger territorial ambitions, and whatever promises it made during negotiations, Taiwan would likely become a staging ground for PLA forces, and thus a target of attacks by the U.S., Japan, and other allies in case of a larger regional conflagration.

The above scenarios are simply exercises in imagination, a way to focus the attention of decision makers and help them prioritize. There are others, but the ones above are, in descending order, the likeliest. I have no pretension of knowing which one will come about, or whether things would turn out as I described them in my contingencies. But it is important to think about these things, and to be aware that the past behavior of the CCP, or the structure of the international system, for that matter, might not be similar to what we have known over the years. With a disruptive, megalothymia and unpredictable leader like Xi Jinping in charge, Taiwan and its allies cannot afford not to be imaginative in their forecasts of the future. The stakes are simply too high.

★ ★ ★

As people stepped outside on the morning of 25 November 2018 the atmosphere in Taipei had what could only be described as a post-Brexit vibe. The streets were oddly empty; breakfast places, usually busy on weekends, were oddly quiet. A few young couples with long faces sat at tables, unenthusiastically munching away at their meals. On TVs above them, Han Kuo-yu, the candidate from the KMT in the Kaohsiung elections who had been victorious in the previous day's nation-wide nine-in-one local elections, was energetically announcing that the first thing he would do upon becoming mayor would be to establish a cross-Strait working group to revive the southern city's supposedly stagnant economy.

The 24 November elections were a major setback for President Tsai and her DPP. In a reversal that was oddly reminiscent of that which had marked the beginning of the "collapse" of the KMT in the year-end 2014 municipal elections, the DPP lost seven of the 13 cities and counties it had held since 2014, and suddenly found itself with only six. The political map, meanwhile, showed mostly blue across the nation – a major comeback for a party that many had thought was history after 2016. There was much reason to disagree with that hubristic assessment of the KMT's fortunes. After all, this was a party that had suffered many setbacks in the

What's next? 2019 and beyond **183**

past, chief among them the loss of the Chinese Civil War and relocation to Taiwan, as well as democratization. This was a party that had had decades to establish grass-roots networks and install powerful ruling families and factions around the country, and it was those families and networks – which failed to mobilize in 2014 amid almost universal discontent with the Ma Ying-jeou administration – that engineered the party's comeback in the 2018 elections.

For the DPP, a mix of hubris and complacency since 2016 was the key reason for its highly disappointing performance in the local elections. Some DPP mayors and county commissioners had appeared to be on cruise-control, and overall, despite a slowly reviving economy since Tsai had taken the helm in 2016, ordinary Taiwanese did not feel any wealthier. (A sense that one has more money in his or her wallet, rather than overall GDP growth figures, is an important element of public mood regarding how well an economy is doing. This is true worldwide, even in China.) There is also evidence that disgruntled public servants, angered by the Tsai administration's pension cuts, voted in bloc against DPP candidates to punish the party. Impatient, voters decided that four years of DPP rule in municipalities had not yielded the hoped-for results; so they turned to the opposition, with the hope that new faces would be able to deliver more (in DPP-controlled municipalities where the mayors performed well, worked hard, and reached out to different parties and factions, as in Taoyuan and Hsinchu City, the DPP candidates successfully held their mayorships). That also was true in the city that offered the most unexpected setback for the DPP, in Kaohsiung. There, the favorite, Chen Chi-mai (陳其邁) of the DPP, was pitted against Han, a politician with little experience, a populist who ran a less-than-stellar campaign platform that included erecting a 'love Ferris wheel" in the city, drilling for oil on Taiping Island in the South China Sea, and banning all political protests.

And yet, Han beat Chen by a considerable margin. This was a clear indication that the DPP, which had ruled the city for the previous two decades, had ossified, that new ideas – a shock to the system – were needed. The upset was reminiscent of the surprise results in Taichung and Taipei in 2014, two cities where the public had grown fatigued with long periods on uninterrupted KMT rule. Han's rising star also tapped into dissatisfaction among retired civil servants and members of the armed forces who had seen their pensions cut by the DPP; the wave of Han supporters, most of them in the older age brackets, also tended to be more socially conservative (e.g., in their opposition to same-sex marriage) and from within the lower-middle-class bracket, therefore likelier to find Han's promises of "great fortunes," even if those were founded on flimsy and often self-contradictory ideas, more appealing. Worryingly, the Han wave also unleashed darker forces within society, resulting from early 2019 in an epidemic of online threats against any Han critic, including those within the KMT, as well as physical intimidation of various politicians and members of the public.

Perhaps more worrying than a KMT comeback (at least for the green camp), was the likelihood that Beijing would use this outcome to its advantage. No sooner had the tallies of the votes in Kaohsiung and Taichung been made public than

184 The road ahead

the newly elected politicians announced their intention to abide by the "1992 consensus" and establish cross-Strait working groups to attract Chinese tourism and renewed investment. Once again, would-be KMT candidates began flirting with the idea of signing a "peace agreement" with China, an idea that had been floated – and just as quickly discarded, in the face of strong public opposition – before (Yu and Wang 2019).

It was clear that the transformed political map would make it easier for Beijing and willing partners in Taiwan to bypass the central government and isolate the municipalities that remained under DPP control. What this created, therefore, was an environment that was more conducive to the "Lebanonization" of Taiwan discussed earlier in this book. There was no doubt that Beijing will not waste a second in trying to bring benefits to those municipalities so as to set an example in the lead-up to the general elections in 2020. Thus, while voters voted mostly for pragmatic and very local matters, the results inevitably had an impact on national and cross-Strait policy. Taiwan did not turn "pro-Beijing" on 24 November, but its voters helped create conditions that added to the DPP's headaches in dealing with the China issue.

As discussed in Chapter 3, the DPP's poor showing also exacerbated calls within the green camp for someone other than Tsai to run on the party ticket in the 2020 elections. Following protocol, Tsai stepped down as party chair on election night and both Chen Chu (陳菊) and Premier William Lai submitted their resignation (Chen Chu eventually stayed at her post, whereas Lai was replaced by Su Tseng-chang [蘇貞昌], with Chen Chi-mai, defeated in Kaohsiung, becoming his deputy). As a result, Tsai's control of her party was eroded, which opened the possibility that more "radical" elements within the green camp would thenceforth guide the party's policy. Many "deep greens" have accused President Tsai since 2016 of being too slow on reform, too soft on China, and too careful in seeking to expand Taiwan's presence abroad. The emergence of a possibly more "radical" party head, however, was averted in the chairmanship elections held in January 2019, when Cho Jung-tai (卓榮泰) defeated You Ying-lung (游盈隆). Cho stood for continuity, whereas You had appealed to "deep green" – and more "extremist" – voices in the party.

William Lai's decision in March to challenge Tsai for the nomination as the party's candidate in the 2020 presidential election created another potential fork in the road for the DPP. As many saw it, the bitter contest would inevitably set the tone for the future DPP. Moreover, a Lai victory would have turned Tsai into a lame-duck president for the reminder of her term, while giving hawks in the CCP and the PLA more ammunition to crack down on Taiwan, given Lai's image as an "independence worker," in contrast with the more cautious Tsai. A more radical leadership at the DPP could have sabotaged the well-calibrated foreign policy that the Tsai administrated has implemented since 2016. While undoubtedly satisfying to elements within the "deep green" camp who sought a more activist foreign polity and greater emphasis on a Taiwan-centric nomenclature, such a departure from a pragmatic foreign policy would almost certainly have cost Taiwan many of

What's next? 2019 and beyond   **185**

the unofficial allies who have agreed to work more closely with it in recent years. The result would conceivably have been greater international isolation and greater justification for Beijing to clamp down on Taiwan "separatists."

In the end, and amid accusations by Lai supporters that the selection was unfair, Tsai secured the nomination, an outcome which no doubt proved reassuring to Taiwan's partners within the international community.

Taiwan's partners abroad, the U.S. chief among them have repeatedly signaled that they welcome Tsai's cautious, predictable, and gradualistic approach to policy making, and would welcome more of the same in the future. This view has been affirmed by Washington's expanding engagement with Taiwan on various issues since 2016, from religious freedom to a free and open Indo Pacific to other projects under the U.S. Department of State's Global Engagement Center (GEC), which has included more direct government-to-government, Track 1.5 and Track 2 interactions.

As discussed in previous chapters, the Tsai administration's reform efforts, while slow in certain areas, were complicated by structural conditions within the agencies in need of reform, resistance by conservatives within the system, and the appointment of officials who, like Tsai, favored a more gradual approach to reform. In areas where reform was a priority, Tsai put her foot down and results were much quicker in materializing, as with pension reform, for example. One area where Tsai will need to pay more attention is the old practice of pleasing the elders, which as discussed earlier prevents the empowerment of new blood in politics and results in wastage the country simply cannot afford. Such practices, highly unethical if not altogether corrupt, *must* come to an end.

The 24 November elections created new, unexpected challenges for the remainder of the first Tsai administration, which seemed to find in those the inspiration it needed to reinvent itself and better address that which Taiwanese voters were looking for in their leaders. All of this was survivable, provided that Taiwanese society and policy makers heeded the warnings and realized that democracy requires vigilance. For the DPP, the results were a reminder that it cannot afford to be complacent, not when forces that seek to undermine Taiwan's sovereignty, and its liberal-democratic system, are unflagging in their efforts. It was also a reminder – to the DPP and the KMT – that public perception that "the system" and the two main political parties are "equally bad" can create an opening for populist outsiders who presume to have the solution to fix everything. The explosion of support for Han Kuo-yu, who mere months after his election was quickly assuming quasi-messianic stature, was an example of what can happen when a sufficient number of voters become disillusioned with the elite and longstanding governance – in this case, mostly stagnant economic growth for more than a decade. Han's solution is to recognize the "1992 consensus" and to strengthen business and investment ties; his success in making this claim has so far relied on amnesia, as this is little more than heated up KMT policy under Ma Ying-jeou, which proved unable to boost economic growth significantly, while once again creating various opportunities for the CCP United Front apparatus to penetrate Taiwanese society (as it became clear

186 The road ahead

that the KMT would be voted out of office in 2016, Beijing blamed the failure of its policy to win over the Taiwanese to lack of effort by Chinese officials to ensure proper distribution of economic benefits to the Taiwanese and accused some of its leading officials, such as former ARATS chairman Chen Yunlin [陳雲林], of corruption) (Chiu 2015). Although Han belongs to the KMT, he is very much an outsider within the organization, using it to propel himself to power. The party, in turn, used him, in what I would argue was a Faustian deal, to rebuild its appeal. The similarities with Donald Trump and the Republican Party in the U.S. are hard to miss and, arguably, equally worrying (Hochschild 2016; Packer 2013). The "lost decade," and the view that only a political "outsider" can resurrect the nation, is also reminiscent of the conditions that led to Alberto Fujimori's election in Peru in 1990. Throughout the 1980s, Peru suffered a significant drop in real GDP per capita accompanied by high inflation, along with the widespread view that the two parties that held power during that decade were highly corrupt (Kenney 2004). As the Peru case has demonstrated, an outsider president coupled with a legislature that remains in the hands of traditional parties can lead to conditions that favor a coup, or self-coup initiated by the president, as Fujimori did in 1992.

The problem for both the Tsai and Ma administrations is that whatever their approach to reviving the economy, in the end hardworking ordinary Taiwanese have on the whole not felt any wealthier, while cost of living has continued to rise.

The Han "wave," which is partly the result of mythmaking, has also fueled a dangerous polarization, if not "tribalism," in Taiwanese politics that threatens to erode the middle ground occupied by President Tsai and moderates in both the DPP and KMT. In such an environment, it is easy to imagine the kind of negative campaigning that would occur in the lead-up to the 2020 elections. The frequency and viciousness of attacks online and in the blue media against whoever criticizes Han has reached disturbing proportions and risks sparking escalatory cycles of retaliation which, if unchecked, could become socially destabilizing. Many of those attacks, furthermore, have been fueled by constant disinformation, which was spread by a triumvirate of blue media that have become the functional equivalents of mouthpieces for the Han camp (Sung 2019). There is reason to believe that a share of the online activity in support of Han Kuo-yu, which has included swarming on social media, death threats, and the intimidation of children of Han's critics, originates outside Taiwan. The change in tone and language style certainly support this contention, but further research needs to be conducted by law enforcement and academia to corroborate this claim. And to date, Han and his administration have failed to distance themselves from such behavior or to condemn its excesses. Additionally, amid Han's rise, more moderate voices within the KMT have gone mostly silent, leaving the space for politicians like Han who are advocating for a less cautious approach to Taiwan's relationship with Beijing. Calls for Han to run in the 2020 elections were also accompanied by threats against other prospective candidates in the party, contributing to an atmosphere of fear and to a sense of historical inevitability, one in which Han has no choice but to run in the election.

Polarization is a destructive force that undermines the kind of moderation where the interests of both the "green" and "blue" camps overlap – what I have long argued constitutes Taiwan's main strength and resilience. The more the center is eroded, the likelier it is that more radical voices on either side of the spectrum will hijack the nation's politics. If we are correct in our assessment that the CCP has realized that the mainstream DPP and KMT will never give Beijing what it wants, it then follows that the Chinese will place its bets on political "outsiders" who are willing to challenge the system and to undo the traditional party/government structure should they get elected. Han's near-total disregard for central government authorities and dismissal of the MAC's warnings during his visit to Hong Kong, Macau and China in late March 2019, during which he held meetings at the United Front-linked Liaison Office of the Central People's Government in the Hong Kong S.A.R. (中央人民政府駐香港特別行政區聯絡辦公室) and with Liu Jieyi (劉結一) of the Taiwan Affairs Office, (Yeh 2019) was also in line with Beijing's ongoing efforts to bypass Taipei and work directly with amenable partners in Taiwan, both at the municipal and grassroots level, elected and not (Central News Agency 2019). Han reportedly didn't provide an itinerary or list of scheduled meetings to the MAC. According to Liu, the "1992 consensus" has contributed to the happiness of the people of Kaohsiung.

Meanwhile, the early months of 2019 seemed to indicate that the CCP would continue to operate along the lines of scenarios #1 and #2 discussed above. There were renewed rumors that China would soon lure another of Taiwan's official diplomatic allies, this time the Solomon Islands, as China ramped up its influence efforts in that increasingly important region of the Pacific Ocean – and it did, twice, in September 2019, adding Kiribati to the list, while threatening that a Tsai re-election in 2020 would result in China stealing all of Taiwan's remaining allies. More Taiwanese artists meanwhile were forced to state publicly that they identified themselves as "Chinese," including Ouyang Nana (歐陽娜娜), the daughter of KMT spokesman Ouyang Long (歐陽龍), possibly in retaliation for his comments about the unviability of "one country, two systems" for Taiwan (*Apple Daily* 2019). And during the National People's Congress in March once again purported representatives of Taiwan, such as Chinese People's Political Consultative Conference (中國人民政治協商會議) member Ling Yu-shih (凌友詩), spoke up using scripts that had evidently been drafted by Beijing. According to Taiwanese authorities, Ling was a member of the China Taiwanese Association, a private organization established to "serve as a bridge and link between the CCP and Taiwanese compatriots." Taipei retaliated by fining her NT$500,000 and threatening to cancel her household registration in Taiwan, although she has been a resident of Hong Kong for several years (Miao and Wang 2019). Ling was also one of the individuals who served as a "character witness" for the CEFC's Patrick Ho, whose case is discussed in Chapter 2.

Expectations that Beijing would tone down its rhetoric and reduce tensions in the Taiwan Strait so as to avoid giving President Tsai and the DPP an advantage in the 2020 elections did not materialize. Xi Jinping's address to "Taiwanese compatriots" on 2 January had made it clear that Beijing has become tone deaf regarding the

188 The road ahead

preferences of the Taiwanese and that it would only work with counterparts in Taiwan who bend to its will (*United Daily News* 2019). The 4,254-character address – about 2,400 characters longer than its predecessor from 1 January 1979 – checked all the usual tropes, with Xi droning on about "unwaveringly resolving the Taiwan question;" the completion of "reunification" as a "historic task" for all Chinese on both sides; "cross-Strait reunification as an irresistible historical trend;" "compatriots across the Strait are all Chinese who share a natural kinship and national identity that can never be changed by anyone or any force;" and "the peaceful and stable development of the cross-Strait situation and the progress of cross-Strait relations are the tide of the time that can never be stopped by anyone or any force."

The platitudinous ramblings of the CCP leader would not have been complete without some revisionism. Over the past seven decades, Xi said, China and Taiwan have "reached the '1992 consensus,' [which is] based on the 'one China' principle" under "the basic principles of 'peaceful reunification' and 'one country, two systems.'" Left unsaid was the fact that, for one thing, the so-called consensus does not exist and that whatever verbal agreement was reached between negotiators between the two sides in 1992 was (1) a party-to-party affair which left out the Taiwanese people and (2) contained an agreement to disagree on what "one China" means, with the KMT insisting on "different interpretations." Also missing was the admission that the Taiwan side never agreed to the "one country, two systems" formula offered by Beijing, not to mention the fact that the said formula has been disastrous for Hong Kong.

Xi then promised that the social system and way of life in Taiwan would be fully respected, and the private property, religious beliefs, and legitimate rights and interests of Taiwan compatriots would be fully protected after "peaceful" reunification is realized. What with Hong Kong, Tibet, and Xinjiang, the nearly total subservience of Chinese media to the CCP, control of the Internet, rampant surveillance, Orwellian "social credit" system, the mass arrests of lawyers, activists, Christians, intellectuals, and others who do not toe the party line, only a fool would take Xi's promise at face value.

The same held for Xi's proposal for "institutional arrangements" for the peaceful development of cross-Strait relations, whereby Beijing and Taipei would conduct "democratic consultations" on cross-Strait relations and the future of the nation. One can ask, do not such bodies already exist, in the form of the Mainland Affairs Council and the Taiwan Affairs Office? Given Beijing's constant warping of democratic principles and the inflexibility of the center-rules-all CCP model, such negotiations would inevitably lead to losses for democratic Taiwan. And here again, whatever agreement was reached would, using the Hong Kong model as an example, almost inevitably be ignored by Beijing after a certain period of time. It is also very clear that "political parties and all sectors on both sides of the Taiwan Strait," who under the arrangements "may recommend representatives to conduct extensive and in-depth democratic consultation on the basis of the common political foundation of upholding the '1992 consensus' and opposing 'Taiwan independence'" would exclude a large number of people in Taiwan – a majority of them, in fact.

Unsurprisingly, Xi made no promise to renounce the use of force against Taiwan, though he noted that "Chinese do not fight Chinese," which presumably would mean that when the missiles rain down on Taiwan, those who declare themselves "Chinese" would be spared the horrors of destruction and loss of family members. Xi also said that the threat of force does not target "compatriots in Taiwan," but only "the interference of external forces and the very small number of 'Taiwan independence' separatists and their activities." Xi said nothing about the majority of Taiwanese who favor the "status quo," who, in other words, do not support unification. His remarks revealed the CCP's continued inability, or refusal, to admit that its Taiwan "problem" is a much larger one, one that stems from clashing values and the embrace, almost universal, of liberal democracy by the Taiwanese, whether they be "green" or "blue," and regardless of their views on the "1992 consensus." In other words, if the CCP were to use force against Taiwanese "separatists," it would have to kill a whole lot of people, not just "a very small number" of "separatists." Needless to say, the notion that "separatism" or the desire to maintain one's sovereignty is somehow the result of manipulations by "external forces" is utterly preposterous, a complete misreading of the choices that the Taiwanese have made for decades.

Xi then urged young people across the Taiwan Strait "to shoulder important tasks with courage, be united and friendly with each other, and strive for a better future hand in hand." Whether the omission of not-so-young people means that older people on both sides need not be friendly to each other is anyone's guess. But what is certain is that China's track record on friendliness has been severely lacking, what with the barrage of attacks on Taiwanese artists on the Internet, the ugly Chinese nationalism on display, time and time again, on university campuses worldwide – not to mention the threat of force just reiterated by Xi. The CCP's definition of Taiwanese friendliness is subservience. Bow to our will, become complicit in the Chinese dream as defined by the CCP, and though shalt not be threatened.

Once again, it was clear that the CCP is the greatest impediment to the peaceful resolution of conflict in the Taiwan Strait. It is its rigidity, its lack of imagination, and refusal to face reality, not "Taiwanese separatists," that stands in the way of some sort of peace. Since 1979, the CCP and the Chinese people have had many occasions to better understand Taiwanese society and the complexities of its democratic system. Xi's painful regurgitation of old tropes in his 2 January address tells us that either the CCP has not learned a thing, or it has, but, cornered by its own rhetoric and ideology, it cannot admit otherwise lest such an admission reveal its fraudulence to the Chinese people.

Former Chinese Taiwan Affairs Office deputy director Wang Zaixi (王在希) later observed that Xi's address had redefined the "1992 consensus," in that it now incorporated not only the two sides agreeing to "one China" but added that the two sides should proactively seek "national unity." Without those two conditions, Wang said, there was not "1992 consensus" (Lee 2019). In other words, any candidate who affirmed his or her support for the "1992 consensus" leading into the 2020 elections would, perforce, be agreeing to abide by Beijing's strict definition

190 The road ahead

and would be expected to actively work toward unification. Just stating one's support for the "consensus" would no longer be sufficient.

Xi's unyielding rhetoric was a boon for President Tsai, who had yet to regain her footing following her party's defeat in the 24 November elections. After initial hesitation, her strong response was celebrated in many circles, both in Taiwan and abroad:

> Over the past two years, Taiwan has faithfully fulfilled its duty as a member of the regional community, actively contributing to cross-strait and regional peace and stability. We do not provoke, but uphold our principles. We have suffered many forms of suppression, but have never abandoned our fundamental position and commitments regarding cross-strait relations. I want to remind the Beijing authorities that a superpower must act with the demeanor and take the responsibility of a superpower, and international society is watching China to see if it can make changes and become a trustworthy partner. The "four musts" are the most basic and crucial foundations that will determine whether cross-strait relations develop in a positive direction.
>
> A so-called "spiritual union" should be built on mutual respect and understanding, with governments on both sides of the strait handling issues regarding the people's welfare pragmatically, such as the urgent swine fever epidemic we are now facing. Pressuring international corporations to change their designation for Taiwan won't bring about a spiritual union, nor will buying off Taiwan's diplomatic allies or circling Taiwan with military aircraft and naval vessels.
>
> *(Office of the President, Republic of China 2019)*

Xi's equating in his speech of the "1992 Consensus" with the "one country, two systems" formula was an act of revisionism, which also put the KMT in a difficult position. In the days that followed Xi's address, various KMT politicians were forced to echo President Tsai's condemnation of that statement by emphasizing that with the exception of ultra-marginal pro-unification groups, "one country, two systems" has very little appeal among the Taiwanese.

Meanwhile, there were fears that amendments to the Fugitive Offenders Ordinance (逃犯條例) and the Mutual Legal Assistance in Criminal Matters Ordinance (刑事事宜相互法律協助條例), proposed by the Hong Kong Security Bureau (保安局) on 13 February could have an additional chilling effect on the ability and willingness of Taiwanese to travel to the Special Administrative Region, once considered the "safest" destination for Taiwanese in China (*Liberty Times* 2019). The amendments, proposed in the wake of the 2018 "suitcase murder," in which a resident of Hong Kong was accused of killing his partner in a Taiwan hotel, were expected to be passed by Hong Kong's legislature that summer. Once implemented, this could have permitted the arrest of Taiwanese crime suspects in the territories of Macau and Hong Kong and their extradition to China proper, where they would face prosecution and imprisonment.

Following revisions proposed to Hong Kong's two Ordinances (the "Extradition Bill"), Taiwanese nationals accused of the crime of subversion – a category which by design has been loosely defined by the Chinese regime – could now be detained upon entering Hong Kong and sent to China to face prosecution. Given that the Law purports to cover the jurisdictions of Macau, Hong Kong, and Taiwan, the alleged crimes need not even have been committed in China proper for a suspect to be seized in Hong Kong and disappeared into the Chinese legal system. Consequently, any Taiwanese academic, activist, artist, or former politician accused of violating Chinese law (this includes anyone who advocates democracy or Taiwanese independence) would no longer need to have been in China proper when the alleged "crime" was committed to face prosecution in China; entering Hong Kong would be enough.

Furthermore, according to a version of the revision proposed by the Security Bureau, the temporary arrest and transfer of a suspect would be ordered by the chief executive of the HKSAR government and would not be subject to usual reviews by the Legislative Council. The interpretative nature of the National Security Law, and the loose definition of the various "crimes" that can be committed against the state, empowers zealous officials to act preemptively; once a decision is made to detain the suspect of an ideological "crime," it becomes very difficult for the system, and ultimately for the central authority in Beijing, to de-escalate, as this would constitute a loss of face. Such dynamics very likely account for Lee Ming-che's fate (discussed in Chapter 2). In September, the Taiwan Affairs Office confirmed that another Taiwanese national, Morrison Lee (李孟居), had been detained in China on suspicions of "engaging in criminal activity harmful to national security" (Lee, Chung and Hetherington 2019).

The Bill backfired for both the Hong Kong government and Beijing, sparking mass protests on a scale not seen since 1997 and which, as of this writing in October 2019, showed no sign of abating. A disproportionate and often violent response by riot police and pro-CCP triads, which resulted in many of injuries, thousands of arrests (with rumors that some detainees may have been raped while in prison), the firing of thousands of tear-gas canisters and the introduction of water cannons turned the streets of the former British colony into a war zone. Not even a global propaganda/disinformation campaign by Beijing seeking to discredit the protesters as "rioters" and "terrorists," or the threat of intervention by the PLA or the People's Armed Police, succeeded in deterring the thousands of Hong Kong protesters.

World opinion, meanwhile, turned against Beijing, even after Carrie Lam (林鄭月娥), the embattled Hong Kong chief, removed the controversial extradition bill, by which time the protests had become about something much larger – the very future of governance in Hong Kong. In Taiwan and elsewhere, pro-CCP elements threatened, and sometimes assaulted, Hong Kong students on school campuses and tore down Lennon Walls that had been erected to support the protesters. The situation in Hong Kong, which caught the attention of officials in Washington, D.C., also had the effect of elevating Taiwan's prominence and role as a democracy in the region.

192 The road ahead

Amid all this, one politician who benefitted from the unrest was President Tsai, whose popularity, having hit a new low following the 14 November debacle, divisions within her party, and an embarrassing scandal surrounding cigarette smuggling by her security detail in August 2019 (Lin and Lee 2019), rebounded. The crisis in Hong Kong seemed to justify her defiance of Beijing, while sealing the deal once and for all on the viability of "one country, two systems" in Taiwan, which as Xi had made clear in his 2 January address, was the one and only offer on the table for "peaceful unification." Han Kuo-yu, her opponent from the KMT who months earlier had seemed unstoppable, began to self-destruct and appeared to have alienated much of the mainstream KMT. Many in the party, it would seem, regretted the primary's outcome, which had selected Han over more seasoned politicians and Terry Gou (郭台銘), the business tycoon who, spurned, for a while flirted with the idea of running as an independent candidate (with backing from Taipei Mayor Ko's party) only to abandon that plan and to cancel his KMT membership. As Tsai's numbers rose, the KMT seemed in the grip of another existential crisis, divided against itself and unable to control the populist forces which Han's emergence had unleashed.

Regardless of what happens in the 2020 elections, the new leadership had well remember the lessons of Taiwan's recent past: hubris, or a careless cross-Strait policy, will inevitably be met with resistance and the promise of democratic retribution such as the Sunflower Movement of 2014. In other words, Taiwan's democracy, flawed, exposed to populism and unexpected swings though it may be, and buffeted by Chinese "sharp power," also holds the resilience that has allowed this nation to survive many past challenges.

References

Apple Daily (2019) "歐陽娜娜涉「獨」】二度表忠起作用？ 共青團中央撐：兩岸一家親," 24 March. https://hk.news.appledaily.com/china/realtime/article/20190324/59405081.

Central News Agency (2019) "韓國瑜澄清不丹人傻傻的 證實會港中聯辦主任," 23 March. www.cna.com.tw/news/firstnews/201903220309.aspx?fbclid=IwAR0Nb5yFj9Ii3z6Wa6Rwdx96aJsSCsIuZ0hJ2nUVoyUPDaHNFqcKfVNADsU.

Chiu, Pei-fen (2015) "「對台工作完全錯誤」 習近平點名批判陳雲林," *Storm Media*, 4 September. www.storm.mg/article/64359.

Hochschild, Arlie Russell (2016) *Strangers in Their Own Land: Anger and Mourning on the American Right*, New York: The New Press, 2016.

Kenney, Charles D. (2004) *Fujimori's Coup and the Breakdown of Democracy in Latin America*, Notre Dame: University of Notre Dame Press.

Lee, Hsin-fang, Chung Li-hua and William Hetherington (2019) "Details Sought as Morrison Lee's Detention Verified," *Taipei Times*, 12 September. www.taipeitimes.com/News/front/archives/2019/09/12/2003722126.

Lee, Zhong-wei (2019) "前國台辦官員：國民黨一中各表不是真「九二共識」," *United Daily News*, 26 February. https://udn.com/news/amp/story/7331/3665189.

Liberty Times (2019) "黃之鋒警告！ 台灣人赴港旅遊恐成下個李明哲," 15 February. https://news.ltn.com.tw/news/politics/breakingnews/2699747.

Lin, Chang-shun and Lee Hsin-Yin (2019) "13 Officials CAL Staffers Indicted in Cigarette Smuggling Scandal," *Focus Taiwan*, 23 August. http://focustaiwan.tw/news/asoc/201908230016.aspx.

Miao, Zong-han and Flor Wang (2019) "Taiwan Citizen Fined for Taking up Political Post in China," *Focus Taiwan*, 15 March. http://focustaiwan.tw/news/afav/201903150011.aspx.

Office of the President, Republic of China (2019) "President Tsai issues statement on China's President Xi's 'Message to Compatriots in Taiwan'," 2 January. https://english.president.gov.tw/News/5621.

Packer, George (2013) *The Unwinding: An Inner History of the New America*, New York: Farrar, Straus and Giroux.

Sung, Wen-ti (2019) 宋文笛：偶然言中》「寇謐將」評韓國瑜引起的 2019 藍綠大混戰," *Liberty Times*, 9 March. https://talk.ltn.com.tw/article/breakingnews/2721692.

Tu, Aaron, Lin Ching-chuan and William Hetherington (2018) "PRC Funding of Campaigns Probed," *Taipei Times*, 23 October. www.taipeitimes.com/News/front/archives/2018/10/23/2003702864.

United Daily News (2019) "全文／習近平首提五原則 探索一國兩制台灣方案," 2 January. https://money.udn.com/money/story/5603/3569712.

Wen, Gui-hsiang (2019) "宗教自由對話在台舉辦 總統：台美堅實夥伴關係," *Central News Agency*, 11 March. www.cna.com.tw/news/firstnews/201903110181.aspx.

Yeh, Hui-hsuan (2019) "陸委會證實 韓國瑜下午將和國台辦三任劉結一會面," *United Daily News*, 25 March. https://udn.com/news/story/7238/3716952.

Yu, Hsiang and Flor Wang (2019) "KMT May Not Reverse Law on Peace Pact Referendum: Chairman," *Focus Taiwan*, 20 February. http://focustaiwan.tw/news/aipl/201902200024.aspx.

INDEX

16+1 initiative 56
1992 Consensus 6, 9–11, 16–18, 20–21, 26–27, 35, 44, 98, 184–185, 187–190
228 Massacre 71, 122
311 base 45
800 Heroes 50, 153
85°C coffee chain 114

Abe, Shinzo 104, 124–128, 130–131, 134
Act Governing Relations Between the People of Taiwan Area and the Mainland Area 4, 6; amendments to 163
Air Canada 39–40, 141
Akama, Jiro 130
Alibaba 42
All China Lawyers Association 85
Allison, Graham 81
All-Nippon Airways (ANA) 40
American Institute in Taiwan (AIT) 103, 107, 112–113
Amnesty Act 74
An, Fengshan 21
Anti-Secession Law 12, 179
Apple Daily 25
Ashe, John 56
Asia Cement Corp 156
Asian Development Bank (ADB) 132
Asian Financial Crisis 8
Association for Asian Studies 36
Association for Promotion of Chinese Culture (CAPCC) 45, 47
Association for Relations Across the Taiwan Straits (ARATS) 6, 10, 21, 186

Association of East Asian Relations, Taiwan 130
Association of Southeast Asian Nations (ASEAN) 28, 104–105, 139, 144
Association of Taiwan Investment Enterprises on the Mainland 48
Australia 31, 39, 54, 104–105, 131, 139, 163
authoritarianism 13, 20, 22, 39, 41, 46–47, 62, 86–90, 92–95, 102, 110, 131, 143, 151–156, 164, 167, 175, 177

Bahrain 32
Baidu Tieba, 25, 42
Bamboo Union 49, 50, 128–129, 163
Bashi Channel 59
Beidaihe 92
Belt and Road Initiative (BRI) 22, 54, 56, 84–85, 87, 104, 124, 132–133, 138, 143, 145
Bio, Julius Maada 85
Blair, Dennis 133
Blue Sky Alliance 50
Bo, Xilai 56, 90
Bolton, John 107
British Office 142
Brownback, Sam 104
Burkina Faso 29
Bush, George W 114–115
Bush, Richard 19, 126

Cambodia 32, 88, 139
Cambridge University Press 36
Canada 13, 31, 38–39, 140–141

Index 195

Canadian Trade Office in Taipei (CTOT) 141
Catholic Patriotic Association 145
CCP *see* Chinese Communist Party (CCP)
Center for Peace and Development Studies (CPDS) 46
Central Election Commission (CEC) 161
Central Military Commission (CMC) 60, 63, 83, 90
Chad 55
Chan, Andy Ho-tin 55
Chan, Melissa 54
Chang, An-le 49–50, 52, 128
Chang, Fu-tang 53
Chang, Wei 49, 128
Chen, Chi-mai 183–184
Chen, Chu 184
Chen, Fu-hai 59
Chen, Shui-bian 5, 11, 22, 69, 72, 74–75, 98, 101, 114, 152, 157
Chen, Yunlin 186
Chiang, Ching-kuo 52
Chiang, Kuo-ching 158
China x, 3–23, 25–46, 48–65, 69–76, 79–96, 98–108, 110–115, 118, 122–135, 138, 140–146, 151–152, 158, 163, 167–168, 171–175, 177–184, 187–192; and blacklisting of Taiwanese artists 41–42; and censorship 36–38, 87; and century of humiliation 79; and Chinese Dream 83, 92–95; cyber attacks from 22, 45, 89–90, 111; and debt-trap diplomacy 84–86, 138; declaration of ADIZ in East China Sea 80, 133; espionage by 22, 52, 89–90; extradition of Taiwanese nationals to 32–33; and nationalism 42, 95; peaceful rise of 22; pressure on international companies 37–40; and strategic periphery 82; tourism to Taiwan 8, 22, 27–28; and trade war with the United States 62, 93, 100, 124, 166, 180
China Association for Friendly International Contact (CAIFC) 45, 47
China Central Television (CCTV) 46
China Council for the Promotion of Peaceful National Unification (CCPPR) 53
China Energy Fund Committee (CEFC) 46–47, 55–56, 140, 187
China Merchants Port Holdings 85
China Model 14, 56, 86
China National Tourism Administration (CNTA) 28
China Peace Development Association 53
China Quarterly 36

China Taiwanese Association 187
China Unification Promotion Party (CUPP) 13–14, 16, 49, 51–53, 71, 104, 108, 128–129, 163
China-U.S. Exchange Foundation 45–46
Chinese Civil War 12, 183
Chinese Communist Party (CCP) 3, 10–12, 14–18, 21–23, 26, 36, 38, 43, 45, 46–56, 60–62, 64–65, 69, 79, 81–82, 85, 87–96, 99–100, 110–111, 117, 123, 128–129, 145–146, 151, 158, 163, 167–169, 173–174, 177–192, 184–185, 187–189, 191; and 19th Party Congress 18, 22, 60, 82, 91; Politburo Standing Committee 92
Chinese Nationalist Party *see* Kuomintang (KMT)
Chinese Politics in the Xi Jinping Era 92
Chinese Ryukyu Study Society 128
Chiu, Tai-san 157
Chou, Tzu-yu 4, 41
Chu, Eddie 49
Chu, Eric 3, 9
Chu, Judy 113
CITIC Group 55
Citizen Congress Watch 160
Civil Aviation Administration of China (CAAC) 38–39
Civil Servants Election and Recall Act 160
civil society xi, 16, 75, 87–88, 90, 92, 94, 103, 112, 143, 146, 152, 164, 173
Communist Party school 54
Communist Party of the Soviet Union (CPSU) 178, 181
Communist Youth League of China 41
Community of Democracies 143
Comprehensive and Progressive Agreement for Trans-Pacific Partnership (CPTPP) 132
Concentric Patriot Association of the ROC (CPAROC) 51, 129
Confucius Institutes 22
content farms 44
Cook, Tim 87
COSCO Shipping Corp 29
Council of Asian Liberals and Democrats (CALD) 143
Council of Grand Justices 159
Council of Indigenous Peoples (CAP) 156
CPC Corp Taiwan 55
Crimea 51, 81, 87, 180
Criminal Code 163
Cross-Strait Development Forum 53
Cross-Strait Media People Summit 44
Cross-Strait Services Trade Agreement (CSSTA) 8, 151

196 Index

Cross-Strait Taiwan Guangdong Exchange Association 51
Cui, Tiankai 108
Cultural Revolution 18, 36, 91
Cyber Security Law (China) 37–38
Czech Republic 55–56, 140, 155

Dai, Leon 42
Dalai Lama 27
death penalty 157–158
Deby, Idriss 55
Democratic Progressive Party (DPP) xi, 3–4, 9, 11, 16–17, 26–27, 29, 46, 50, 70, 74–75, 88, 95, 98–99, 101, 125, 129, 131, 151–154, 156–161, 163–164, 171, 178, 182–187; deep-green segment of 69–76, 184; democracy xi, 5–6, 13–14, 16–17, 19–20, 23, 33, 39, 43, 46–47, 49, 52, 56, 61, 71, 85–90, 99, 101, 112, 128, 130, 135, 141, 144, 151–155, 158, 160–165, 167, 169–170, 172, 175, 178–179, 185, 189, 192–192
Democracy in Crisis 46
Deng, Xiaoping 18, 20, 22, 91, 95, 168
Diamond, Larry 165
Diaoyutai islands 129, 180
Diba Facebook Expedition 25
digital silk road 87
diplomatic truce 17, 26, 28–36
direct democracy 159–161
disinformation 43–47, 50, 61, 72, 87–88, 103, 138, 154, 160, 173, 178, 186, 191; and LGBTQI rights 44, 160–161
distant-water fishing 161–162
Dominican Republic 29, 112
DPP *see* Democratic Progressive Party (DPP)

East Asian Olympic Committee (EAOC) 37
East Asian Youth Games 37
East China Sea 35, 80, 123–124
East Coast Rail Link (ECRL) 84
Eastern Theater Command 45
Easton, Ian 63
Economic Cooperation Framework Agreement (ECFA) 8
Economy, Elizabeth 93–94
Ecuador 32
Eight Honors and Eight Shames 25
eight-point proposal 19
Election Study Center 14
El Salvador 17, 29, 31, 43, 111–112
European Association of Taiwan Studies (EATS) 37
Everything Under the Heavens 95

External Propaganda Bureau (EPB) 46
Ezrahi, Yaron 15

F-16 Viper 115
F-22 126–127
F-35 117
Facebook 25, 44, 47, 54, 161, 169
Faith and Hope League 160
fake news *see* disinformation
Falun Gong 42
Fang, Fenghui 90
foreign agents bill 163
Formosan Association for Public Affairs (FAPA) 170
Four Seas Gang 49
France 13, 31, 93, 140
Free and Open Indo-Pacific (FOIP) 104, 131–132, 145
French, Howard 95
Fu-Jen University 146
Fujian Provincial Communist Party School – Taiwan Social Elite Class 54
Fujimori, Alberto 186
Fukushima Prefecture 131
Fukuyama, Francis 95
Futenma Air Station 127

Gadio, Cheikh 55
Gap 38
Gardner, Cory 111, 113
General Association of Chinese Culture (GACC) 71
Germany 31, 33, 93, 140, 143
Ghost Island News 44
Global Cooperation and Training Framework (GCTF) 103–104, 130, 133, 142–143, 173
Global Engagement Center (GEC) 185
Global Taiwan Institute (GTI) 170
Global Times 51, 61, 128
Gou, Terry Tai-ming 192
Grayling, A. C. 46, 151
Greater Taipei Stability Power Alliance 160
Great Firewall 25
Greenpeace 161–162
Guam 81, 127
Gui, Minhai 33–34
Guo, Boxiong 90
Guterres, Antonio 56

Hambantota Port 85
Han, Kuo-yu 46, 161, 182, 185–186, 192
Henoko Bay 126–127
Hille, Kathrin 44

Ho, Han-ting 52
Ho, Patrick Chi-ping 55–56, 187
Holy See *see* Vatican
Hong Kong 9, 14, 18–19, 28, 34, 38, 42, 48–50, 54–56, 61, 76, 88, 99, 128, 181, 187–188, 190–192; and extradition bill 190–191; protests in 14, 18, 76, 88, 191
Hong Kong, Macau, and Taiwan Affairs Committee 48
Hong Kong Foreign Correspondents Club 55
Hong Kong National Party 55
How Democracies Die 46, 169
Hsiao, Bi-khim 160
Hu, Jintao 22, 25, 100, 168
Hu, Qiaomu 50
Hu, Shiying 50
huadu 13
Huang, Huang-hsiung 154
Huang, Kuo-chang 160–161
Huawei 110, 141
humanitarian assistance and disaster relief (HADR) 133
Human Trafficking Prevention Act 162
Hun, Sen 32, 88
Hung, Hsiu-chu 9, 13

Ikea 38
India 15, 31–32, 39, 79–80, 88, 104–105, 111, 131, 139–140, 180; relations with China 32
Indigenous Defense Submarine 117
indigenous rights 156–157
Indo-Pacific x, 29, 80, 111, 133, 135, 185
Indo-Pacific Strategy 104–105
Industrial Technology Research Institute (ITRI) 133
Institute for National Policy Research (INPR) 105
Interchange Association (Japan) 130
International Civil Aviation Organization (ICAO) 35, 142, 173
International Cooperation Development Fund (ICDF) 132
International Covenant on Civil and Political Rights (ICCPR) 158
International Journal of Taiwan Studies 37
International Politics 36
Interpol 33, 35–36, 142, 173
Isa, Dolkun 33
Israel 140, 169

Jade Mountain 61
Japan x, 10, 12, 15, 20, 27–28, 31, 37, 40, 42, 56, 79, 80–81, 93, 95, 104–105, 117, 122–135, 138–139, 142–146, 157, 179, 181–182
Japan Airlines (JAL) 40
Japan Infrastructure Initiative (JII) 132
Japan International Cooperation Agency (JICA) 132
Japan Self-Defense Forces (JSDF) 126, 130, 133–134
Japan-Taiwan Exchange Association 129–130
Jiang, Yi-huah 165
Jiang, Zemin 19, 168
Jordan 32
Journal of Asian Studies 36
Journal of Chinese Political Science 36

Kadeer, Rebiya 27
Kadena Air Base 126–127
Kan, Shirley 115
Kenya 18, 32
Khan, Sulmaan Wasif 80
Kim Il Sung 128
Kim Jong Un 82, 112, 128
Kinmen 58–59
Kiribati 29, 111
Ko, Simon Shen-yeaw 37
Ko, Wen-je 46, 52, 75, 192
Korean Peninsula 79, 81–82, 102, 124, 167, 179
Kovrig, Michael 141
Kuomintang (KMT) 3, 8–9, 12–14, 16–17, 46, 51, 53, 70–72, 75, 98–99, 122, 129–131, 134, 152, 154–156, 161–161, 163–164, 171, 178–179, 182–188, 190, 192
Kutesa, Sam 55

Labor Standards Act 162
Lai, William Ching-te 74, 132, 184
Lam, Carrie 191
Landbridge Group 29
Law, Nathan 49
Lee, Ching-yu 34
Lee, David 70
Lee, Ming-che 33–34, 71, 191
Lee, Morrison 191
Lee, Teng-hui 23n1, 114
Legal Environment Report of the "Belt and Road" Countries 85
Legislative Yuan xi, 3, 8, 50, 164; and committee of achievers 169
Levitsky, Steven 46, 169
Li, Cheng 91–92
Li, Eric X. 86
Li, Keqiang 84

198 Index

Li, Kexin 53, 108
Li, Wenhui 49
Liaison Office of the Central People's
  Government in the Hong Kong SAR 187
Liaoning aircraft carrier 101
Liberal Democratic Party (LDP) 127
Liberal International 143
Lin, Ming-cheng 52
Lin, Shirley Syaru 15
Line 44, 161
Ling, Yu-shih 187
Liu, Jieyi 187
Liu, Shih-chung 113
Lo, Andrew 55

M503 air route 17, 60
Ma, Xiaoguang 10
Ma, Ying-jeou xi, 5, 8, 16–18, 23, 26, 35, 49,
  53, 55, 114, 130, 144, 151–152, 157, 165,
  183, 185–186; summit with Xi Jinping
  in Singapore 21
Macau 38, 187, 191
Mahatir, Mohamad 84, 88
Mainland Affairs Council (MAC) 21, 26,
  58, 187–188
Malaysia 44, 84, 143
Maldives 88
Manes, Jean 31
Mao, Zedong 91, 128, 167
Margarita Island Port 29
Marine Corps Air Station Futenma 126
Maritime Disaster Prevention Center
  (MDPC) 133
Maritime Security Initiative (MSI) 111
Marriott 38
Martial Law 5, 122–123, 154, 170
Marut, Christopher 103
MassResistance 159
Mattis, Jim 104–106, 113
Mattis, Peter 48
McGregor, Richard 126
Medtronic 38
Meng, Hongwei 36, 173
Meng, Wanzhou 141
Mercedes 38
meritocracy 14, 86
Ministry of Defense (Japan) 125
Ministry of Foreign Affairs (Japan) 125, 132
Ministry of Foreign Affairs (Taiwan) 104,
  130–131, 143, 170
Ministry of Justice Investigation Bureau
  (MJIB) 142, 179
Ministry of National Defense (Taiwan)
  60–61, 173
Ministry of State Security (MSS) 91, 182

Minzner, Carl 93
Monaco, Nick 25

Nathan, Andrew 80
National Committee of the Chinese
  People's Political Consultative
  Conference (CPPCC) 44, 48, 187
National Defense Authorization Act
  (NDAA) 106–111, 117, 174
National Development Council 172
National Endowment for Democracy
  (NED) 17, 47
National People's Congress (NPC) 14
National Security Act (Taiwan) 52, 131;
  amendments to 163
National Security Bureau (NSB) 164, 173
National Security Council (NSC) 70, 173–174
National Sun Yat-sen University 144
National Taiwan University 48
National Unification Council 11
Netease 42
New National Security Law (China) 14,
  33, 191
New Party 13–14, 16, 52–53, 71, 108,
  128–129
New Power Party (NPP) 75, 160
New Southbound Policy 105, 132, 139,
  143–145, 162, 167
New Zealand 54, 139
Nigeria 32
No Other Love 42
North American Free Trade Agreement
  (NAFTA) 141

Obama, Barack x, 98, 115
Office of the U.S. Trade Representative
  (USTR) 118
Okinawa 80, 126–129
one China 8–9, 19, 26, 30, 32, 35, 38,
  41, 54, 101–102, 107, 113–114, 130,
  141–142, 144, 188–189
one country, two systems 14, 16, 19, 34, 44,
  50, 99, 181, 187–188, 190, 192
one generation and one stratum 48, 57
Organized Crime Prevention Act
  (Taiwan) 52
Orwellian nonsense 40
Ouyang, Long 187
Ouyang, Nana 187

Panama 29, 112
Peaceful Integration and Development
  Forum 53
peaceful unification 19, 99, 188; historical
  inevitability of 30, 63

Index 199

Pei, Minxin 91
pension reform 45, 50, 152–155, 158, 185
People's Armed Police (PAP) 182
People's Daily 52
People's Liberation Army (PLA) 12, 19,
  21, 30, 45, 59–64, 81, 84, 90, 100, 106,
  108, 114, 117, 124, 126, 133–134, 174,
  178–182, 184, 191
People's Republic of China *see* China
Perry, Katy 42
Peru 186
Pew Research Center 62
Philippines 28, 32, 50, 139, 144, 180
Phoenix TV 61
Political Donations Act (Taiwan) 52
political warfare 13, 17, 26, 47–48, 51, 54,
  61, 87, 128–129, 138, 162–165, 179, 192
Pompeo, Mike 103
Presbyterian Church of Taiwan 159
Prospect Foundation xii
PTT Board 45

Quad 105, 142
Quanzhou 61

Razak, Najib 88
Regional Religious Freedom Forum 104
Republic of China (ROC) 4–7, 9, 11–12,
  26, 32, 37, 71, 73, 98
Rigger, Shelley 141
RIMPAC 111
Road to Unfreedom 168
Rosneft, 55
Royce, Ed 113
Royce, Marie 107, 112
Rubio, Marco 31
Rwanda 155
Ryukyu Independence Study Association 128
Ryukyus 81, 128

same-sex marriage 44, 158–161, 183
Sao Tome and Principe 29
Schriver, Randall 115
Scobell, Andrew 80
Second Island Chain 28, 81, 85
Senkaku islands 123–124, 129, 180
Severe Acute Respiratory Syndrome
  (SARS) 35, 143
Shanghai Canxing Trading Co 48
Shanghai City Cross-Strait Cultural
  Exchange Promotion Association
  48–49
Shanghai Cultural Association 48
Shanghai Flight Information Zone 60
Shanghai Voice of Dream Media 48

Shangri-La Dialogue 105
sharp power *see* political warfare
Sherman, Brad 113
Sierra Leone 85
Silk Road 82
Sing! China: Shanghai-Taipei Music
  Festival 48–49
Singapore 21, 50, 82, 105, 112, 131, 139, 157
Six Assurances 107, 109
Snyder, Timothy 87, 168
Socialist Conception of Honors and
  Shames 25
soft power 16, 23, 103, 144, 171
Solih, Ibrahim Mohamed 88
Solomon Islands 29–30, 85, 111, 187
Song, Zhongping 61
South Africa 155
South China Morning Post 61
South China Sea 12, 38, 56, 64, 80–81, 84,
  102, 111, 133, 167, 180, 183
South Korea 4, 27–28, 104–105, 117, 131
Spain 33, 37
Spavor, Michael 141
special state-to-state relationship 11, 23n1
Springer Nature 36
Sri Lanka 85
Star Fire Secret Unit 52
Strait Forum 44
Strait of Miyako 59
Straits Exchange Foundation (SEF) 6,
  21, 34
Su, Chi 8
Su, Tseng-chang 184
subversion 33, 162–165, 191
Summer Universiade 35–36
Sunflower Movement xi, 8–9, 41–42, 50,
  70, 151, 192
Sung, Vivian 42
Swaziland 29

Taichung City Cross-Strait Business and
  Trade Association 53
taidu 13
Tainan Cross-Strait Exchange Promotion
  Association 51
Taipei Economic and Cultural
  Representative Office (TECRO) 107, 171
Taiping Island 64
taishang 48, 163
Taiwan: and diplomatic allies 28; erosion
  of sovereignty 8, 19, 34, 43, 69, 134, 178,
  185; general elections of 2016 9, 16, 20,
  25, 27, 29, 44, 71, 125, 152, 158–159;
  general elections of 2020 xi, 3, 20, 30, 59,
  74–75, 161, 178–179, 184, 186–187, 189,

192; and Japanese colonial rule 12, 122; Lebanonization of 51, 184; low birthrate in 172–173; nine-in one elections (2018) 46, 52, 154, 158, 161, 182–185, 190, 192; and outlying islands 12, 58, 60; polarization in 43, 74, 168–170, 186–187; and tourism 27–28

Taiwan Affairs Office (TAO) 10, 21–22, 26, 49, 51, 53, 56–57, 61, 163, 187–188, 191

Taiwan Air Defense Identification Zone (ADIZ) 59

Taiwan Allies International Protection and Enhancement Initiative Act *see* Taipei Act

Taiwanese Chinese Heart 54

Taiwan External Trade Development Council (TAITRA) 139–140

Taiwan Foundation for Democracy (TFD) xii, 14, 20, 104, 164

Taiwan International Workers' Association (TIWA) 162

Taiwan-Japan Relations Association 130

Taiwan People's Party 46, 192

Taiwan Red Party 53–54, 163

Taiwan Relations Act (TRA) 20, 72, 100, 105–107, 109–110, 114, 116–117, 134

Taiwan Security Act 108

Taiwan Strait: median line in 60; PLA transits in 59–60, 101; status quo in 4–6, 11, 20–21, 31, 69, 72, 79, 82, 98–99, 106–107, 124–125, 174, 189; Third Crisis 20–21, 126; US Navy transits in 101, 114

Taiwan Travel Act 106–108, 114

Tamaki, Denny 127

Tencent 42

Thailand 28, 32–33, 139

Thinking Taiwan Foundation x

thirty-one incentives 45, 48, 56–58

Thomas G. Thompson port call at Kaohsiung 110

three new links 59

three middles and the youth 48

three noes and one without 11

Thucydides trap 81

Tiananmen Square massacre 36

Tibet 18, 27, 36, 38, 57, 104, 146, 188

Tillerson, Rex 102–103

Tōhoku earthquake 123, 131

Tokyo Olympics 37, 74

track-two diplomacy 21, 130, 135, 142, 185

Trade and Investment Framework Agreement (TIFA) 118

transitional justice 154–156

Trans-Sabah Gas Pipeline (TSGP) 84

Treaty of Mutual Cooperation and Security Between the United States and Japan x, 125–126

Trudeau, Justin 39, 140–141

Trump, Donald, J. x, 82, 85–86, 98, 100–102, 104–108, 112–113, 115–117, 127, 141, 186; arms sales to Taiwan 115–117

truth and reconciliation 155

Tsai, Ching-hsiang 157

Tsai, Eng-meng 44

Tsai, Ing-wen: criticism of 4, 20, 34, 51, 70–71, 75, 184; defeat in 2012 elections xi, 9; election of 9, 16, 20, 25, 41, 64, 71, 74, 98, 125, 152, 159, 186; inauguration of xi, 3, 53, 59, 69, 71; policy statements 3–7, 10, 47, 175; telephone conversation with Donald Trump 101–102; transits in Houston and Los Angeles 113; transits in Paraguay and Belize 113

T&T Supermarket 38

Tung Chee-hwa 55

Turkey 32

Twitter 25, 47

Uganda 55

Ukraine 81, 180

United Airways 40

United Arab Emirates 32

United Front Work Department 46, 48, 53–54, 185

United Kingdom 31, 140, 142–143

United Nations Educational, Scientific and Cultural Organization (UNESCO) 173

United Nations General Assembly 31, 56, 142, 173

United States-Mexico-Canada Agreement (USMCA) 141

University of Salamanca 37

U.S.-China Cultural Exchange Society 53

U.S. National Counterintelligence and Security Center 89

U.S. Department of Defense 62, 104–106, 108, 111, 118

U.S. Department of State 102–103, 108, 111–113, 162, 185

U.S. National Aeronautics and Space Administration's Johnson Space Center 114

U.S.-Taiwan Business Council 115–116

Vatican 145–146

Voice of the Taiwan Straits 45

waishengren 70, 74, 168
Wang, Chin-pu 53
Wang, Daohan 10
Wang, Ding-yu 159
Wang, Ping-chung 52–53
Wang, Yang 44
Wang, Zaixi 189
Want Want China Times 44
WeChat (Weixin QQ) 33, 44
Weibo 38, 61
Wenzao Ursuline University 146
White Terror 71, 122, 154
Wong, Alex 105
Wong, Joshua 49
World Games 36
World Health Assembly (WHA) 35, 142, 173
World Internet Conference 87
World Trade Organization (WTO) 20, 40
Wu, Jianguo 52
Wu, Joseph 70
Wu, Nien-chen 42

Xi, Jinping x, 9, 11–12, 14, 18, 20, 22, 26, 48, 50, 53, 56, 60, 63–64, 69, 79–80, 82, 84, 90–92, 99, 102, 124, 139, 146, 167, 178–180, 182, 187; anti-corruption campaign 90–92; at Mar-a-Lago 102; and megalothymia 95, 182; removal of presidential term limit 92; summit with Ma Ying-jeou in Singapore 21; telephone conversation with Donald Trump 101–102; Xi Jinping Thought 82, 91
Xiamen 44
Xinjiang Autonomous Region 27, 57, 99, 104, 146, 188; and re-education camps 14
Xu, Caihou 90

Yameen, Abdulla 88
Ye, Jianming 55–56
Yeh, Jiunn-rong 50
Yiu, Edward 49
Yok, Mu-ming 53
Yu, Zhengsheng 48, 53, 57
Yueyang City Intermediate People's Court 33

Zara 38
Zeman, Milos 55
Zhang, Nianchi 10
Zhang, Yang 90
Zhang, Zhijun 53
Zhao, Vicky 42
Zhao, Xiaozhuo 106
Zhou, Hongxu 52–53
Zhou, Yongkang 90
Ziblatt, Daniel 46, 169
ZTE 110

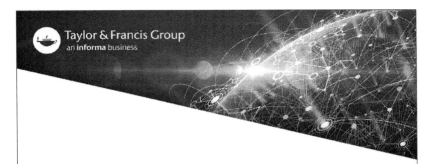

Taylor & Francis eBooks

www.taylorfrancis.com

A single destination for eBooks from Taylor & Francis with increased functionality and an improved user experience to meet the needs of our customers.

90,000+ eBooks of award-winning academic content in Humanities, Social Science, Science, Technology, Engineering, and Medical written by a global network of editors and authors.

TAYLOR & FRANCIS EBOOKS OFFERS:

- A streamlined experience for our library customers
- A single point of discovery for all of our eBook content
- Improved search and discovery of content at both book and chapter level

REQUEST A FREE TRIAL
support@taylorfrancis.com